ESSAYS IN EUROPEAN HISTORY

Selected From the Annual Meetings of the
Southern Historical Association
1988-1989

Volume II

MCA

ESS

Edited by

June K. Burton
Carolyn W. White

University Press of America, Inc.
Lanham • New York • London

European History Section of the
Southern Historical Association

Copyright © 1996 by
University Press of America,® Inc.
4720 Boston Way
Lanham, Maryland 20706

3 Henrietta Street
London, WC2E 8LU England

Library of Congress Cataloging-in-Publication Data

Essays in European history : selected from the annual meetings of the
Southern Historical Association, 1988-1989 /vol II. / edited by
June K. Burton and Carolyn W. White
p.   cm.
"Co-published by arrangement with the European History Section of
the Southern Historical Association"--T.p.verso.
includes bibliographies.
1. Europe--History--1789-1900. 2. Europe--History--20th century. I.
Burton, June K. II. Southern Historical Association. European
History Section.
D353.E87   1996   940.2--dc20   96-37939 CIP

ISBN 0-7618-0316-5 (cloth: alk. ppr.)
ISBN 0-7618-0317-3 (pbk: alk. ppr.)

Co-published by arrangement with the European History Section of the
Southern Historical Association

The paper used in this publication meets the minimum requirements of
American National Standard for information Sciences—Permanence
of Paper for Printed Library Materials,
ANSI Z39.48—1984

Contents

iii

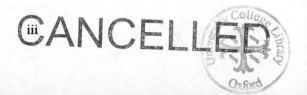

PART II. THE 1989 ANNUAL MEETING (LEXINGTON)

PREFACE

These essays are presented through the initiative and support of the European History Section of the Southern Historical Association. Since the publication of Volume I in 1989, the members of the Section have observed with astonishment the changes that have transformed contemporary Europe. Indeed the Berlin Wall was dismantled during the annual meeting in Lexington. We hope the essays presented here will help to place these momentous events in historical context.

Significant changes in American higher education have also occurred since 1989. The *Essays* have survived state prorationing and several budget crises. The editors appreciate the patience of the contributors and the financial support of the European Section.

We thank especially Donna Walker and Ann Lee for their technical expertise. This volume is dedicated to the memory of Joe Thompson of the University of Kentucky

June K. Burton
The University of Akron

Carolyn White
The University of Alabama in Huntsville

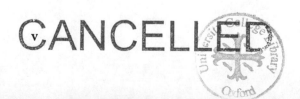

The University of Akron Department of History
and
The University of Alabama in Huntsville Institutional Sponsors

Part I. The 1988 Annual Meeting
Norfolk, Virginia

The Joseph J. Mathews Address

FROM MACRO- TO MICROHISTORY: A JOURNEY OUT OF SEASON

Enno E. Kraehe

If I may, I would like to begin with a little history. This organization, the European Section of the SHA, was founded in Memphis in 1955. Since then there have been thirty-two luncheon speakers, and I have heard twenty-five of them. It is a distinguished list, and I take this opportunity to thank you for your invitation to join this illustrious group.

No doubt you have been wondering what in the world I was going to ramble on about under the umbrella-like title I have chosen. I wondered too at the time. I only knew that I was ill-prepared to do what is expected of a speaker in this situation, that my path through history has not been the usual one. In the normal course of events one does a detailed dissertation on a more or less narrow topic, then progresses to books of larger scope, including perhaps a Western Civ. text, and finally, in a few distinguished cases, fills a presidential address with sweeping conclusions acquired in a lifetime of ever-expanding horizons. My own course, I fear, has been exactly the reverse, beginning with the abstract and universal and ending with-- maybe I should put that proceeding to--the concrete and particular. I know I really shouldn't bother you with the story of my life, even this limited segment of it, but I think it's in the by-laws of the European Section somewhere that a charter member has a special claim on your indulgence. And besides, my dues are paid up for life!

Beyond that there were two more immediate reasons for choosing the title I did. The first was a paragraph in the preface of my volume on the Congress of Vienna, wherein I sang the praises of what I half-facetiously called "microhistory." At the time I had the model of macro-and microeconomics in mind and only meant to convey the notion that broad historical generalizations are no better than the accuracy of the facts on which they are based. How dumb can you get? What I had really done was to hand the reviewers an opening-- fortunately only a few took advantage of it--for their own virtuoso perorations on the subject. "Microhistory without macrohistory is blind," I was told in one piece. And didn't I know that "the historian must play the roles of commentator, interpreter, and judge?" said another. Since I thought the book fairly bristled with interpretations and judgments--some of them pretty wild, in fact--I had to conclude that the expression "microhistory" had upstaged the substance of the work. And so, although I used it in a fit of absentmindedness, I was stuck with it, and I have ever since been compelled to reflect further on the issues it raises. While in this state of mind I attended the Joseph J. Mathews address given to this group last year by William H. McNeill. Most of you will recall that sterling talk, which was devoted to the historiography of Arnold Toynbee. It was clear that Toynbee was not only the subject of the book McNeill was working on but also the dazzling inspiration behind his own career as a historian. Now you can't get any more macro- than Toynbee's six volume *A Study of History* with its ecumenical erudition and majestic accounts of the rise and fall of some twenty-one civilizations according to regular patterns that amount to laws of history.   McNeill vividly recounted the excitement he felt as a graduate student at Cornell at the discovery of Toynbee, and his eloquence left no doubt that he still feels that excitement.

It was a feeling that I could well appreciate, for I too had received my baptism in history at the hands of a grand-scale macrohistorian. Perhaps the only peer that Toynbee had in this particular genre. The hero in my case was Oswald Spengler, whose ponderous *The Decline of the West* was for all its difficulty a best seller in the years between the two world wars--a popularity as remarkable as that of Paul Kennedy's *Rise and Fall of the Great Powers* is today. Kennedy, however, with all his caution, modest, and tentativeness, will never appeal to the young. Now compare Spengler. "It is not," he says, "merely a question of writing one out of several possible philosophies but of writing *the* philosophy of our time. This may be said without presumption." Or again: "All genuine historical work is philosophy unless it is mere ant-industry." Now *that's* how you appeal to a bookish eighteen-year old ready to reject establishment historiography even before I had had a college course in Western Civ. (Actually, I haven't had one yet.)

The real kick, though, was intellectual. To refresh your memories, Spengler identified some seven cultures (in contrast to Toynbee's twenty-one):   Egyptian, Chinese, Hindu, Graeco-Roman, Arabic, Mexican, and our own Western, each an organism like any other with a characteristic and necessary life cycle. By disregarding linear time and lining the life courses up side-by-side you could discern common features characteristic of the childhood, youth, maturity, and old age of each and thereby predict what lay ahead for us: for example, military dictatorship like that of the Caesars, the drying up of great art, the golden age of engineering and imperial administration, and the victory of the parasitic megalopolises over the life-giving countryside. Capitalism and socialism were two sides of the same coin, vulgar materialism, and would succumb together. And so on. This was widely regarded as pessimism, and it is true that Spengler's own heroes were the Michaelangelos and Beethovens of the West and not the engineers whose inevitable reign was beginning. As I read the master, however, he was simply an objective viewer making scientific estimates of the future, but unlike Marx, say, or Hegel, predictions that could be empirically based on half a dozen models we already had before us. These were the basis for true scientific objectivity as opposed to the anthropocentric wishful thinking of Marxism.

Continuing my personal confession, I was as an undergraduate, a student possessed, often toting around campus the heavy one-volume edition (the English one, I should add; I didn't read German then), quoting opinions to captive listeners and citing colorful passages to bolster whatever argument I was making at the time. This wasn't terribly effective on dates, but it was the way in which I resolved to be a historian no matter how much ant-industry was necessary to get the union card. I can't remember when the fever left me. Perhaps the ant-industry was the indicated antibiotic, or maybe, like the great cultures themselves, I just outgrew certain traits in the natural unfolding of my own life-cycle.

In either case what bothered me was the relationship between the lives of human beings, their daily concerns and specific motivations, as revealed in micro-research--these on the one hand--and the grand patterns on the other. It was easy to impute objective existence to the former even if interpretations might vary, but what was the ontological habitat of the patterns? For reasons too complex to go into here I finally concluded that it could only be in the eye of the beholder. And indeed, most of Spengler's admirers in his day and since have said: "Yes, he is wrong but what a masterpiece he wrote, a beautiful and harmonious poem." They lost me there. I cannot imagine a historian taking that as a compliment, or think of him as not seeking, within his limits, a true account of reality. Even poets and painters seek that.

So the majestic contours of half a dozen cultures faded from mind. What remained, however, was an abiding fascination with the philosophy of history, not as an exercise in charting the grand patterns but in the metaphysics and epistemology of it all. How do we know the past? What is the nature of historical explanation, the validity of historical knowledge? R. G. Collingwood and Friedrich Meinecke became the new gods. Both were radical historicists, as you know, arguing, like Spengler himself, that all knowledge and being are understandable only in history. For Collingwood it was the historical past living on in the present subconsciousness of the historian that made possible the conscious recovery of the past. Meinecke was the more extreme relativist, holding that everything was individuality obedient to its own laws. "Everything is in flux. Give me a place where I can stand," he cried out in anguish. This was Spengler in microcosm, a focus on particulars but still with mental categories shaped by the historical process itself and as Meinecke said, providing no objective ground on which to base judgments independently of historical conditioning. That was disturbing too, but in the meantime my ant-like industry went on apace, bringing in time a Ph.D., a congenial academic employment, a number of articles, and several trips to European archives. The archives were eye openers. It was like Keats first looking into Chapman's Homer or the first time a microscope exposed the beauty and teeming life in stagnant water. Here were the tangible remains of concrete reality. At last I could do what I thought all historians did: find out what was there--a few working hypotheses perhaps but no large preconceptions.

Or so it seemed. In fact, I found that most of my generation of German historians, at least in this country, had a program in mind or let us say a "conceptual framework." (As you know, preconceptions are bad, "conceptual frameworks" are good.) They were trying to find the roots of national socialism, to establish a direct connection between Bismarck and Hitler, royal authoritarianism and Nazi totalitarianism. As a corollary, interest focused on the putative weaknesses of German liberalism, and we all know the answers they found. Liberals had a defective concept of freedom, preferring Hegel to natural law. Too many liberals were docile state officials rather than independent business entrepreneurs--one of the few compliments I ever heard applied to business men by academics. The liberals did not try to make common cause with the masses. They made "fatal compromises" with the Prussian state (and please note that Prussia is at the center of everything), accepting under Bismarck continued authoritarianism thinly disguised as constitutional government. The authoritarian elites, moreover, sought salvation in aggression and war. Eckert Kehr, the first German to explain foreign policy as a function of *Innenpolitik*, was raised from oblivion to the pantheon of heroes.

It is not my intention to disparage the foregoing. On the contrary, I share some of these views, and we are the richer for all the studies the program has inspired. The point here, however, is that it is a program, that the standards applied to Germany are derived from American, British and French norms, that this framework is a priori and not the result of empirical study of Germany or of comparable practices at other times and places, or of the choices realistically available to the participants in their concrete settings. Events are not seen in their unique wholeness but as examples or illustrations of something else.

But I need not dwell on this; the model is already on its way out, the victim in fact of the challenges posed mostly by younger historians working in painstaking detail at the micro-level. Indeed, most historical revisionism comes about in this way, subjecting the early macrohistorical conceptualizations, usually politically partisan, to empirical scrutiny. Notice, for example, how the speculative Leninist and Hobson explanations of imperialism have been routed by the micro-explanations of Robinson, Gallagher, Fieldhouse et al. Or I could cite my own work on the Congress of Vienna, which had it been available when Henry Kissinger wrote his *World Restores*, might have saved him a few pratfalls. To cite but one example, using the best monographs of the time, Kissinger erected an elaborate theory of legitimacy on Metternich's profound cunning in merely pretending to mediate peace with Napoleon in 1813 the better to persuade the allies to fight the war on his ideological terms. Very original and impressive, but since we now know that Metternich's negotiations were utterly sincere, if he had any ideological goal for Europe, it would have to have been Bonapartism--as indeed it was. This last is a generalization too, but what it lacks in brilliance it makes up in compatibility with the facts.

Now I don't think anybody would quarrel with the proposition that the validity of a generalization depends on factual accuracy at the micro level, that one builds castles from the ground up. Nevertheless, the world seems to consider broad synthesis the superior calling, the achievement most recognized in awarding prizes and tenure. I do too provided that harmony exists between the macro-and micro-levels, and the patterns do not merely reflect the mind's yearning for coherence and order. Wouldn't we all rather be a Newton, a Kepler, or a Darwin than a Tycho Brahe or a Louis Agassiz? Oh, the grandeur of it all! And don't we all have colleagues in the social sciences who loftily think of us historians as fact finders, food gatherers, as it were, while they themselves are the food processors making our hard kernels and roots fit for human consumption. Of course, more often than not, the processor removes all the flavor and nutrients along the way.

In some ways, though, these attitudes reflect older models. While our satellites circle the globe in the grip of Newtonian mechanics, here on earth center stage is occupied by the nucleus of the atom--quantum mechanics, indeterminacy, and the quest for ever tinier particles. And in biology do the Nobel prizes go to the great system makers or to the builders of double helixes? Even music taps out this beat. In my youth, my Spengler years approximately, the great artists--Paderewski, Artur Schnabel, Fritz Kreisler, Leopold Stokowski--were towering romantics belting out glorious masses of music, more intent on the overall effect than the faithful reproduction of each note or the composer's directions. (It was great; I loved it.) Then came the triumph of Toscanini, Heifetz, and Rubinstein. They were moving too but made their points with clarity, precision, reverence for every single note. Currently conductors like John Mauceri and David Lawton (scarcely household names) are making careers by performing Verdi's operas with an attention to the master's metronome marks that even Toscanini never dreamed of--and might even have considered pedantic.

Now I am not arguing here that micro- is necessarily better than macro-, only that the pursuit of it is not an inferior calling, and this in regard to both the final product and the intellectual powers demanded by the technique. In view of the emphasis I have placed on facts you might well conclude that I wish to revive the simplistic positivism of a century ago, which viewed the historian as an objective scientist of the past, collecting and ordering facts so that they could speak for themselves. This optimistic view has been represented in our own time most consistently by Maurice Mandelbaum, who believes that the historian has direct access to facts that are objectively given in the record. A nice compliment to our craft, to be sure, but I fear the opposite is the case. On this matter I stand with Collingwood, who insists that what we examine directly is only *evidence* from which the facts, the actual events, must be inferred. Actually the events themselves do not exist at all or at least no longer exist; they must be reconstructed the way an astronomer, say, much of the time must deal with light rays emitted by stars that become extinct an aeon ago.

Similarly, most particle physics depends on inferring fleeting events from the traces left on photographic plates. To the extent that the mind of the historian is thus unavoidably the instrument for establishing what the particular facts are or were, the historical enterprise is subjective.

The central question, therefore, is not whether the technique is subjective but whether the results are or need to be. Our century has generally answered this question in the affirmative--sometimes with despair as in the case of Meinecke, sometimes joyfully. Why joyfully? I can't speak for everybody, but I think it's because of a sense of liberation: if everything is relative, why strain so hard to pursue the literal truth? This conviction is the open door to the programs alluded to earlier, to all the agendas for social change, to the pursuit of special interests, whether relevant to public concerns or not, whether trivial or important to human understanding. The most fastidious historians have taken the trouble to spell out their biases. I think, for example, of Koppel Pinson's *Modern Germany: A History*, a book by the way that I abandoned as a text years ago only because of the cumbersome topical organization. Aware that he was criticizing some well established and not inhumane attitudes, he explicitly warned in the preface that the book reflected the point of view of a mid-twentieth century liberal who deplored the course of German history. Nothing wrong with that as far as it goes, but when an author modestly says (in contrast to Spengler's arrogance) that this is only one among many possible ways of looking at the subject, he is really passing the choice among viewpoints along to the reader, who most likely knows less than he about the subject.

If people like Pinson represent a bashful kind of historical relativism, Marxism is the strident opposite. It is the one twentieth-century school that rejects subjectivism with a vengeance, insisting instead on the objectivity of the historical process, to which it has the key. The governments of Eastern Europe would hardly maintain their historians in relative comfort in posh institutes if they did not believe that their high priests were indeed charting the way to an inevitable future--though things are changing now that the paved road of the dialectic is filling up with potholes. In any case, Marxism's pseudo-objectivity is in reality just another brand of the subjectivism that marks our century.

But once again I would like to submit a minority report, this time to argue that the active role of the historian in making the past intelligible does not necessarily foreclose the attainment of stable and enduring results approximately on a par with any other kinds of knowledge the human race possesses. Physical science, to be sure, has the advantage, in some cases but not all, of being able to isolate its objects of study and to repeat experiments, but otherwise its results are no less the product of human creativity without their being regarded as hopelessly subjective. In the realm of human affairs explaining how we know the present is to me more difficult than explaining how we know the past. At the commonsense level we take for granted that the passage of time will dull partisan passions, bring out vast stores of data unavailable at the time the events occurred, and provide what we call perspective.

Perspective--that's what it's all about, the reason why the public at large has any interest in history at all. Microhistory is not to be confused with narrow specialization. It pertains mainly to the research function of the historian, not the training of his intellect, which requires the greatest possible range of experience. I deplore, for example, the narrowness of our current graduate programs. For similar reasons I consider it folly to fragment our professional societies as we have done in recent years--and continue to do. The current interest in comparative history is well placed, but in truth the best historical judgments have always incorporated the wisdom gleaned from countless comparable cases, whether expressly mentioned or not.

Medical schools are measured in part by the number of beds they have, that is to say the variety of cases they can provide to their students. History is not much different. Instead of worrying whether it is a science or an art, we might compare ourselves to doctors, or for that matter to lawyers and engineers. Sorry. I know that's a depressing thought, but let me explain. Though they are more or less learned in scientific principles of one kind or another, their primary function is to establish the truth in a particular case. Is this the right site for a bridge? Is this prisoner guilty of this particular crime? What did he know and when did he know it? Does this patient here have leukemia or something else? I dare say that all of us in this room, as victims, would be eagerly awaiting answers to these questions, not theories about what is generally true. For the historian, of course, the stakes are seldom so high, certainly never a matter of life and death, but if they were, I doubt that we would want to stray as far from the micro-record as casually as we now feel called to do.

Now I haven't told much that you haven't heard before, ever since Ranke urged us to try to write history *wie es eigentlich gewesen*. I have only put the package together in a different and exceedingly personal way. Before closing this odyssey, however, it behooves me to return to Spengler and ask whatever happened to him. Well, he died in Munich in 1936 at age 56, *persona non grata* to the Nazis. They thought he should have recognized in Hitler the great Caesar of the West. Instead he saw only a cheap politician sharing the vulgarity of the democratic masses and openly contrasted him with the heroic figures of the Junkers. Since then interest in Spengler has persisted at a modest but steady pace, rising noticeably in times of doom and gloom. A German named Manfred Schroeter wrote numerous books on Spengler from the 1920s into the 1960s and even earned a Festschrift for his efforts. In this country H. Stuart Hughes published a small book on him in 1952 as the Cold War heated up. Currently a graduate student at Virginia is trying to assess the accuracy of Spengler's prophecies, but he is not in my department. My role is merely to give him an occasional aspirin to keep the fever down. Lately the reviewers of Paul Kennedy's book on the great powers sometimes cite Spengler in stressing the common theme of pessimism.

In the history of thought Spengler is most often lumped with Germany's other cultural pessimists, who huddled on the political right and promoted elitist authoritarian causes. The evidence, however, is derived more from his political tracts, which were indeed reactionary, than from The Decline of the West itself. An exception, however--and a major one it is--is Claude Levi-Strauss in France, who considered Spengler his own inspiration in the founding of structuralism. From my vantage point on the anthill these matters don't concern me much any more. But I can tell you this: as between Spengler's rigorously consistent determinism and Toynbee's feckless hope that religious morality might bail out the West after all, give me Spengler any time.

Selected Papers

FRANZ VON PAPEN AND THE ANSCHLUSS

GEORGE O. KENT

Franz von Papen remains a controversial figure in modern German history, and several contentious episodes punctuate his career of more than four decades. The Anschluss[1] is one of them. This essay, part of a projected biography of von Papen, explores his activities as Hitler's special envoy in Vienna and concentrates on the foreign policy aspects of that mission. In particular, it examines Papen's role in achieving the Austro-German agreement of July 1936, and attempts to gauge the importance of this agreement to the Anschluss of 1938.

When the news of Chancellor Dollfuss' death and the failure of the Nazi Putsch in Austria reached Berlin on July 25, 1934, the German government was thrown into a major crisis[2] According to an eyewitness account, Hitler and his entourage at Bayreuth were in a state of indescribable confusion which, following the Roehm crisis of the previous month, shook the regime to its very foundations.[3] In addition, Hindenburg was seriously ill, and Hitler feared that conservatives who wished to restore the monarchy might exploit the President's death. With Italian troops positioned at the Brenner to protect the Austrian independence, the outbreak of war appeared a real possibility. In this confusion, Hitler turned to Putzi Hanfstaengl and exclaimed, "I have it! Papen is the man. What was it you called him two years ago, Hanfstaengl? *Ein Luftikus* [an airhead]. And [add] Catholic. . . to the bargain. He would talk his way around those priests and nuns in Vienna until they don't know whether they were going or coming."[4]

The next day, Hitler sent for Papen and asked him to undertake a special diplomatic mission to Vienna to restore German-Austrian relations. According to Papen, Hitler told him that he "was the only man who could restore such an appalling and dangerous situation. 'We are faced' he said, and I [Papen] can still hear his hysterical voice, 'with

a second Sarajevo.'"[5]   After a lengthy discussion in which Papen
specified his conditions for accepting the assignment, Hitler agreed to
Papen's terms and Papen agreed to undertake the mission.[6]

Papen's appointment was announced on July 27, even before the
Austrian government had agreed to accept the appointment.[7] The
Austrians, not surprisingly, were suspicious of Hitler's motives and not
at all happy with Papen's nomination. At a ministerial council on July
27, the Austrian Vice-Chancellor, Starhemberg, expressed his lack of
sympathy for Papen personally and his preference for a professional
diplomat. Starhemberg was concerned that, as a Catholic, Papen would
be able to win over to Naziism those groups in Austria that had been
previously unsympathetic to Nazi Propaganda.   Minister of Trade
Stockinger agreed with Starhemberg and added that in his view Papen
was a great intriguer. In the end, the Council delayed its decision to
accept Papen's appointment.[8] At the August 7 session of the Council,
Foreign Minister Berger-Waldenegg reported that the Austrian delay in
accepting Papen's appointment received favorable comment abroad but
that French and Italian officials believed that the agreement could not
be delayed any longer and should be granted within a week. According
to confidential reports, the Roehm affair had severely undermined
Papen's position; he had accepted the assignment to Vienna to
reestablish his prestige.[9] During the Council's subsequent discussions,
Chancellor Schuschnigg reminded the members that Papen had bitterly
attacked the late Chancellor Dollfuss in two speeches in 1933, then
vowing that Germany would fight Austria until Dollfuss was deposed.
In the end, however, the ministerial council agreed to Papen's
appointment.[10]

A reading of the minutes of the council's meeting explains why the
Austrians felt they had to accept Papen's appointment. What is less
clear are Papen's motives for accepting himself the Vienna appointment
when he knew that his acceptance would serve Hitler at a time when
the Fuhrer's position at home and abroad was extremely precarious.
Less than a month after two of Papen's closest collaborators had been
murdered and he himself had barely escaped a similar fate, Papen was
apparently ready to aid in rehabilitating the reputation of the very man
who had been responsible for these events. Papen's own justifications
for his action, as presented in his memoirs, are revealing:

The situation was serious and he [Hitler] appealed to my patriotism .
. . the most urgent task was to prevent, if possible, a complete
breakdown in Germany's relations with the outside world . . . after
the disgraceful events of June 30 [my acceptance] would be to many
people an incomprehensible act . . . but a statesman with a true
sense of responsibility must sometimes be ready to face the unjust
censure of his friends . . . I must not let personal resentment
influence my decision . . . disillusioned as we were by internal
developments, it seems all the more necessary to prevent a
catastrophe in our international relations . . . I felt it my duty to
salvage something from the wreck, whatever criticism and
misunderstandings might be directed at me personally. There was
no way of proclaiming effective public opposition to the Nazis'
policies, so the next best thing was to work quietly in the
background and risk the odium of one's friends.[11]

About his ideas regarding future German policy toward Austria, Papen
wrote:

It was clear that the only long-term policy I could follow was the
historical path of eventual union [between Germany and Austria] . . .
I was fascinated by the magnitude of the task and the possibility of
providing a modern interpretation of Bismarck's policies. It seemed
to me a task of European importance. The increasing threat from
Communist underground movements in every Western European
country, and their unmistakable intention of disrupting the whole
social order by world revolution made it seem to me imperative to
rebuild the Central European dyke. That was the decisive factor in
my acceptance of the Vienna post.[12]

Papen's statement about the Communist threat was clearly written
to appeal to readers of the 1950s, the height of the Cold War, when his
memoirs appeared. However, other elements of his views, especially
that union with Austria would represent "a modern interpretation of
Bismarck's policies," appealed not only to Papen but to all German
nationalists, steeped as they were in the concept of *Mitteleuropa* and
Germany's mission in the Balkans. The incorporation of Austria
appeared the first step in fulfilling this mission.[13] These views
reflected those traditionally held by the Army and the Foreign Ministry,
both of which advocated a peaceful penetration of southeastern
Europe.[14] Papen also managed to gain Hitler's support for his (Papen's)
approach to union with Austria by stressing that a peaceful settlement
of the Austrian question would enable Germany to continue its internal
consolidation and its rearmament.[15] Papen believed in an evolutionary

policy which, by removing Austrian fears of direct German intervention, would, through cultural and economic cooperation, eventually lead to a voluntary and peaceful union of both countries.[16]

When he arrived in Vienna on August 15, 1934, Papen blamed his cool reception on the Austrians'misunderstanding of his previous actions in connection with the fall of Bruening and Hitler's accession to power.[17] In Papen's own words, the Austrians "suspected [him] of having trapped the Vatican into signing the Concordat, and of being a 'Catholic in wolf's clothing' against whom everyone must be on his guard."[18] In particular, Papen faced two major obstacles: the Austrian Nazis and the Catholic Church. The former were in a state of complete disarray following the unsuccessful July Putsch and were split into a moderate and radical wing. The moderate Nazis consisted primarily of younger and more recent party members who were fully agreed with Papen's evolutionary approach. The radicals were the Austrian Nazi Party's "old guard" who opposed any cooperation with the existing government and stressed the needs of their own party against those of the German NSDAP.[19] Throughout his tenure in Vienna, Papen consistently supported the moderates, and although many Germans favored the Austrian radicals, Papen's conciliatory policies prevailed and eventually led to the restoration of relations between the two countries that was reflected in the German-Austrian agreement of July 1936. Papen later wrote in his memoirs that he saw it as his duty "to prevent radical elements in the Nazi Party both in Germany and Austria, from pursuing a policy which would be likely to lead to international complications."[20]

The Austrian Catholic hierarchy's opposition to Papen was based on the bishops' belief that Hitler was bent on destroying the Church in Germany and that Papen, as a prominent Catholic layman, might be able to turn the Catholic elements in Austria against the Schuschnigg regime. The Nuntius in Vienna strongly distrusted Papen, and Cardinal Innitzer of Vienna refused to receive Papen for two years.[21] Papen was never able to overcome the opposition of the Austrian clergy to his mission, although he was later instrumental in arranging a meeting between Hitler and Innitzer soon after the Anschluss.[22]

Papen's method of achieving union by evolutionary means had two dimensions, domestic and foreign. On the domestic level, he planned to influence the various elements of the Austrian national opposition-- including the dissatisfied soldiers of the Heimwehr, the disgruntled members of the Christian Social Party, the avid supporters of a "Greater

Germany," and the moderate Austrian Nazis.

To achieve this goal, Papen developed a wide network of Austrian friends and supporters. Prominent among them were the former general and director E. Glaise-Horstenau of the Austrian military archives, the editor Anton Rohan of the *European Review*, the editor Friedrich Funder of the *Reichspost*, Austrian Nazis such as Gilbert in der Maur and Arthur Seyss-Inquart, and other prominent personages from the arts, the business world, and industry. Papen was able to enlist these individuals in his cause by stressing their common interest, background, and goals. To Friedrich Funder--no friend of the Nazis-- Papen presented himself as a victim of Hitler by recalling the events of 1934. To Austrian business leaders, he stressed the advantages of Austro-German economic cooperation. To Austrian Nazis, he mentioned his long-standing nationalist sympathies, to Catholics, his role in bring about the Concordat, to the Austrian aristocracy, his passion for hunting, and to the Austrian officer's corps, their common experiences in the first World War. During his four years in Vienna, these influential friends helped to shift Austrian public opinion from a position of rigid opposition to Hitler to a more tolerant attitude supporting an evolutionary solution to the Austrian problem.[23]

In the area of foreign policy, Papen's aims were to keep other powers from interfering in Austro-German affairs, to neutralize Austria's protector, Italy, and to improve relations between Germany and Austria, so that a peaceful union between the two could eventually result. Because Papen saw unification as a long-range goal, the immediate task, in his view, was cooperation and not confrontation.[24] The Austrian government continued, however, to see Papen's role differently. According to Berger-Waldenegg, Papen pursued only one aim from the day he arrived in Vienna: to soften up (*sturmreif*) Austria for a German take-over.[25] As early as October 1934, Papen attempted to restore Germany's influence by proposing a German-Austrian treaty of friendship, but the Austrian foreign ministry rebuffed him.[26]

Despite the rejection, Papen continued to advocate an evolutionary course, and subsequent event in Europe favored this approach, at least in the short run. Germany's accelerated armaments program and France's attempts to establish an anti-German coalition induced Hitler to defer for the moment any plans for Anschluss. When Papen went to Berlin in early 1935, Hitler told him that German foreign policy for the next two years would have to be low key and that he should undertake nothing that could be construed as interference in Austrian domestic affairs.[27] To reduce tension between Germany and Austria, Papen suggested a halt to German press attacks on Austria. Goebbels ordered the German press to comply, and, in a speech on May 21, Hitler stated that "Germany neither intends nor wishes to interfere in the internal affairs of Austria, to annex Austria or to conclude an 'Anschluss'".[28] It cannot be determined whether Hitler's inclusion of this conciliatory phrase was a result of Papen's influence or not, although Papen claims in his memoirs that it was.[29]

Back in Vienna, Papen again proposed a bilateral agreement to Schuschnigg. This time the Austrian chancellor asked him to submit "a detailed proposal" for such an arrangement.[30] On Papen's next visit to Berlin, he refrained from spelling out the details of his conversations with Schuschnigg, mentioning instead only something about "furthering the understanding between Austria . . .[and Germany] through conversations with [Schuschnigg] . . . and perhaps Starhemberg . . ."[31] Hitler once again told Papen "that at present nothing should be done which would be [calculated] to bring the Austrian problem into the limelight."[32] Despite this warning, only a week later Papen submitted a draft of a bilateral agreement to the Austrians, emphasizing that it "was entirely . . .[his] own proposal, although . . . admittedly . . .[he had] been fully authorized . . . to negotiate with the Austrian Government on all questions . . ."[33]

It took the Austrians two and a half months to respond to Papen's proposal with one of their own.[34] A comparison of the Papen and Austrian drafts of the agreement shows that the Austrians had generally accepted the essence of Papen's proposal, which formed the basis of the subsequent Austro-German agreement of July 1936.[35]

According to the terms of this agreement, the two governments recognized and affirmed each other's legitimacy. The Germans denied any desire to interfere in the internal affairs of Austria, and the Austrians that their country was a German state. There were further provisions regarding economic cultural, and press relations, emigre problems, tourist traffic, and procedures for adjusting grievances and complaints.[36]

Schuschnigg's motives for concluding the Agreement were twofold. He wanted to avoid any provocation that might result in a forceful German takeover of Austria, and he hoped that through closer economic cooperation with Germany, Austria would overcome her severe unemployment problem and would recover from the deep economic depression. Essentially, Schuschnigg was delaying, believing that the European balance of power would be more favorable to Austria in a few years.[37]

On the German side, the aid of the agreement was to remove the Austrian problem from the international scene, legalize the Austrian Nazi Party so that it would be able to agitate more forcefully for the Anschluss and, by expanding Austro-German cultural relations, weaken and undermine Austria's identity.[38]

Austria's readiness to sign such an agreement seems to have been the result of the Austrian government's realization that Mussolini might be too preoccupied with Ethiopia to continue to protect Austria's independence.[39] When Papen saw Hitler shortly after receiving the Austrian draft, Hitler agreed that Papen should continue negotiations with the Austrians but should also exercise considerable restraint in his future conversations.   Papen seems to have followed Hitler's instructions, because no discussions took place for the rest of the year. Then, early in January, 1936, Mussolini announced to Hassell, the German ambassador, that, as far as Italy was concerned, Germany and Austria should settle their own differences in the future, a statement clearly indicating the end of Italy's guarantee of Austrian independence.[40] Neurath informed Papen of Mussolini's change of policy and advised Papen to let the Austrians make the first move to negotiate a pact with Germany.[41]   However, the Austrians, still reluctant to conclude a bilateral pact with the Germans, suggested instead that an Austro-German settlement be made part of an anti-Jewish Freemason front that would include Germany, Italy, Austria, and Hungary.[42]   Papen expressed some skepticism about the appropriateness and feasibility of such a scheme, but when Schuschnigg later proposed a joint Austro-German declaration for "the protection of German interest," it became clear that Papen's evolutionary policy was working.[43]

In May 1936 Guido Schmidt, Schuschnigg's foreign policy advisor and later secretary of foreign affairs, asked Papen about a resumption of bilateral talks and Papen expressed his willingness to do so.[44] In a subsequent conversation, the Austrian Chancellor indicated that he was prepared to include certain members of the Austrian Nazi Party in his government and to discuss restoring normal relations with Germany.[45] When Papen told Hitler about these negotiations, the Fuehrer urged a continuation of talks and even said that he would be willing to meet with an Austrian negotiator.[46] No such meeting took place, because Papen and Schuschnigg were able to conclude the negotiations themselves; they signed the German-Austrian Gentlemen's Agreement on July 11, 1936.[47]

The Agreement was, without a doubt, an important step in reconciling Austria and Germany after the failed Putsch of 1934; it was also the major achievement of Papen's Austrian mission. That the Austrians were driven by necessity to sign the agreement is clear, but it is also true that Papen advocated the resumption of normal relations and the signing of such an agreement long before Germany's move in the Rhineland and Mussolini's preoccupation with Ethiopia made the agreement essential for Austria. The Agreement was also an important step in the implementation of Papen's policy toward Anschluss. He had been successful in shifting public opinion in Austria toward Germany, and then events had intervened to persuade Mussolini that the Austrians and Germans should be left to settle their grievances themselves. Papen was then instrumental in convincing Schuschnigg to accept the moderate Austrian Nazis, the so-called National Opposition, into his government and to sign the Austro-German Agreement. Once in the government, Papen intended the Nazis to play the role of the Trojan Horse, i.e., to undermine the government from within until it was ripe for Anschluss.[48] The Austro-German Agreement thus eliminated the Austrian problem from the international scene and gave Hitler time to prepare for the Anschluss at a time of his own choosing. In recognition of Papen's role in achieving this goal, Hitler conferred the rank of ambassador on Papen.[49]

The July Agreement represented the high point of Papen's tenure in Austria; his influence thereafter declined substantially as Goering, leader of the Four-Year-Plan, increasingly stressed Austro-German economic cooperation. Papen's chance to participate again in the *Grosse Politik* came in September 1937, on the occasion of Mussolini's visit to Germany, when Papen suggested, with Hitler's concurrence, that in exchange for German support for Mussolini's foreign adventures, Mussolini should agree to closer German-Austrian economic and military cooperation.[50] At subsequent meetings between Papen, Goering, and Mussolini, the Duce expressed considerable sympathy for Germany's position as long as Austria's independence was formally recognized. These talks thus enabled Papen to further distance Austria from Italy and to reinforce Mussolini's abdication of his role as Austria's protector. Shortly thereafter, Britain and France declared themselves in favor of a peaceful resolution of the Austrian problem, thus virtually eliminating any threat of foreign intervention in an Anschluss between Austria and Germany.[51]

There were discussions in Berlin about the incorporation of Austria into the Reich, primarily for strategic and economic reasons, as early as November, 1937, and it was at this time that Papen suggested to Schuschnigg that he meet with Hitler.[52] Hitler himself states that he decided in January of 1938 "to bring about the self-determination of the 6 1/2 million Germans in Austria in one way or another."[53] At the same time the radical wing of the Austrian Nazi party planned to incite disturbances in Austria and if necessary to assassinate Papen as a convenient excuse for a German invasion.[54] (The plan for Papen's assassination, known as the Tavs Plan, was found with other incriminating documents in January 1938 by the Austrian police among the papers at Nazi Party headquarters in Vienna).[55] When Schuschnigg was told about the Nazi plans to incite mass riots, he believed that this information would give him an important advantage in a meeting with Hitler. When Papen extended an official invitation on January 26, Schuschnigg accepted.[56]

In the midst of preparations for this historic meeting, Hitler decided to replace several of the older, more conservative members of the armed forces and the diplomatic corps with more pliable and younger Nazi Party members. In the course of these changes, Papen was recalled from Vienna and his mission was terminated.[57] Papen's reaction was one of complete surprise. His first thought was that it was essential to deposit "copies of all . . .[his] correspondence with Hitler in a safe place, so that they could not be destroyed by the Gestapo."[58] His assistant Wilhelm von Ketteler did in fact take these documents to Lichtenstein for safekeeping.[59] Disappointed and angry about his dismissal just at the time when his plans for the meeting were about to be realized, Papen went to see Hitler at Berchtesgaden where he persuaded the Chancellor to let him return to Vienna and to participate in the forthcoming meeting. Although the major outlines of the Hitler-Schuschnigg meeting at Berchtesgaden on February 12, 1938, are well-known, Papen's role in the final preparations for the Anschluss is somewhat obscure.[60]

After Papen and Schuschnigg returned to Vienna, Papen helped Schusschnigg draft a face-saving communique,[61] but the two later fell out over the implications of the Berchtesgaden meeting and Schuschnigg's subsequent speech.[62] In this speech, Schuschnigg in a vain attempt to reaffirm Austria's independence called for a plebiscite. Hitler, who considered this move a violation of the Berchtergaden agreement, was furious and directed the charge d'affaires in Vienna to lodge a protest.[63] When the Austrians rejected it, Hitler asked Papen to intervene, and the latter, no longer in an official capacity, talked privately to Schmidt, the Austrian foreign secretary. Papen suggested first that the plebiscite be postponed. When Schmidt rejected that, he proposed a change to the text, but this was also not accepted by the Austrian official. When Papen reported this to Berlin, Hitler asked him to come to the Reich Chancellery the next day.[64]   According   to Papen, everything at the Chancellery was in chaos. Hitler raved and ranted and threatened to invade Austria unless the Austrians called the plebiscite off immediately. Papen was able to calm him. For a while it looked as though a peaceful solution might be found. Then Goering took over, arranged for the Austrian Nazis to request German military intervention,[65] and on March 10, Hitler ordered military operations to start two days later.[66] On March 13, Hitler ordered Papen to meet him in Vienna. An official Nazi Party announcement over the German radio broadcast the news that "The Fuehrer has received Minister Franz von Papen into the National Socialist German Worker's Party in appreciation of his valuable services and has awarded him the Gold Medal."[67]

We now know that the Anschluss was but a step in Hitler's drive to the East. At the time, there was widespread popular enthusiasm for the Anschluss both in Austria as well as in Germany. A great majority of Austrians and Germans believed that the incorporation of Austria into the Reich was the fulfillment of an age old dream for Greater Germany that had eluded Bismarck.

Papen played a detective role in bringing about the Anschluss. Against considerable odds, he managed to strengthen the moderate wing of the Austrian Nazi Party and to induce Schuschnigg to let them enter the government. From the very beginning of his ambassadorship, Papen sought a bilateral agreement with Austria. Taking advantage of favorable conditions in the European balance of power, he was able to achieve it. He was also instrumental in arranging the fateful Hitler-Schuschnigg meeting at Berchtesgaden in February 1938, which laid the ground work for the subsequent Anschluss.

Papen's Austrian policy was from the very beginning aimed at a peaceful, evolutionary, and voluntary incorporation of Austria into the Reich, and in his approach he had the support of a considerable number of Austrians. That the Anschluss came sooner and in a somewhat different form from the one Papen had envisaged, was due more to the immediate circumstances and to Hitler's reaction to Schuschnigg's call for a plebiscite than to anything else. In 1938 Papen, like most of the old-line German conservatives, refused (or was unable) either to recognize Hitler's real goals or that Hitler was using him and other conservatives to achieve them.

ABBREVIATIONS

DGFP   *Documents on German Foreign Policy 1918-1945* 19
vols., (Government Printing Office, Washington, D.C., 1949-83)
HHStA Haus-, Hof-, und Staatsarchiv, Vienna
IMT   International Military Tribunal, *Trial of the Major War
Criminals*, 42 vols., (Nuremberg 1947-49)
Memoirs Franz von Papen, *Memoirs*, (London 1952)
Schmidt Prozess *Der Hochverratsprozess gegen Dr. Guido
Schmidt*, (Vienna 1947)

NOTES

1. For a discussion of the term "Anschluss," see G. Botz, "Der Ambivalente
'Anschluss' 1938/39.   Von   der   Begeisterung   zur   Ernuechterung,"
Zeitgeschiehte, 6.Jahrg., Heft 3, Dez. 1978, 91-109.
2. For the events in Austria in July 1934, see N. Schausberger, *Der Griff
nach Oesterreich*, (Vienna, 1978),. 265ff and G. Jagschitz, *Der Putsch*, (Graz,
1976) passim.
3. "Ein Begleiter Papen's schilderte die Verhaeltnisse wie sie am 26. Juli
in der Umgebung Hitlers geherrscht haben, als total beschissen...er haette noch
nie gesehen, dass die Leute die Hose so voll gehabt haetten wie hier..."
(Tauschitz an Berger-Waldenegg, Berlin, 21.   August 1934, Hornbostel
Nachlass, HHStA, Vienna).
4. E. Hanfstaegl, *Unheard Witness*, (Philadelphia, 1957), 277.
5. F. V. Papen, *Memoirs*, (London, 1952), 338.
6. According to Papen, he insisted on the following conditions: Habicht
would be dismissed. The German Nazi Party would not interfere in Austrian
internal affairs.   Austria's union with Germany would be achieved by
evolutionary methods and not by force, and his mission would end as soon as
normal relations had been established. Also, he would report directly to Hitler
and not to the Foreign Minister. (*Memoirs*, 340-41). For Hitler's letter to
Papen of July 26, 1934, see DGFP, C III, doc. no. 123 and for a different
assessment, J. L. Heinemann, *Hitler's First Foreign Minister*, 107.
7. DGFP, C III:235, fn. 3.

8. *Protokolle des Ministerrats der Ersten Republik,* (Vienna, 1986), Bd. 7, Protocol of July 27, 1934, 662-72.

9. According to a report by M. Hemberger, the former Berlin correspondent of the *Prager Presse,* the *Wiener Tag,* and the *Stunde,* Papen was supposed to go first as ambassador to the Vatican; this fell through, however, when the Vatican refused to accept him. According to Edgar Jung, whom Hemberger knew personally, Papen felt very insecure in Germany after his Marburg speech, and desperately wanted to go abroad. He had no standing whatever in Germany and did not have the confidence of Hitler. (Unsigned Memo of August 8, 1934, Hornbostel Paper, HHSTA, Vienna). According to another report (cf fn. 3), Papen hesitated to accept the post in Vienna because he did not have Hitler's full confidence after the murder of Jung and Bose. Hitler was supposed to have assured Papen of his confidence but added, that "only in Papen's Office and certainly without his (i.e., Papen's) knowledge, things were not as they should be." There were also rumors of attempts on Papen's life by the SS in retaliation for his Marburg speech and to create tension between Germany and Austria.

10. "Minutes of the Austrian Ministerial Council of August 7, 1934," Oesterr. Verwaltungsarchiv MRP 961/1. Vienna.

11. *Memoir,* 338-40.

12. Ibid., 346. Although Papen presents himself in this episode as the savior of western civilization, I think it is likely that he accepted the appointment because he was unwilling to be relegated to the sidelines.

13. DGFP, D I no. 196, esp. p. 374; C III no. 167, Encl. 2. No. 186. N. Schausberger, "Zur Vorgeschichte der Annexion Oesterreichs," Anschluss 1938, 2-3. According to G. Jagschitz, "The '*Anschluss*' was still the final aim of German foreign policy and Papen was therefore instrumental in fulfilling nationalsocialist expansion interests though he was more flexible and more discriminating than his predecessor." "Zwischen Befriedung und Konfrontation," *Das Juliabkommen von 1936,* 158. See also G. Messersmith Affidavit of August 30, 1945, IMT, xxx, 2385PS:295ff, esp. 296-97.

14. F. Mueller, "Franz von Papen und die deutsche Oesterreichpolitik," *Tirol und der Anschluss,* (Innsbruck, 1988), 357-83, esp. 360 and notes.

15. Ibid., 364 and fns. 42, 43, 44.

16. *Memoirs,* 347.

17. Ibid., 351. According to Theodore Hornbostel, director of the Political Division in the Austrian Foreign Ministry,' Papen was coming to Vienna as the "boykottierte Friedensbote" and the "Steigbuegelhalter Hitlers." (Schmidt Prozess, 171).

18. *Memoirs,* 351.

19. F. Mueller,"Franz von Papen," 369-70.

20. *Memoirs*, 347. For Hitler's dismissal of Leopold, the leader of the Austrian radical Nazis, see E. A. Schmidl, *Maerz 38. Der deutsche Einmarsch in Oesterreich*, (Vienna, 1987), 78-79.

21. E. Weinzierl-Fischer, "Oesterreichs Katholiken und der Nationalsozialismus," II, *Wort und Wahrheit* 18 (8/9, August/September 1963):497.

22. Ibid., 508.

23. F. Mueller, "Franz von Papen," 364-65; on Funder see DGFP, C IV no. 428, p. 854. Rebuffed by the Austrian Catholic hierarchy, Papen renewed his friendship with bishop Alois Hudal, whose Nazi sympathies were well known and who, in his book *Die Grundlagen des Nationalsozialismus*, (Leipzig 1936), had tried to reconcile the beliefs of the Roman Catholic Church with the ideas of the Third Reich. For Papen's views on Hudal's book, see A. C. Hudal, *Foemische Tagebuecher*, (Graz, 1976), 134-36.

24. N. Schausberger, *Der Griff nach Oesterreich*, 309 and footnotes; *Memoirs*, 346ff.

25. Berger-Waldenegg's testimony in the *Schmidt Prozess*, 287 and Hornbostel's testimony, ibid., 171.

26. Ibid.

27. IMT, 28, 1760PS:270.

28. DGFP, C IV:174.

29. *Memoirs*, 361.

30. DGFP, C IV no. 111:217 and Neurath's comments.

31. Ibid., no. 197:422.

32. Ibid.

33. Ibid., no. 203:434. *Memoirs*, 362ff. That Papen often acted independently, is shown by a note from Koepke to Hassel, "All this, of course, will not prevent Herr von Papen from suggesting . . . to the Austrians [proposals] on his own responsibility, as before . . . (C IV:422-23).

34. DGFP, C IV no. 319:676-78. In his *Memoirs*, 362. Papen claimed that he had reminded Berger-Waldenegg on September 9 of their conversation of the previous July, "and informed the Foreign Minister that Hitler had expressed his approval of my proposal." I could find no record of this conversation or of Hitler's approval. See also, *Schmidt Prozess*, 168/1 and Schuschnigg, *Ein Requiem*, 245ff.

35. *Memoirs*, 363. DGFP, C IV:678.

36. Ibid., C V, Editors' Note, 755-60.

37. For Schuschnigg's view, see his *The Brutal Takeover* (London, 1971), 139-146.

38. Schausberger, *Der Griff nach Oesterreich*, 352.

39. Cf. DGFP, C IV no. 349:725.

40. Ibid., no. 485:975. See also G. Weinberg, *The Foreign Policy of Hitler's Germany* (Chicago, 1970) 1:264 ff.

41. DGFP, C IV, no. 515:1030-31.

42. Ibid., no. 556:1127.

43. Ibid., no. 586:1191.

44. Schmidt Prozess, 35/1, 661/1,2. *Memoirs*, 368.

45. Ibid., 369. DGFP, C V, no. 304:499.

46. Ibid., no. 321:537.

47. Ibid., nos. 351, 357, 369, 371, 389, 395, 401, 407, 408, 415, 423, 424, 426. *Memoirs*, 369-70. Weinberg, op. cit. 1:268-69.

48. See Dodd's interrogation of Papen, 3413PS, 3414PS at Nuremberg, unpublished; also Schausberger, *Der Griff nach Oesterreich*, 352, and *Memoirs*, 376.

49. Ibid., 372.

50. DGFP, D I, no. 1:1-2; no. 252:458-59. Weinberg, op. cit., 2:279-83.

51. F. Mueller, "Franz von Papen," 374, fn. 104. For the Hitler-Halifax meeting, see DGFP, D I, no. 31; for the Hossbach Memorandum, ibid., no. 19, and Schausberger, *Der Griff nach Oesterreich*, 421-24 and fn. 100. Weinberg *Foreign Policy*, 2:283.

52. Schausberger, *Der Griff nach Oesterrich*, 492 ff.

53. Ibid., 504. fn. 46. Weinberg,Foreign Policy, 2:287-89 and fns. 117-25.

54. L. Hohenecker, "Der Kampf um Oesterreich im Jahre 1937," in *Oesterreich in Geschichte und Literatur*, 12 May 1968, 265.

55. Schausberger, *Der Griff nach Oesterreich*, 508 ff.

56. Ibid., 511. *Schmidt Prozess*, 557.

57. Schausberger, *Der Griff nach Oesterreich*, 516; IMT, 16:349-50.

58. *Memoirs*, 407, 424.

59. Conversation with H. V. Halem in Schauu, Lichtenstein, 21 June 1987. Wilhelm von Ketteler, who, together with Jung and Bose, had been Papen's assistants in Berlin, had followed Papen to Vienna and had, apparently, been in touch with Catholic anti-Nazi groups in Vienna. A few weeks after the *Anschluss*, Ketteler's body was pulled from the Danube and it was later established that he had been murdered by the SS. H. Graml, "Vorhut konservativen Widerstands. Das Ende des Kreises um Edgar Jung", in H. Graml, Ed., *Widerstand im Dritten Reich*, (Frankfurt a. M., 1984), 172-82.

60. For the different versions of the Berchtesgaden meeting and Papen's role, see *Memoirs*, 409-21; K. V. Schuschnigg, *Ein Requiem in Rot-Weiss-Rot*, (Zurich, n.d.), 37-52 and *Im Kampf gegen Hitler*, (Vienna, 1969), Weinberg,

Foreign Policy, 2:291-92, fn. 135.

61. Text in *Documents on International Affairs*, 1938, 2:47-48.

62. DGFP, D I, no. 327. *Memoirs*, 421, 423-24. See also Schuschnigg *Im Kampf gegen Hitler*, 224; and W. J. Leavey, "Hitler's Envoy 'Extraordinary' - Franz von Papen: Ambassador to Austria, 1934-38 and Turkey, 1939-44," unpublished Ph.D. dissertation, St. John's University (New York, 1968), 141.

63. DGFP D I, no. 341. *Schmidt Prozess*, 380ff. D. Wagner, G. Tomkowitz, *Anschluss*, (New York, 1971), 47. *Anschluss 1938* (Vienna, 1988), 245.

64. *Memoirs*, 426-27. Wagner, Tomkowitz, 47-48.

65. Ibid., 96ff. DGFP, D I, Editors' Note, 568.

66. IMT, 9:296-99. *Anschluss* 1938, 302-04.

67. Quoted by Wagner, Tomkowitz, 215.

THE UNIVERSITY OF VIENNA AND THE *ANSCHLUSS*

JOHN HAAG

Long before March 1938 most of its students and faculty regarded the University of Vienna as a German institution, not an Austrian one. Intellectually, Anschluss had taken place long before the Ides of March. Starting in the 1870s a growing number of Austrian intellectuals began to worship at the shrine of Pan-Germanism, uncritically accepting its ideals of *macht*--success at any price--and war as the "creator of all things." The ignominious collapse of both the Dual Monarchy and the Hohezollern-Bismarckian Reich in November 1918 did little to redirect these energies. If they were not in the Catholic or Marxist *Lager*, Austrian *deutschnational* intellectuals continued to believe that only a fusion of the German-speaking territory of the defunct Habsburg state with the German Reich could save the German *Volk*.

The German pacifist Friedrich Wilhelm Foerster, who taught briefly in Vienna before 1914 (and found himself the object of violent protests by his *volkisch* students) summed up this situation in his memoirs.

> Austria's greatest misfortune was her rootless intellectuals, who for more than fifty years were befuddled [*benebelt*] by the successes of the Hohenzollern Reich, its power, technology and science, and who thus no longer had any inkling of the true German mission in Europe or of the deep nature of it links with the Slavic world. Instead of directing their intelligence to this goal, they knew nothing but a Pan-German intoxication and hatred against the Slavs....[1]

The defeat of 1918 led to a brief flurry of reform movements at most Austrian *Hochschulen*, particularly at the University of Vienna. Many of the reform organizations, including those of the Social Democrats, enjoyed a large increase in membership. Yet these were essentially illusory transformations, and many of these new members were political opportunists (*Konjunkturmitglieder* or *Kartoffelmitglieder*) who quickly dropped out when it became clear by the fall of 1919, at the latest, that the basically authoritarian nature of Austrian academic life was not going to change. An ominous sign of growing disaffection during this time of hope was the highly successful boycott in November 1919 of the celebrations of the first anniversary of the Republic by both faculty and students.[2]

The *Deutsche Studentenschaft* was founded in the spring of 1920 at the University of Vienna. While it shared the same name as the Pan-german student organization created at Wurzburg in the summer of 1919 and was in fact a component part of it, the University of Vienna's Deutsche *Studentenschaft* shared none of the liberal and democratic ideals that could still be seen--if only imperfectly at times--in the Wurzburg entity. Vienna's *Deutsche Studentenschaft* was from birth an aggressively racist and chauvinistic organization. It appeared in April 1920 as a result of savage antisemitic riots, and until it was banned by the Dollfuss regime in August 1933 it set the tone for much of Viennese student life--brutal, demagogic, and bloodily confrontational.[3]

Student *Krawalle* were nothing new in Vienna, dating back centuries, but since the 1880s they had taken on bloodier forms as the new political culture of illiberalism flourished under the brilliant and unscrupulous Georg von Schonerer. Starting in the 1880s German-nationalist *Burschenschaften* concentrated on attacking the growing pro-Habsburg Catholic student groups, the *Cartellverband* (CV), while after 1900 it was increasingly the Jewish students (particularly Zionists, but also Social Democrats as well, many of whom were of Jewish origins) who had to defend their rights against the terror of the duelling fraternities. The duelling fraternities continued to attack the Catholics, but it was clear even before 1914 that the task of warring against Catholics, Jews, and Marxists all at once was a hopeless proposition. The coming of war in 1914 brought a *Burgfrieden* among all student groups, but by 1916 the Catholics and duelling students had reverted to their traditional hatreds and were organizing an antisemitic, anti-Marxist coalition that was officially announced to the public in June 1918 and would last with few minor interruptions until 1932.[4]

After 1920, Jews, Marxists, liberals, pacifists, and democrats as well as Catholics who did not accept the Pan-Germanism of their academic elders found themselves without protection--*vogelfrei*--at the University of Vienna and other Austrian *Hochschulen*. The case of Ernst Karl Winter is instructive in this regard. A conservative Catholic

Monarchist and believer in a separate Austrian identity, Winter never had his *Habilitation* approved at the University of Vienna despite his undoubted intellectual brilliance. Winter's cardinal sin was his belief in a separate Austrian identity and his stubborn rejection of the idea of *Anschluss*. Winter's intellectual independence incurred the permanent emnity of Professor Othmar Spann, the uncrowned king of the University. Without an accepted *Habilitationsschrift*, an academic career remained closed to Winter.[5]

The entire Jewish minority found itself frozen out of the academic profession by 1923. With a few exceptions in the Medical Faculty, even the most brilliant Jews were excluded from teaching careers by the simple expedient of an unwritten faculty rule of denying *Habilitationen* to Jewish candidates. A secret organization called the *Deutsche Gemeinschaft*, which included as members many prominent senior faculty, was able to frustrate the careers of not only Jewish but ideologically unacceptable non-Jewish faculty members as well. Lists of "crooked" (*ungerad*) faculty were circulated by this organization, which exercised immense power at the University of Vienna in the 1920s.[6]

Not only organizations but also individuals were able to mold the University of Vienna in an intolerant image after 1918. The dermatologist Gustav Riehl, Rector of the University for academic year 1921/22, was able with considerable effort to exclude Jewish talent from his First Dematological Clinic. Upon his retirement in 1926, he was able to pass the Clinic on to his successor *judenrein*--an amazing achievement in view of the fact that Jewish physicians had for decades excelled in the area of dermatology.[7]

Antisemitism and anti-Marxism took tangible form not only in the violence of the *Deutsche Studentenschaft* but in the appearance of the National Socialist movement at the University of Vienna. Already in the early 1920s the Viennese press called the racist students *Hakenkreuzler*, but few of them were members of the insignificant Austrian NSDAP. Indeed, as early as 1919 a National Socialist student group was in existence at the University, but this organization was composed almost exclusively of Sudeten Germans with little if any contacts to the Nazi movement in Munich.[8] Not until 1926 was a Nazi student organization chartered at the University of Vienna.[9]

By 1929, the University of Vienna had become virtually an enclave of the Third Reich within Red Vienna. The tradition of academic autonomy, the inviolability of *Hochschulboden*, permitted the most violent outrages against Jewish and other "unacceptable" students to take place under the auspices of the *Deutsche Studentenschaft*. Only rarely did University officials take vigorous action to restore order. Ironically, it was during academic year 1928/29 that the last Rector who made a serious attempt to halt the Nazi tide appeared on the scene--the "*Friedensrektor*" Professor Theodor Innitzer.[10]

The attitude of the faculty toward the bloody *Krawalle* was, with few exceptions, a negative one. Even the most militantly *volkisch* faculty members regarded these riots as manifestations of an unfortunate gutter mentality, a crude *Radauantisemitismus* that could only tarnish nationalist ideals. Yet faculty censure was essentially passive, and it is significant that from 1920 to 1933, when these riots occurred at the University of Vienna (and virtually all other Austrian *Hochschulen* as well), few voices other than those of a handful of Social Democratic faculty members were raised in public protest against these bloodly confrontations.

Typical of the majority conservative faculty response to violence were the comments made by the Dean of the Vienna Law Faculty Professor Alexander Hold-Ferneck during one of the bloodiest student disturbances of the interwar years, that of November 1929. Appearing before a group of rioting students, Hold-Ferneck in no way condemned the ongoing bloody attacks on Jews. Instead, he noted the difficulties this kind of antisemitism was creating for the academic authorities who, while they were fully in sympathy with the goals of the *Deutsche Studentenschaft*, felt that its violent methods were creating difficulties for the nationalist cause. Hold-Ferneck began his address by calling for three cheers for the D S. He ended it not by calling for an end to the riot but by cautioning the rowdies simply not to "be so awkward" in their actions.[11]

By the late 1920s, Austria was well on the road to civil war. The burning of the Palace of Justice in July 1927 resulted not only in many casualties but in the reemergence of the *Heimwehr* movement and a growing belief that the Austrian Right could soon crush Marxism and create a Fascist Corporate State. The universities--whose radical antisemitism and anti-Marxism had diminished in intensity from 1925 through 1927--now consciously rekindled the flames of violent nationalism. The November 1929 riots far exceeded anything before. Female students were brutally attacked if they wore bobbed hair (*Bubikopf*), a sign of defiantly "un-German" feminine assertiveness. At the Anatomical Institute on the Alserstrasse, the lecture hall of noted

Jewish professor Julius Tandler was demolished. The Nazi students broke into the dissection rooms throwing scalpels, parts of cadavers, and anything else they could find against the Jewish and other "un-German" students.[12]

The situation deteriorated dramatically after 1929. In April 1930, the University's Academic Senate announced an ordinance for student political representation by "Nations." This harkened back to the medieval notion of academic self-government--not abolished in Vienna until 1849. In real terms it was almost totally directed against the Jewish student minority. "Aryans" were now regarded as the only true student citizens of the University with the Jews and other "aliens" merely granted the rights of barely tolerated guests.[13] When the Austrian constitutional court declared this internal regulation invalid on a technicality in June 1931, the University erupted in an explosive outburst of antisemitic violence that also disrupted a Rotary International convention that happened to be taking place at the same time. As Austria and Germany plunged deeper into depression, the Nazification of the student body of both countries accelerated. At the convention of the Deutsche Studentenshcaft in Graz in 1931, the Nazis succeeded in capturing the leadership of the organization--the first major institution in Germany to fall to the Nazis.

A culture of violence was pervasive at the University of Vienna in the 1930s. The friend-foe world extended beyond the occasional bloody *Krawalle*. Students walking to their classrooms every day passed by the announcement cases of various fraternities, the Nazi, Social Democratic and Communist parties, and the *Deutsche Studentenschaft*. Bulletins and posters mercilessly attacked ideological opponents, while the propaganda of the Nazi student organization specialized in scurrilous antisemitic caricatures.[14]

At times the underlying violence burst forth with sudden drama. In 1932, Professor Gustav Alexander of the medical faculty was shot dead by a demented patient. The same year, Professor Othenio Abel was the target of an assassination attempt by an embittered faculty colleague, whose aim was fortunately poor so that Abel remained uninjured.[15] In neither case were political motives at work, but the message was clear. The University was no longer a tranquil sanctuary. The tensions and demented behavior of the "real world" now brutally penetrated academic precincts. The climax of this violence was the murder of the eminent philosopher Professor Moritz Schlick at the University on June 22, 1936. Here too the motives were more personal than political, but

Schlick had by the late 1920s become a symbol of progressive, even radical ideas and was much hated by conservatives because of the anti-traditional implications of the thinking of his Vienna Circle. Few on the political Right shed even crocodile tears upon hearing of Professor Schlick's violent end.

Schlick had come to Vienna in 1922 largely as a result of the efforts of the mathematician Hans Hahn, one of few Social Democrats on the faculty. Within a few years Schlick would be condemned as a Jew (which he was not, being a descendant of the famous Ernst Moritz Arndt) and as an advocate of free-thinking and atheism. Schlick recognized the threat posed by Nazism and despite his liberal ideals was willing to work with the lesser evil of Austro-Fascism and offer his services to the Dollfuss regime.[16]

The basic mood at the University of Vienna from 1933 to 1938 was one of watchful waiting. Most faculty and students believed that Austria's fate was out of its own hands. The increasingly powerful German *Reich* would in the final analysis determine the future of a generation of young men and women for whom the present was full of difficulties and frustrations. While surviving many took out "insurance policies" for what they saw as the inevitable *Anschluss* to Hitler's Germany. One such individual was Theodor Vieter. Born in 1907, Vieter was active in Catholic student politics at the University of Vienna as a member of the monarchist *CV* fraternity "Rudolfina," using his political skills to become chairman of the Katholisch-Deutsche Hochschulerschaft Osterreichs. This post became a stepping-stone to his first job in 1929, that of secretary to the Christlichsozial delegates to the Bundsrat, a post he held until the abolition of political parties in 1934.

Veiter made a name in the early 1930s as a publicist, criticizing democratic institutions in the Christian Social newspaper *Reichspost*. He placed his political bets on a shrewd peasant, Engelbert Dollfuss, who in 1934 made Veiter--a fellow "*CV-Bruder*"--a political editor in the Government Information Office (Amtliche Nachrichtenstelle). While working for the Catholic-dominated anti-Nazi Dollfuss regime, on June 19, 1934, Theodor Veiter joined the illegal Nazi party, Breitenfeld local branch, as applicant no. 14,391. His cover name was "Dr. Theodor Innerer." By the time Dollfuss was killed in the botched Nazi coup attempt of July 25, 1934, Vieter was a full-fledged member of the underground Austrian Nazi Party, an "*Illegaler*." Theodor Veiter played his double game in 1936 becoming president of the

International Catholic Students' Organization "Pax Romana." In August 1937, the Pope awarded Veiter the Knight's Cross of the Order of St. Gregory.[17]

While few became as adroit in their opportunism as Theodor Veiter, many conservative Austrian intellectuals were able to rationalize their belief that an *Anschluss* between their impoverished state and the prosperous, respected German Reich was quite compatible with their own religious and moral values. Whatever excesses had occurred in Germany--the bloody purge of June 30, 1934, for example--were to be explained by the fact that while some of his underlings were indeed capable of thuggery, Adolf Hitler himself was a many of truly noble motives. The University of Vienna historian Heinrich Ritter von Srbik held firmly to this belief throughout the 1930s. Writing to fellow-historian Oswald Redlich a few days before the signing of the July 1936 Austro-German Agreement, Srbik described Hitler as "an unusual man in whom millions have a blind trust." Srbik glanced back at the bloody purge of June 30, 1934 in Germany as well as the failed Nazi putsch of July 25, 1934 in Austria, describing these events as "ghastly" but hastening to add that the victims of the Rohm purge had after all been "highly unworthy human beings."[18]

Despite immense evidence of the bloody nature of the Nazi regime thrown almost daily into their faces, most bourgeois Austrian intellectuals stubbornly held to the belief that the "true" Germany simply could not be guilty of the atrocities ascribed by German emigres and the foreign press. Typical of this desperate need to continue to believe in the essential decency of Germany after 1933 appears an incident involving the Austrian composer Anton von Webern.

Webern went to Spain in 1936 to conduct the world premiere of Alban Berg's violin concerto. Soloist Louis Krasner was Jewish and assumed that he and Webern would take the usual route from Vienna to Spain, namely through Switzerland. But Webern insisted on traveling an indirect route through Germany to get to Switzerland. When the train stopped in Munich, Von Webern--a withdrawn, shy man who was certainly not the convivial beer drinking type--invited Krasner to accompany him to the train station dining room for a beer. The beers were ordered and consumed in total silence. In the train after it crossed the German-Swiss frontier Webern asked his Jewish colleague, "Na, Krasner! Hat Ihnen jemand 'was getan?" (Well now, Krasner, were you injured in any way?). Webern had proven to himself, if not to Krasner, that in the "true" Germany Jews were not mistreated and that

the atrocity stories were in fact fabrications.[19]

It was not a real--and messy--world that Austrian intellectuals were drawn to in the 1930s but rather a *Wunschbild* of an ideal, much better reality. It was, as Klaus Breuning has pointed out, the "vision of the Reich" that deeply inspired German, particularly Catholic German, and Austrian intellectuals in the 1920s and 1930s.[20] These reactionary Utopias made a profound impression on academic youth. At the University of Vienna, the lectures of Professor Othmar Spann and his disciples made social and political Romanticism the dominant ideology of bourgeois intellectuals from about 1921 through the mid-1930s.

Spann's ideal was the *Standestaat*, a new-feudal authoritarian regime in which the proletariat was respectful of and obedient to its social superiors. More importantly, intellectuals in Spann's perfect Platonic society enjoyed immense prestige and were close to the centers of power. Spann and his University of Vienna disciples, Walter Heinrich, Jakob Baxa, Johann Sauter and others regarded the that was the basis of the neo-feudal ideology as the only authentic social science theory compatible with the German spirit.[21]

A curious mood of illusion and unreality prevailed in Viennese academic life on the eve of *Anschluss*. While it was almost universally acknowledged that Nazi Germany would place increasing pressure on Austria, few of the individuals whose lives and careers would be shattered in the event of annexation made serious plans for such an eventuality. The Jewish biologist Professor Hans Przibram, offered a position in the United States by his former assistant, Paul Weiss, then at the University of Chicago, refused the offer, finding it impossible to believe that "Austria could sink into barbarity."[22] Another case of astonishing blindness in the face of a clear and present danger was the attitude taken by Karl and Charlotte Buhler, who were both threatened because of their Social Democratic sympathies and Charlotte's Jewishness. Yet when offered positions in the United States in 1937, they declined, believing that Austria would somehow be able to remain free.[23]

By late 1937, tensions were clearly rising in Vienna. The July 1936 Austro-German agreement had opened the floodgates for Nazi influences, already deeply rooted at the University, where many students and faculty were prepared for the day when they would be privileged *Volksgenossen* in a glorious Third Reich. The changed psychological mood of late 1937 was most dramatically revealed in a strike of medical students that enlisted both Marxist and Nazi students in protests against a government plan to lengthen the period of medical study. The strike was a success, closing down the University and forcing the regime to make major concessions.[24]

By the first weeks of 1938, a ban on public manifestations of political allegiances--first issued by Rector Ernst Spath in September-- was being totally ignored by most students. As the 1937/38 winter semester drew to a close, many students increasingly neglected their studies in the belief that great events were soon to transpire. Many of the University's Nazi students were active members of the *SA* or *SS*, those in the latter organization being organized in *SS-Standarten* 11 and 89 of the *Allgemeine SS*. They now spent much of their time in the fraternity houses of *Burschenschaften* that had for several years been closely allied with the NSDAP despite the fact that their parent organizations in the Reich had been banned since 1935.

Just as the tradition-minded fraternities had earlier supported the underground Nazi cells, during the last months of Austrian independence a harmonious relationship between the generations appeared in the support given militant National Socialist students by their parents, many of whom were sympathetic to the movement without actually having joined it. The sons of Professors Othmar Spann, Hans Ubersberger, Othenio Abel and Karl Gottfried Hugelmann were all dedicated Nazis. All of them received varying degrees of emotional and material support from their "non-political" academic fathers. In the tense weeks before the *Anschluss*, the homes of Professors Hans Eppinger, Wilhelm Falta and Hans Spitzy served as quarters for Nazi student cells because of their proximity to the University.[25]

The naming of Arthur Seyss-Inquart as Minister of the Interior, a direct result of the Hitler Schuschnigg meeting held at Berchtesgaden on February 12, 1938, opened the floodgates of Nazism. The announcement of a sweeping amnesty for political prisoners on February 16 was followed up the next day by a directive from Minister of Instruction Hans Pernter that extended the amnesty to political infractions committed by secondary school and *Hochschul* students.[26] University Rector Spath continued the losing struggle he had waged since September against the Nazi student offensive, banning on February 24 any display of flags in black, white and red colors, the colors of Nazi Germany.[27] The Rector's directive was almost totally ignored as students could be seen in classrooms and hallways wearing *Hakenkreuz* pins, enthusiastically greeting one another with "Heil

Hitler!"

In the seemingly inevitable and inexorable Nazi sweep of Austrian higher education a few signs of resistance appeared on the eve of *Anschluss*. One was the attempt on the morning of March 9 by a representative of the illegal Social Democratic intellectuals' organization to establish ties with the *Hochschul* branch of the Vienna Fatherland Front organization.[28] While doubtless a sincere gesture, this attempt to forge a united anti-Nazi front was clearly too little and certainly too late.

March 11, a Friday, was marked by dramatic events in the streets of Vienna. That morning on the Florianigasse in the Josefstadt district bloody clashes took place between members of the *CY* fraternity "Austria" (Chancellor Kurt Schuschnigg's own *Verbindung*) and about ten *SA* men. The brawl resulted in fifteen casualties for the two groups, some serious.[29] Perhaps the most dramatic and moving event of that March 11 was the march down the Ringstrasse of a heterogeneous group of student supporters of Chancellor Schuschnigg's recently announced call for a plebiscite. Assembling at the University, students from the Socialist, Communist and conservative-monarchist *Lager* chanted "Freiheit fur Osterreich!" openly proclaiming their anti-Nazi yearnings as realistic hopes waned that Austria might preserve its independence.[30]

March 12 witnessed the *de facto* takeover of all Austrian *Hochschulen* by Nazi students and faculty. The University of Innsbruck had already been taken over on March 11 by students in *SS* uniforms who demanded that the current Rector be replaced by historian Harald Steinacker, a scholar in full sympathy with National Socialism. At the University of Vienna, the academic *Machtergreifung* was much less dramatic. Here Rector Spath, not a Nazi but a Sudeten German whose *deutschnational* allegiance few would question, lost no time in sending a letter to Austria's new Nazi chancellor Seyss-Inquart assuring him of the total loyalty of the venerable *Alma Mater Rudolphina* to the new state.[31] During the intoxicating first days of *Anschluss*, it appeared that the University of Vienna and other Austrian *Hochschulen* would receive their appropriate and generous rewards for their long and vigorous partisanship on behalf of the national cause. The first measures of the new, Nazi Austrian administration restored organizations banned in 1933, including the *Deutsche Studentenschaft* and a number of suppressed *Burschenschaften* and *Vereine*.[32] Yet, after the plebiscite of April 10, these non-Nazi bodies were liquidated in a thoroughgoing process of academic *Gleichschaltung*. By the summer of 1938, both the Catholic CV and the *deutschnational* fraternities disappeared, to be replaced by the totalitarian NSDStB, the National Socialist Student League.[33]

At the time of the *Anschluss*, Adolf Hitler snubbed the University-- perhaps the most *echt-Nazi* institution in all of Vienna, granting only a brief audience to all of the new Rectors at the Hotel Imperial on March 17.[34] This was hardly surprising, given Hitler's gut feeling that academics were essentially cowardly fence-sitters and impractical *Stubenhocker* (stay-at-homes), men constitutionally incapable of turning thoughts into deeds.[35] As for the University faculty, the new regime brought much more grief than joy. Probably the individual who received the greatest shock was Professor Othmar Spann, who had looked forward to *Anschluss* for decades, hoping that his own *standisch* theories would change the face of the new and unified German state. Spann celebrated the *Anschluss* with champagne, but glory turned to terror a few days later when the Gestapo appeared on his doorstep. Only the intervention of influential friends secured his release form Dachau.[36]   Another naive University of Vienna professor, the prehistorian Oswald Menghin, agreed to serve as Minister of Instruction in the Seyss-Inquart cabinet, but by May 1938 he had been removed by the ruthless *Gauleiter* Josef Burckel, who compounded Menghin's humiliation by liquidating the Ministry of Instruction.[37] Even the politically agile Theodor Veiter was unable to overcome strong Nazi prejudices against intellectuals; he was arrested, and although influential Nazi friends secured his release, Veiter was unable to be accepted into the NSDAP as a genuine *Alter Kampfer*.[38]

Students too often found the Third Reich quite different in reality from what they hoped. Many of the duelling students now discovered that they had not only lost their colorful *Burschenschaften* sub-culture but were often forced to do something they hoped to avoid as a result of their education, namely physical labor and contact with the working classes. The "socialist" aspect of National Socialism now demanded at least a symbolic bridging of the vast chasms of class suspicion that characterized the dead "system" of pre-*Anschluss* clerical-Fascist Austria. Consequently, some students were now compelled to work in factories and farms in order to shed the arrogant spirit of *Standesdunkel* (pride of place) that had previously alienated them from their fellow German *Volksgenossen*.[39]

The purge of Jewish and politically unreliable faculty members resulted in the intellectual decapitation of a University that even after 1918 had been able to retain much of its pre-1914 reputation. From late March 1938, when the first measures to combat "*Uberfremdung*: were announced to the events of *Kristallnacht* in November, after which they no longer could even enter institutions of higher learning, Austrian Jews and individuals of part-Jewish ancestry were rapidly excluded from all academic life.

On March 17, University faculty and staff swore allegiance to the new state; Jews and part-Jewish *Mischlinge* found themselves excluded. On March 29, further registration of Jews was banned, while those already enrolled were placed in a special category that permitted their expulsion at any time without cause. On April 29, a Jewish *Numerus clausus* of 2% was announced, it being noted that even this limit depended on whether all Aryans were able to register for specific courses. On May 2, Jews were informed they could only enter the University of Vienna with special permission. On October 1, the Jewish quota was reduced to 1% and the right to audit courses was denied to full Jews, while *Mischlinge* retained that privilege.[40]

As a result of *Kristallnacht* in November 1938, Jews were forbidden to enter all institutions of higher learning in the Reich. In Austria, a decree of November 29 forbade all Jews from entering all *Hochschul* libraries. In December 1938, those few Jews who still enjoyed special permission to carry out research in a private capacity in research institutes and libraries had that privilege cancelled. In May 1940 Jewish *Mischlinge* (as well as members of the Czech minority) were banned from entering all institutions of higher learning.[41]

What impact did *Anschluss* have on the University of Vienna? The purge of Jewish faculty virtually destroyed the medical school, with 153 of the 197 faculty members losing their positions. For the entire institution, the senior faculty--many of whom had earned international reputations in their fields--was virtually decapitated for both racial and political reasons. Of 186 full professors and 91 associates in academic year 1937/38, Nazification resulted in only 64 and 27 respectively keeping their positions.[42] Those who fled often were too old to resume their careers in other countries, thus denying the world important work.

Many of those who remained in Austria died in the Holocaust. Incomplete research indicates at least twelve faculty members died in Nazi death camps. At least three and possibly as many as six faculty members committed suicide, most of them in 1938. One of the oldest victims was Dr. Elise Richter, the first woman to receive a doctoral degree from an Austrian university and the first woman to achieve professorial rank in Austria.[43] She died, aged 78, at the "model concentration camp" Theresienstadt, whose first commandant, Dr. Siegfried Seidl, was also linked to the University of Vienna, having joined the Nazi party while studying law there.[44] Theresienstadt also claimed the lives of the biologist Hans Przibram, the neurologist Alexander Spitzer, and the law professors Josef Hupka and Stephan Brassloff.

By 1942 the University of Vienna had been thoroughly *gleichgeschaltet*. The Rector, botanist Fritz Knoll, served as *Führer* of an institution that obeyed the letter but not always the spirit of the laws of the Nazi state. Many faculty members remained morally obtuse to the destructive nature of National Socialism, unable to connect evils in the big picture with events taking place on their own speck of academic soil. Only such an interpretation can explain the 1941 attempt of Professor Viktor Christian, Dean of the philosophical faculty as well as an *SS-Hauptsturührer*, to attempt to halt the deportation to the East of a colleague's Jewish mother-in-law.[45] After Stalingrad, most of the University's students were at the front, with only women and wounded still attending classes on a regular basis. Only after massive military defeats did the faculty show evidence of disillusionment with National Socialism; even then, few seriously considered active involvement in resistance.[46] The liberation of Austria in April 1945 revealed a University of Vienna that had suffered severe physical damage. Less visible, but very likely more significant was the moral decay that had for decades severely weakened the edifice of learning, made a mockery of humane values, and left virtually undefended the liberal ideals of the nineteenth century. These profound human failings made it possible for the *Anschluss* of 1938 to epitomize the modern seizure of power in an ethical vacuum which permitted a malignant inhumanity to flourish and proliferate.

NOTES

1. Friedrich Wilhelm Foerster, *Erlebte Weltgeschichte* 1896-*1953*, *Memoiren* (Nürnberg, 1953), 229.

2. *Arbeiter-Zeitung*, 13 November 1919.

3. John Haag, "Blood on the Ringstrasse: Vienna's Students 1918-33," *Wiener Library Bulletin*, 29, New Series Nos. 39/40 (1976): 29-34.

4. Andrew G. Whiteside, *The Socialism of Fools, Georg Ritter von Schönerer and Austrian Pan Germanism* (Berkeley, 1975), 43-63; *Reichspost*, 15 June 1918.

5. Rudolf Ebneth, *Die österreichische Wochenschrift "Der Christiliche Standestaat"* (Mainz, 1976), 51-52.

6. Wolfgang Rosar, *Deutsche Gemeinschaft, Seyss-Inquart und der Anschluss* (Vienna, 1971), 29-37; Professor Gottfried Haberler, personal communication.

7. Michael Hubenstorf, "Österreichische Ärzte-Emigration," in *Vertriebene Vernunft I: Emigration und Exil österreichischer* Wissenschaft *1930-1940* (Veinna, 1987), 375.

8. See 1919 issues of *Deutsche Arbeiter-Presse*; F. L. Carsten, *Fascist Movements in Austria: From Schonerer to Hitler* (London, 1977), 71-73.

9. Bundesarchiv Koblenz, Sammlung Schumacher 279/I/37.

10. After the *Anschluss*, exiled Austrian Social Democrats in Paris praised Innitzer for his impartiality as Rector of the University.

11. *Neue Freie Presse*, 8 November 1929, a.m.; *Arbeiter-Zeitung*, 8 November 1929.

12. Karl Sablik, *Julius Tandler, Mediziner und Sozialreformer. Eine Biographie* (Vienna, 1983), 299, and contemporary press accounts.

13. Brigitte Fenz, "Zur Ideologie der 'Volksburgerschaft.' Die Studentenordnung der Universitat Wien vom 8. April vor dem Verfasssungsgerichtshof," *Zeitgeschichte*, 5, No. 4 (January, 1978): 125-45.

14. Robert Korber, *Rassesieg in Wien, der Grenzfeste des Reiches* (Vienna, 1939), a notorious antisemitic book that illustrates some of these items.

15. See the Viennese press of 13 April and 1 July 1932.

16. Friedrich Stadler, *Vom Positivismus zur "Wissenschaftlichen Weltauffassung." Am Beispiel der Wirkungsgeschichte von Ernst Mach in Österreich von* 1895 *bis* 1934 (Vienna, 1982), 196-203; Michael Siegert, "Der Mord an Professor Moritz Schlick," in Leopold Spira, ed., *Attentate, die Österreich erschutterten* (Vienna, 1981), 123-31.

17. Ernst Schmiederer, "Ruckversicherung," *profil*, 16, No. 49 (2

December 1985): 60-61.

18. Jürgen Kammerer, ed., *Heinrich Ritter von Srbik, Die wissenschaftliche Korrespondenz des Historikers* 1912-1945 (Boppard am Rhein, 1988), 458-59.

19. Louis Kranser, as told to Don C. Seibert, "Some Memories of Anton Webern, the Berg Concerto, and Vienna in the 1930s," *Fanfare*, 11, No. 2 (November/December 1987): 337.

20. Klaus Breuning, Die Vision des Reiches: *Deutscher Katholizismus zwischen Demokratie und Diktatur* (1929-1934) (Munich, 1969).

21. Erika Weinzierl, *Universität und Politik in Österreich* (Salzburg, 1969), 9-10.

22. Arthur Koestler, *The Case of the Midwife Toad* (London, 1971), 121.

23. Charlotte Buhler, "Die Wiener psychologische Schule in der Emigration," *Psychologische Rundschau*, 16 (1965): 187-88.

24. Erich Witzmann, "Der Anteil der Wiener waffenstudentischen Verbindungen an der volkischen und politischen Entwicklung 1918-1938" (Inaugural-Dissertation, University of Vienna, 1940), 163-64.

25. Albert Massiczek, "Die Situation an der Universität Wien Marz/April 1938," in *Wien 1938* (Vienna, 1978) [Forschungen und Beitrage zur Wiener Stadtgeschichte, 2], 218-19.

26. Wladimir von Hartlieb, Parole: Das Reich. Eine historische Darstellung der politischen Entwicklung in Österreich von Marz *1933* bis März *1938* (Vienna, 1939), 478-80.

27. Massiczek, op. cit., 200.

28. Heinrich Drimmel, "Die katholischen Intellektuellen," in Erika Weinzierl *et al.*, eds., *Kirche in Osterreich* 1918-1965 (2 vols., Vienna, 1966-67): 343.

29. "Blutiger Zusammenstoss in der Florianigasse," *Neue Freie Presse*, 11 March 1938, p.m.

30. Marie Tidl, *Die Roten Studenten, Dokumente und Erinnerungen* 1938-1945 (Vienna, 1976), 23-24.

31. *Neues Wiener Tagblatt*, 13 March 1938, quoted in Christine Klusacek et al., eds., *Dokumentation zur österreichischen Zeitgeschichte 1938-1945* (Vienna, 1971), 28.

32. "Grosse Kundgebung der ostmarkischen Studentenschaft in Wien," *Deutsche Akademiker-Zeitung*, 30, No. 7 (1 April 1938): 9.

33. The fraternities comprising Vienna's *Waffenstudententum* were officially absorbed by the NSDStB in a ceremony at the Grosse Konzerthaussaal on 8 June 1938. See Franz Gall, *Alma Mater Rudolphina 1365-1965. Die Wiener Universität und Ihre Studenten* (3d ed., Vienna, 1965), 191.

34. Gall, ibid., 31; the University itself was visited by *Gauleiter* Josef Burckel that same day, which was briefly noted in the press: "Burckel sprach zu den Studenten," "Bilder vom Tage," *Volkischer Beobachter*, Vienna ed., 18 March 1938.

35. Hermann Rauschning, *Gesprache mit Hitler* (New York, 1940), 45-46.

36. Ernst von Salomon, *Fragebogen [The Questionnaire]*, transl. Constantine Fitzbiggon (Garden City, 1955), 102; Walther Bartz, "Othmar Spann," *Die Neue Weltbuhne*, 34, No. 14 (7 April 1938): 417-22.

37. Radomir Luza, *Austro-German Relations in the Anschluss Era* (Princeton, 1975), 87.

38. Schmiederer, "Ruckversicherung," 61.

39. "Unpaid Work," *Austria To-Day* [London], No. 6 (January 1939), p. iii; "Studenten arbeiten in Grossbetrieben," *Volkischer Beobachter*, Vienna ed., 17 March 1939.

40. "Verweisung der letzten Juden aus den Hochschulinstituten" *Volkischer Beobachter*, Vienna ed., 23 December 1938.

41. Brigitte Lichtenberger-Fenz, "Österreichs Hochschulen und Universitaten und das *NS-Regime*," in *Emmerich Talos*, ed., *NS*-Herrschaft in Österreich *1938-1939* (Vienna, 1988), 269-82.

42. *Statistisches Jahrbuch der Stadt Wien*, new ser., 5 (1938):   177; *Statistisches Jahrbuch der Stadt Wien 1939-1942*, new ser., 6 (Vienna, 1946): 373.

43. Hans Helmut Christmann, *Frau und "Judin" an der Universitat. Die Romanistin Elise Richter* (Wien 1865--Theresienstadt 1943) (Wiesbaden, 1980); Marie-Therese Kerschbaumer, *Der weibliche Name des Widerstands. Sieben Berichte* (Olten, 1980), 19-50.

44. Zdenek Lederer, Ghetto Theresienstadt (New York, 1983), 74.

45. Michael H. Kater, Das "Ahnenerbe" der SS 1939-1945. *Ein Beitrag zur Kulturpolitik des Dritten Reiches* (Stuttgart, 1974), 274; Berlin Document Center, Personalakte Viktor Christian.

46. Radomir V. Luza, *The Resistance in Austria, 1938-1945* (Minneapolis, 1984), in which faculty and students are conspicuous by their almost total absence.

PATRIOTISM AND THEATER POLITICS IN THE SECOND REICH: PAUL HEYSE'S "COLBERG"

JERE H. LINK

The verdict of the literary historian, Helmut Schanze, is severe: he concluded that between 1850 and 1890 German drama was at its nadir and hardly worth studying.[1] He finds three exceptions: dramatists Friedrich Hebbel and Otto Ludwig and composer Richard Wagner. In no study are once popular dramas by Paul Heyse considered seriously. Heyse and contemporaries Emanuel Geibel, Felix Dahn and Gustav Freytag are consigned to the dustbins of neo-classicism and patriotic literature. Is this fair to those writers? Has the modern canon excluded them because they are thought second-rate or because patriotic fiction is now passe? Such questions arise in examining the meteoric rise and total eclipse of the literary star, Paul Heyse.

Born in 1830 to a grammarian of Greek and his well-connected Jewish wife, Paul Heyse became the boy wonder of Berlin salons and later the youngest of the "Northern Lights" called to Munich to grace the court of King Max II. If anything of his is still read, it is one or two of the early novellas, such as the Neapolitan romance *La Rabbiata*. But Heyse, who wrote in every genre, was bitten by the dramatic bug. All his life (he died in 1914) he tried to impress audiences with serious drama, if he could; with one-act topical plays otherwise.

Heyse imitated the neo-classical verse of Platen, the Romantic tales of Tieck, and the worldly tone of both Goethe and Heine. He was eclectic. In the field of drama, like so many rivals, he wanted to write something worthy of Shakespeare or Schiller. For these and other sins the era after 1848 has been branded.epigonal. Fair as an aesthetic judgment, this does not vitiate the cultural significance of the epigones who practiced the historical drama. Heyse's patriotic dramas deserve reconsideration, not because they were particularly good--they now read like bad Schiller,--but rather because they were intimately bound up with the theater politics of the age and the better sort of German patriotism.

To ears schooled on critical, even cynical post-war historiography, it may seem suspect to praise anything about German patriotism. We know all too well the perverse uses to which patriotism may be put. Indeed, Heyse's most enduring content or aesthetic qualities but rather with their place in the lost world of court theaters. Until the 1880s, when private and dramatic success, the patriot play "Colberg" (1865), was exploited for ulterior ends as late as the Nazi era. Yet the play and its stage history before the First World War show that one must guard against assuming continuities between Bismarckian patriotism, Wilhelmine nationalism, and National-Socialist chauvinism. A discussion of Paul Heyse's plays should not begin with their municipal theaters became serious rivals, Germany's court theaters ruled cultural life. The court theaters of Vienna and Berlin, Munich and Dresden, Hannover and Kassel had at their disposal excellent ensembles and budgets as generous as those available to the best theaters in Paris and Italy.[2] The court theaters of Karlsruhe, Mannheim, Braunschweig, Weimar, Darmstadt, and Stuttgart were also prestigious.[3] Playwrights felt that at court theaters the cause of Art was in good hands; the box office usually played less of a role.

Unfortunately, the court-theater system also had its bad side: frivolous aristocratic patrons, meddling princes, and faint-hearted intendants. Opera, ballet, and theater were often treated in that order.[4] The opera ate up profits from the theater; and in Berlin the ballet director had carte blance in 1868 for *any* expense.[5] In spoken theater, the public preferred comedies, French society-pieces, and the classics. To be successful with new pieces dramatists were wiser to serve up the tried-and-true than to experiment.[6]

Another problem was censorship. Though the historical drama was sanctioned, the moralism of official culture sometimes clashed with the aesthetic program of even semi-official dramatists, such as Heyse. One reason was the political sensitivity of princes and courts in certain matters. As the writer Julius Grosse put it:

Our greatest national materials, in which the most powerful forces
and antitheses of our history interact, are for the most part still a
'noli me tangere' today--at least for a large part of the German
people. The fight between Popes and emperors raises no problems
on only a few stages...; also the dramatization of the history of the
last centuries turns up precious few usable themes, since one must
take care almost everywhere in the representation of princes, courts,
etc.[7]

A Prussian cabinet order of 1844 decreed that no members of the
Hohenzollern family, dead or alive, could be depicted on stage without
permission, but there were many exemptions.[8]

Writers like Heyse became adept at pleasing royal tastes. He
corresponded with Ludwig II of Bavaria, dukes Georg and Ernst of
Meiningen, and others.[9] Princes could interfere in their theaters at will,
but most did not, so well did intendants screen and playwrights self-
censor works. Princes liked Heyse because he was socially and
artistically correct--and amenable to manipulation. In 1880 Ludwig II
asked Heyse for an epilogue to his play "Ludwig der Bayer," the
jubilee-piece for the anniversary of the Wittelsbachs. Theater director
Possart said the king wanted a "finale-symphony glorifying the house of
Wittelsbach" with tableaux vivants and an apotheosis.[10]

Relations with princes were complicated by their quirks and desires.
In 1868, having offended Prussian princes with a piece on the French
Revolution, Heyse turned to the women for help. He had one friend
give his piece to Queen Augusta's reader and sent another to speak to
crown princess Victoria; both were women known for more liberal
attitudes.[11] Late in life Kaiser Wilhelm I frequented Baden-Baden to
attend military manoeuvres and take the cure. Karlsruhe's court theater
was expected to drop everything to entertain him. However, since he
was hard-of-hearing, the actors had to scream themselves hoarse.[12] By
all accounts the Berlin royal theater suffered most from royal meddling
and poor intendants. Botho v. Hulsen was only a *Gardeoffizier* before
becoming intendant in 1851; his successor, Baron Hochberg, did not
make a better impression.[13] An observer in Baden noted in 1889: "To
ruin the theater is of course the sovereign right of the ruling
gentlemen,--for which Berlin has give the best proof for decades."[14]

After sixty years of dealing with court theaters, and after receiving
the Nobel Prize for literature in 1910, Heyse still encountered strictures.
In 1913 his play about the Seven Years' War faced difficulties in
Saxony and Prussia. In Prussia it had to surmount the Hohenzollern-

paragraph; Heyse had Friedrich II onstage. But the jibes at Saxony's expense were more serious. A friend in Berlin believed a private theater might accept the piece, but:

> Our court-theater, at the decision-making level, would take umbrage, given considerations it must keep in mind due to its special relationship with the head of state, and that could have consequences which could be very unpleasant. The strongly Prussian spirit which breathes through your piece would not avert the unpleasant consequences here and would even worsen them with our honored neighbors [the Saxons].[15]

On the whole, Prussian critics found the historical drama problematic. Karl Frenzel stated that in France and England such dramas still evoked patriotic response; let a Prussian praise his land, and he finds himself "preaching to deaf ears."[16] Other evidence, however, belied his opinion.

The case of Heyse shows that the right subject and treatment could insure not only box-office success but also perennial favor for a Prussian-patriotic drama. The good luck attendant on "Colberg" cannot be appreciated unless we bear in mind how the North-South chasm in politics affected historical drama.[17] Even before unification Heyse found that his Bavarian plays won less acclaim and caused more headaches than his two Prussian plays, "Hans Lange" (1864) and "Colberg." More than his other dramas, these two pieces held the boards in Germany until the First World War.

Heyse respected and courted Vienna's *Burgtheater*, but neither Prussian piece succeeded there. "Hans Lange" was panned in Vienna, so he informed the Stuttgart intendant that he should postpone his premiere until the Berlin reviews were in: "The success here [Berlin], if all turns out favorably, as I hope, can steal a march on the Viennese, since the theme for patriotic reasons has to resonate more in the North."[18] This play and "Colberg" did well in Berlin. From 1865 to 1899 each logged a respectable fifty-five performances. This was hardly a box-office smash. Wagner's "Tannhauser" played a record 401 times in the same period; Goethe's "Faust," 208 times. And Ernst v. Wildenbruch's patriotic "Quitzows," written in 1888, had played 143 times by 1899.[19] Other factors made Heyse's "Colberg" important in its own right. For instance, its long use as a school text, meant that "Colberg" was more than a staple of the court-theater repertoire; it was a prop of general patriotism.

Written partly in verse, "Colberg" relies on rhetorical effects and the power of historical memory. Its more than fifty years of popularity derived from three factors: the unfaded power of melodrama, the resonance of the patriotic plot, and Heyse's facility with language. The events surrounding the legendary 1806-07 defense of the seaport Colberg were a rallying point in the Wars of Liberation that centered on two heroes, the exsailor Nettelbeck and Major Gneisenau. The conflict reduces to one between French cosmopolitanism and Prussian patriotism. The Gallicized townsmen want to surrender; the loyal Prussians want to defend their city to the death.

Heyse skews the argument for the town's defense with calculated appeals to the cults of Frederick the Great, the martyr of 1809, Major Schill, and others. The heroine Rose is shown reading Schiller, and she meets the fabled Queen Louise in exile.[20] The Peace of Tilsit saves Colberg and all ends on a note of hope in a united Germany where "no foreign oppressor will ever set foot on our holy, beloved soil! But only one thing can bring us this highest grace: a people united as brothers, a nation in arms!" The final allusion to Schiller's "Wilhelm Tell" includes a phrase from the Prussian propaganda war of 1813. The whole play seemed too patriotic to one of its first readers, the Viennese writer Faust Pachler.[21]

Oddly enough, the stage history of this eminently Prussian piece began with threats of censorship from the Berlin intendant, Bismarck and the king. Heyse wanted the piece premiered before a friendly audience, so he chose Berlin's royal theater. Intendant Hulsen complimented Heyse for showing the "true" relationship between people and army, a point he felt South Germans misunderstood.[22] One problem was the anti-French tone, then (1865) taboo in official circles. The stage manager discovered no other contraband but still decided it would be wise to ask Bismarck to review the piece. Heyse joked that he expected no changes in Bismarck's politics, only in his writing style.[23] Someone assured him that Bismarck ("the little he") had more say in such matters than the king ("the big He"); also, Bismarck never stooped to pettiness. Heyse did not feel reassured.

> Not because [Bismarck] has reserved to himself the censorship over pieces from recent history,... rather because even in the great stream of public life in Berlin pettiness and chicanery always swim on top.[24]

His worries proved groundless except in particulars. The piece was officially accepted, with ministerial and royal approval; only "the strong anti-military coloring during the arrest in the first act" would have to be removed; and, indeed several "offensive" lines disappeared.[25]

The first performance was a great success; the four granddaughters of Nettelbeck were all present, and the critics gave their *imprimatur*.[26] Actor, Theodor Doring, who played Nettelbeck, wrote that the piece, while deeply moving, might have had a greater effect had the political climate been better. He added, "In Munich Colberg probably won't be given, since love of Prussia is hard to find there."[27]

The subsequent stage history involved three factors: the friendly attitude of court theaters, political climate, and the play's increasing ties to official culture.[28] The official seal of approval in the North, a potential kiss-of-death in the South, came a few months after the premiere. Heyse's Berlin publishers announced excitedly: "On the king's birthday, day after tomorrow, "Colberg" will be performed at the court theater!"[29] Outside Prussia the piece was helped by the occupancy of several directorships by native Prussians: Edmund Devrient, Gustav zu Putlitz, then a certain Burklein in Karlsruhe; Putlitz's son in Stuttgart; and Otto Devrient in Mannheim. Devrient recalled tales of Colberg from his youth and said tears came to his eyes as he read the piece. Moreover, the Karlsruhe public shared his enthusiasm.[30]

The climate in Stuttgart was anti-Prussian, so Heyse feared that the intendant and director would accuse him of falsifying history to satisfy prevailing political notions in Berlin. The piece was only accepted in Stuttgart after a year's delay.[31] In 1876 Otto Devrient was amazed that "Colberg" had never been performed at the Mannheim court theater, which he ascribed to the earlier anti-Prussian movement.[32] Evidently, one part of Baden did not approve of what another part was doing.

Perhaps "Colberg" was unlucky in being chosen for higher things: it became *the* ceremonial play for such national holidays as Sedan Day, and official birthdays.[33] It was in effect co-opted as a nation-building myth in order to instill loyalty among non-Prussians to the Hohenzollerns. The emperor made a point of telling classicist Ernst Curtius how much he liked the play. On Proclamation Day 1884 he sat through the entire performance, something unusual for royalty. The crown prince left after the first act to go to a ball in Potsdam.[34] In Darmstadt, on the emperor's ninetieth birthday, the writer Otto

Roquette composed a *Festspiel*, replete with a speech relating the
events of "Colberg" to the emperor's early life. Hurrahs and the
national hymn followed.[35] A village veterans club in the Taunus
performed the play in 1908 and 1910, the local pastor adding that the
actors' enthusiasm overcame their lack of talent. National patriotism
motivated the "countless" performances given in the 1913 centenary
year of the Leipzig Battle of the Nations.[36] "Colberg" was one of
Wilhelm II's favorite pieces, according to court intendant Hochberg,
who refused to let any other theater in Berlin stage the piece.[37]

"Colberg" was, of course, not the only patriotic play put to political
uses. Kleist's "Prinz Friedrich von Homburg" was given in the
euphoric 1914/15 season at no less than eighteen court theaters.[38] In
the Wilhelmine era Ernst v. Wildenbruch, not Heyse, dominated the
Prussian scene.[39] Wildenbruch shared the new patriotism under
Wilhelm II; besides, he was related to the Hohenzollerns on the wrong
sides of the sheets.[40] The new emperor's patronage certainly helped
Wildenbruch's success in Prussia.

His claim to popularity rested with plays such as "Die Quitzows," a
stirring patriotic rendering of the 15th-century resistance by the old
nobility to the upstart Hohenzollerns. The play is more nationalist in
tone than the Schillerian "Colberg." The plot is contrived and the
romance overheated.[41] One character ends the apotheosis of
Brandenburg with the cry: "Hohenzollern! Hohenzollern!"

The wild success of the "Quitzows" in north Germany disturbed
older writers, such as Heyse and his friend Ernst Wichert of
Konigsberg:

> I'm convinced [the emperor] belongs completely to the younger
> generation, which has no understanding for us any more. Poetry in the
> service of 'national politics,' of rabid patriotism--that's what is fostered
> by them....I fear we face literary devaluation, if right after Bismarck's
> dismissal political jingoism begins to celebrate its orgies. It seems to
> me that, for the unforeseeable future, it is unlikely that the nation will
> calm down.[42]

Though Heyse's patriotic dramas had political overtones and the
potential for nationalist exploitation, this does not mean that either
Heyse or Wildenbruch was responsible for misuse of their plays. The
shame of "Colberg" was that it later served masters who should have
hated Heyse. National Socialist ministries negotiated for the film
rights to "Colberg"--this, despite Heyse's Jewish background.[43] The

patriotism of Colberg's defense against French imperialism served at
the 1945 premiere to remind the audience that the Soviet army was at
the gates of Kolberg--but too late.[44]

The fate of "Colberg" was in some ways sealed by its close
association with Prussian, later German heroes Queen Louise, Major v.
Schill, Nettelbeck, and Gneisenau. Historical drama reinforced an
uncritical view of the national past; it also gave heroes such as Wilhelm
I and II, Bismarck, and Moltke cult-status by virtue of the close
association of an approved play with official occasions. The irony is
that Heyse and his colleagues were mostly Bismarckians who
disapproved of the ominous turn in German culture under the second
Wilhelm. Moreover, most of them were cosmopolites in debt to French
culture. The anti-French tone of "Colberg" was historically and
aesthetically justifiable, but Heyse in no way wanted to foster sentiment
against France or its culture. Nor did Bismarck or the court in the
play's first years, 1865-1869. In 1870, however, and at later crises that
tone could be misunderstood.

Heyse was appalled at Gustav Freytag, who in January 1871
damned "Colberg" with chauvinist praise and stooped to penning
tasteless war-poems.[45] Heyse also lapsed into jingoism, and intendant
Devrient, in Baden, candidly told him so. Heyse's Francophobic piece
of February 1871 embarrassed Devrient, who laid down a golden rule of
patriotic art: "a patriotic piece must also be a good piece (like
"Colberg"), yes, even better than others, so that patriotism itself can
thereby come more into its own."[46]

Devrient was right, but why were German examples so problematic?
The patriotic pathos of "Maid of Orleans" and "William Tell" began to
seem trite, even to Schiller-cultists like Heyse. The problem was one of
the skewed perspective to which patriot emotion all too easily leads in
writers as well as audiences. A great artist can maintain perspective
and present full, human characters, as does Fontaine in his lovely
Before the Storm, a Prussian-patriotic novel set in 1812-13. Heyse's
Prussians of 1807 are, in comparison, onsidedly good; the Gallicized
antagonist, Heinrich Blank, must be converted before he can be saved.
Such patriotism, akin to religious faith, oversimplifies human nature
and political reality. It is no accident that "Colberg" includes so many
allusions to cult-heroes; like saints, cult-heroes are icons in the national
religion where zeal is patriotism. In the German national cult Colberg
was a holy place; Heyse's play was a bit of hagiography, not art.

Schiller's ideal of the "stage as a moral institution" was undermined later by the triumph of patriotic over aesthetic criteria. Given the nature of the court-theater system, it was easy to co-opt Heyse's "Colberg" into the cult of the Hohenzollerns. New historical dramas depended first on the approval of the prince, ministers and the court intendant; later, they depended on their continued favor. "Colberg" was then doubly holy at official functions; there national heroes fused with political cults.

In the final analysis "Colberg" was fatally compromised by these associations. The Hohenzollerns were disgraced by the Great War, and Prussian patriotism was relegated to the far right. The style of the literary epigones of 1850 to 1890 seemed hopelessly naive and dated in the cynical, polarized Weimar Republic. The canon had changed. Uncritical writers like Heyse yielded pride of place to new cultural heroes such as Holderlin, Buchner and Grabbe, all more complex and critical. Only Kleist and Fontane survived in the canon as Prussian patriots--Kleist, because he was seen as a martyr; Fontane, because his elegant prose saved his patriotism from banality. The case of "Colberg" suggests how Prussian hegemony extended over Germany in cultural matters. It also shows how political exploitation hurts writers and works associated with a discredited regime.

NOTES

1. The historical drama is discussed in: Fritz Martini, *Deutsche Literatur im bürgerlichen Realismus 1848-98* (Stuttgart: Metzler, 1974), 128-29, 206-08, 220-25 passim; Friedrich Sengle, *Das deutsche Geschichtsdrama* (Stuttgart: Metzler, 1952); and Helmut Schanze, *Drama im bürgerlichen Realismus* (Frankfurt: Klostermann, 1973), 2, 19.

2. Max Martersteig, *Das deutsche Theater im 19. Jahrhundert*, (Leipzig: Breitkopf & Hartel, 1924), 406; still the best study. Figures for Paris and Italy include the budgets for several theaters each: Paris 1,008,000 M; Vienna: 498,000 M; Berlin: 420,000 M; Italy: 388,000 M; Munich: 267,420 M; Dresden: 240,000 M; Hannover: 220,000 M; Kassel: 180,000 M; Karlsruhe: 171,430 M; Mannheim: 70,000 M (1851).

3. H. Bruford, *Germany in the Eighteenth Century* (1835) (Cambridge: University Press, 1971), 84 f.; there were about forty-six court and residence theaters (out of ca. 328) in 1901 Germany, Austria and Switzerland, according to the *Schriftsteller-und Journalisten-Kalender*, ed. Emil Thomas (Leipzig: Fiedler, 1901). The problem with counting is the status of the *Kur-* and *Saisontheater*, as well as those theaters receiving court subventions.

4. In 1892 the historian Sybel recalled the efforts of Immermann in the 1830s to reform Dusseldorfs theater. As director he had won over the middle classes to the classics, "...while counts and bankers in the first rows were bored." *HA VI*, Sto-Vol, Sybel, #26, Oberhof, 16 June 1892. The Heyse-Archiv (*HA*) is housed in the Bavarian State Library, Munich.

5. *HA* I33, H. Anna 1868, #8, Berlin 3 Jan. 1868, [2-3], Heyse says the theater has reached its nadir and that everyone puts his hope in the crown prince (later Friedrich III); for now the political morass with France has driven all other interests offstage.

6. *HA* I33, H. Anna 1888, Berlin #345 & #346, 20.1.; #348, 22.2., #350, 24.1.

7. Grosse to intendant Baron v. Gall, Munich, Oct. 1864: Deutsches Literaturarchiv (*DLA*), Schillermuseum (Marbach a. N.), Samml: Hoftheater, Grosse Julius, Z1130.

8. Peter Mertz, *Der König lebt* (Frankfurt: Fischer, 1982), 39-41. The edict was in force until 1918. See Heinrich Stümcke, *Hohenzollernfürsten im Drama* (Leipzig: G. Wigand, 1903), passim, for exemptions.

9. As crown-prince, the mad Ludwig swooned over Heyse's "Elisabeth Charlotte;" as king, he gave Heyse a special commendation for a piece on the Franco-Prussian war. In 1902 Heyse claimed (bourgeois pride) that he had

the training of police forces in Tangier by French officers had been requested by the Maghzen itself.

French reaction to Spanish distrust was astonishment in light of their previous accords.[13] Jules Cambon, transferred from Madrid to Berlin as French Ambassador, had described Spain as "a field of battle." He was not wrong. Nevertheless, leading officials of the Spanish government, King Alphonso, Prime Minister Maura, Foreign Minister Allendesalazar, and Spanish ambassadors in major European capitals worked in tandem with the French, if indeed cooperation was uneasy. Therefore, when as Hafid's advances against Aziz continued to succeed and when he attempted to send delegations to each of the major European capitals for formal diplomatic negotiations, Hafid's representatives were not received formally or informally in Madrid anymore than they were in Paris. When on August 27, 1908, Aziz finally gave up his fight, Spain had already agreed with the French on what became a combined French-Spanish note spelling out both countries terms for recognition of Hafid as the legitimate Sultan.[14]

The note contained the terms under which both countries would accept Hafid's accession to the Sultanate, but these were such that they would be quite acceptable to all those of the European community who had signed Algeciras. France and Spain stood simply as the guarantors of Algeciras, something dictated by that very Act accepted by all powers. Moulai Hafid was to accept Algeciras, as had the previous Sherifian government, including the safeguard of all foreign interests in Morocco, all treaties and obligations concluded by previous Moroccan sovereigns, and all debts previously contracted by Aziz. Hafid was to accept regulation of damages caused by the Casablancan troubles as those damages might be decided by a special commission, was to enter into relations with foreign governments on the basis of international law, make in this regard his intentions known publicly and officially, and calm all agitation throughout his empire by publicly disavowing any continuation of holy war. Security and liberty of communications around all ports and along the main routes to the interior were to be assured.   Finally, an "honorable regulation" of Aziz's personal situation was to be accepted as well as that of Aziz's functionaries.[15] Hafid, quite wisely, would concur with these demands. Recognition as the legitimate Sultan was worth a mass. The other powers agreed with the conditions laid down in the joint note, since it was obvious that these protected their own commercial and financial interests along with the welfare of their respective nationals.[16]

skewed by greater number of performances in 1880s and '90s.

20. Paul Heyse, *Colberg* (Stuttgart: Cotta, 1903), 19th edition; Schiller allusion in Act 1, sc. 6 (pp. 18-19). The quotation is from act 5, sc. 11.

21. *HA I*33, Li-Z, Pachler Faust, #26, Berlin, 3 Oct. 1865.

22. *HA I*33, Kug-Kur, Kugler Clara, #104, Berlin, 5 Oct. 1865, [2].

23. Ibid., #106, Berlin, 11 Oct. 1865. Bismarck was then in Biarritz.

24. *HA I*33, Kug-Kur, Kurz Hermann 1864-67, #54, München, 19 Oct. 1865.

25. *HA VI*, Di-Ebner, Düringer Philipp, Berlin, 3 Nov. 1865 and 23 Dec. 1865. Düringer, with the artistic-technical department, sent Heyse reports on this premiere.

26. The satirical *Kladderadatsch* lambasted the intendancy for cowardly misgivings, as did the *Münchener Neueste Nachrichten*, where Heyse's old friend Grosse controlled the feuilleton. *HA VI*, Hertel-Hertz 1875, Hertz Wilhelm, Berlin, 11 and 15 Jan. 1866.

27. *HA VI*, Di-Ebner, Döring Theo., Berlin, 19 Jan. 1866.

28. Factors coincided to make the play a success in Königsberg, where the director lengthened the title to "Die Helden von Colberg." *HA VI*, Wend-Wichert (1889), Wichert Ernst, #8, Konigsberg, 31 Jan. 1866.

29. *HA VI*, Hertel-Hertz 1878, Hertz Wm., Berlin, 20 March 1866. "Colberg" was given at the height of the Franco-Prussian war in Berlin: ibid., Berlin, 14 Aug. 1870.

30. Edmund Devrient (1801-77) reigned 1852-70 as director/intendant at Karlsruhe. His son Otto (1838-94) went to Weimar to direct (1873), became artistic director at Mannheim (1878), and in 1884 transferred to Oldenburg. Reaching Berlin in 1889, he lasted only a year (1889-90) midst the stormy theater politics under Wilhelm II. *HA VI*, Cla-Dev, Devrient E., Karlsruhe, 11 Dec. 1865.

31. *DLA* (Marbach), Samml: Hoftheater, Heyse Paul, Z1137, Munchen, 7 Jan. 1866; 20 Dec. 1867.

32. Ibid., Devrient Otto, Mannheim, 31 July 1876.

33. Ibid. (Lazarus letter, above); *HA I*33, H. Anna, 1884, Berlin, #301 14 Jan. and #302, 2 Jan. 1884; *HA VI*, Rod-Sax, Roquette Otto, #21, Darmstadt, 23 March 1887; *HA I*33, H. Anna 1889, #377, Berlin, 11 Oct. 1889; and *HA VI*, Wend-Wichert, Wendt Gustav, Karlsruhe, 27 Oct. 1890. In Berlin the court theater performed it regularly on Sedan Day; and in Karlsruhe it capped the celebration of Moltke's ninetieth birthday (1890).

34. *HA I*33, H. Anna 1884, #302, Berlin, Jan. 1884.

35. *HA VI*, Rod-Sax, Roquette, #21, Darmstadt, 23 March 1887.

36. *HA VI*, Ka-Ko Kaiser (Pfarrer), Altwelnau i. T., 12 March 1910 (the latter performance was for the emperor's birthday); *HA I*33, Heyse-Kohut,

Jacoby Daniel, #70, Munchen, 9 Dec. 1913.

37. *HA I*33, Heyse Anna 1889, #377 Berlin, 11 Oct. 1889.

38. Mertz, *König*, 38, 42.

39. Mertz, *König*, 76; on the "Quitzows," see 77, 86 passim. See also Kathy Harms, "Writer by Imperial Decree: Ernst von Wildenbruch" in *Imperial Germany*, eds. Volker Dürr, Kathy Harms and Peter Hayes (Madison, WI: University of Wisconsin Press, 1985), 134-48, esp. 139.

40. Later rector of the University of Berlin, Erich Schmidt summed up Wildenbruch's reputation in 1891: "Wildenbruch has barred me, a dubious cantonist, from a private foretaste of his new Hohenzollern seven-acter, already endowed with imperial privilege; it's supposed to be very vigorous and action-packed, say the initiated." *HA VI*, Sb-Schm, Schmidt E., #49, Berlin, 1 Jan. 1891; but Wilhelm II once reprimanded Wildenbruch when in 1903 he publicly crticized the new grand duke of Weimar: Helmut Reichold, *Bismarcks Zaunkönige* (Paderborn: Schoningh, 1977), 243.

41. The heroine Barbara, bastard daugher of the Polish king, at one point throws herself into the arms of Dietrich v. Quitzow with the immortal line: "Mein Held! Mein Herr! Mein Gott!" (Act 2, sc. 6): Ernst v. Wildenbruch *Gesammelte Werke* (16 vols.), (Berlin: G. Grote, 1914), 9, 147-324 ("Die Quitzows").   Predictably, "Quitzows" was considered "too Prussian" in Thuringia and the South: Harms, "Wildenbruch," 144.

42. *HA VI*, Wend-Wichert (1889), Wichert E., #362, Berlin, 24 Feb. 1889.

43. *Staatsbibliothek* (E. Berlin), *Stiftungsakten*, Btl. 108 (1914), Akten betreffend: das Testament Paul Heyse's und das im Juli 1930 erfolgte Ableben der Frau Anna verw. von Heyse; Btl. 115, *Stiftung* to Lloyd-Film GmbH (Berlin), Weimar, 22 July 1936; ibid., Bl.63, Lloyd to Lilienfein (secretary), Berlin, 2 June 1936 on Goebbels' dilatoriness in processing permission to use "Kolberg;" Bl. 62, Lilienfein to Lloyd, Weimar, 23 April 1936 on Heyse's half-Jewishness, which, Lilienfein points out, has not hindered the booksellers.

44. I am indebted to Prof. Richard Wires, Ball State University, for information about the making of "Kolberg." My sources suggested that the film should have been ready for the invasion of France; but Goebbels tampered with the script and evidently insisted that the epic be done in technicolor; whence the delays. For other details see: David Welch, *Propaganda and the German Cinema, 1933-1945* (Oxford: Clarendon Press, 1983), 221-33.

45. *HA VI*, Hertel-Hertz 1875, Hertz Wm. 1870-75, Berlin, 5 Jan. 1871.

46. *HA VI*, Cla-Dev, Devrient Ed., Karlsruhe, 27 Feb. 1871.

THE FRENCH REVOLUTION AND REVOLUTIONARY VALUES IN BELLE EPOQUE OPERA

ANDRE SPIES

During the 1890s, Parisian opera librettists appropriately capitalized on the centenary of the French Revolution by drawing themes from this "military era which is always sympathetic, and very much in style at the moment."[1] Such topical material could have been incorporated into the opera in any number of ways; in practice, the librettists' selections of incidents and outcomes from the panorama of French Revolutionary history inevitably had political implications. That the Revolution became increasingly important as symbolic ground for the discussion of contemporary political issues during the decade of its centenary is well known to modern historians. Paul Farmer, begins his study of Third Republic historiography by asserting that:

> The controversy over the history of the Revolution is distinguished from other unsettled historical problems in that judgments on the Revolution serve as the locus of almost all the divisions of opinion in France on the problems of modern life. Historical interpretations are inseparably joined to alignments on contemporary politics, to corresponding opinions on such questions as the inter-relationships of the state, the individual, religion, society and classes, and to corresponding evaluations of nationalism, tradition and the Church.[2]

Not surprisingly, the historical operas performed at the Opéra-Comique during this period endorsed certain aspects of the French revolutionary tradition while repudiating others. As we might also expect, the implicit ideological content of these operas served the political interests of the moderate republicans in power. Can we conclude that the Opéra-Comique functioned as an effective and important political arm of the government? If so, how can we account for the apparent failure on the part of contemporaries, including both supporters and critics of the government, to acknowledge the political role of this highly prominent cultural institution?

Bourgeois patrons of the Opéra-Comique shared with the aristocratic clientele of the Opéra the conviction that opera neither did nor should broach serious ideas of any kind. Nearly everyone connected with the two institutions, including not only government administrators but established critics, impresarios who selected the repertoire and even most librettists and composers, proclaimed the incorporation of social or political issues into the opera to be the height of bad taste. This attitude led dissident, socially conscious writers such as Emile Zola to compare the art form to a warm bath of melody that empties the mind while promoting digestion, "a sensual pleasure multiplied . . . by the decors, the staging, and the dances."[3] Most critics were of the opinion that librettos had little impact on the audience, who were supposed to judge performances on the basis of the music, the decors, and the virtuosity of the singers. Saint-Saens complained bitterly about opera subscribers who boasted of never paying the least attention to the words. And the composer Alfred Bruneau estimated that Opéra audiences understood only one syllable in ten of Wagner's *Siegfried*, even in French translation.[4]

As a result, one school of music sociologists has concluded that occasional references to social or political issues functioned simply as "local color" intended to stimulate choreographers, musicians, and designers. In other words, topical ideas were the functional equivalent of exotic fashions in clothes, or the promotion of a new dance craze.[5] This approach represents a healthy reaction against an earlier generation of scholars--Bekker, Crosten, Combarieu--who looked for ideological overtones in every operatic reference to topical social or political issues. Yet now we have come full circle. Professor Fulcher has convincingly identified the political subtext of French Grand Opéra during the July Monarchy. She demonstrates that the political implications of operatic plots, costuming, and staging were widely discussed among both supporters and critics of the government, to the extent that some productions came to be perceived and evaluated as reflections of "the nation's image."[6]

The Third Republic administered the opera according to the same system that had been successful under the July Monarchy, of appointing and supervising directors who exploited the opera for their own profit. In exchange for yearly subsidies approved by the Assemblée Nationale, the government gained administrative control over the budget and the day-to-day affairs of the opera. Impresarios selected the operas to be performed, but they owed their positions to the Ministry of Public Instruction. Each new or renewed appointment was the occasion for renegotiation of the *cahiers des charges*, which defined the general nature of the relationship between the state and the director, and the specific terms of each concession, including the genres of works that might be presented.[7] Unlike the July Monarchy, however, the Third Republic carefully abstained from direct interference in the ideological content of the repertoire. It transformed the opera from an instrument of government propaganda to a more effective hegemonic apparatus which unobtrusively conveyed common-sense messages submerged in the bath of sensual pleasures.

For the Opéra-Comique, the centenary of the French Revolution was an obvious source of topical local color, and the Centennial Exposition of 1889 was a marketing triumph. Though inferior to the Opéra in prestige and in the size of its state subsidy, the Opéra-Comique regularly attracted opera aficionados from Paris and the provinces. It produced what was arguably the best opera in the world at this time, including all the new works of any importance. The Opera, on the other hand, was just a museum of music under the Third Republic. It catered to aristocratic relics of earlier regimes who insisted on hearing again and again the old warhorses that had been fresh and exciting under the July Monarchy and Second Empire.[8] The Opéra demonstrated its contempt for the centennial by declining to introduce a new production even for the hordes of visitors to Paris. The comparatively bourgeois Opéra-Comique, meanwhile, drew record crowds to 101 performances of *Esclarmonde* in 1889. Though vaguely patriotic, Massenet's new opera did not have a revolutionary motif. But a few years later, in 1893, a successful peasant rebellion in Leo Delibes' *Kassya* inaugurated a series of librettos that recreated the social conflicts and the political incidents of the Revolution.

At first, librettists deflected the ideological content of their operas by placing the revolutionary material in distant times and places. For instance, *Kassya*, with a libretto by Henri Meilhac and Philippe Gille that censures the aristocracy while portraying popular political action in a favorable light, takes place in mid-nineteenth-century Galicia. The countryside is being ravaged by a plague of banditry, horse stealing, and arson, all condoned by the local count. The neighboring seigneurs despise the peasantry and laughingly approve when the count arranges to conscript the fiance of a peasant girl who has caught his eye.[9] Proud of their rank and position, the nobility boast that pleasure is the only guide to their behavior.[10] The count raises taxes so high that the peasant hero's father is forced off his land.[11] When the hero returns from the army, he leads a band of armed peasants against the chateau where the local lords have apparently been singing, drinking, and playing ever since the beginning of the second act. After defeating them, he assures the peasantry that it will have nothing further to fear from the nobility, who will henceforth be subject to the laws or go into exile.[12]

Two years later, in 1895, the Opéra-Comique produced Edouard Lalo's *La Jacquerie*, with a libretto by Edouard Blau and Simone Arnoud about the armed peasant revolts of the fourteenth century. A peasant hero, who has been trying to better himself by acquiring learning in Paris, is forced to flee to the countryside after defending a poor man mistreated by a nobleman. The futility of his love for the local seigneur's daughter has made him a revolutionary and convinced him that the nobility does nothing but evil. "They take the earth and its fruits that God gave to us," he says, (II:i). But the hour will come when a young, ardent, strong people will break their chains; in order to obtain victory over their oppressors, they have to unite like brothers, to learn to sacrifice their self-interest in the interests of all the peasants of France.[13] The political program advanced on behalf of the Jacquerie by the librettists--the right to approve new taxes, legal equality and the renunciation of noble privileges, abolition of the *taille* and *corvée*-- anticipates in detail the revolutionary initiatives of 1789-91. But in contrast to the successful direct action in *Kassya*, the confrontation between the peasantry and nobility in *La Jacquerie* teaches the dangers of violent political activity. When, despite the hero's attempts to intervene, the peasantry murders the count and burns his chateau, the swift defeat of its just cause ensues.

Peasant heroes superseded noble heroes on the Opéra-Comique stage at at time when the perceived community of interests between peasant producers and bourgeoisie had become one of the cornerstones of Third Republic politics.[14] In *La Jacquerie*, symbolic affirmation of the electoral alliance between bourgeoisie and peasantry gained color and substance from oblique references to the Revolutionary tradition. Librettos that directly drew on the Revolution for plots and characters and that addressed much more explicitly the unresolved political issues soon followed.

When Godard's *La Vivandière* (libretto by Henri Cain) and Cahen's *La Femme de Claude* (libretto by Louis Gallet) appeared in 1895 and 1896, the Third Republic had survived for more than twenty years-- longer than any other nineteenth-century French regime. Yet intransigent opposition from anti-republicans on both the right and left continued to threaten its existence. The frightening strength of the right had recently manifested itself once again in the Boulangist movement; and the Dreyfus Affair was just over the horizon. A recently concluded alliance with Russia had broken France's diplomatic isolation, but the Republic continued to be oppressed by memories and fears of Prussian militarism. Under the circumstances, the centennial of 1793-94 was a public relations coup. Commemoration of the military victories of those years permitted beleaguered Belle Epoque republicans to borrow some prestige from their political ancestors' triumphs over Prussia and over domestic opponents of the republic as well. Opéra was the ideal vehicle for recreating the music and pageantry of this martial era.

Godard's *La Vivandière*, the most successful of the French Revolutionary operas, celebrates the military triumphs of 1794. Act I opens with a chorus of peasants and servants cursing their local marquis and cheering on the passing Army of the Rhine. The hero is a younger son of the seigneur and the only member of the family loved by the common people. Having been forbidden by his father to marry a girl of no family, he leaves home to join the republican army. The soldiers' evident bravery, cheerfulness, camaraderie, and filial devotion, the mutual respect and love between soldiers and officers and especially their success in important battles against invading Germans all combine to show the republicans in the best possible light. The next year, Cahen's *La Femme de Claude* reinforced the idea that the republican army was the guarantor of French sovereignty. The action of the opera begins with a Republican general confidently defending Lorraine from invasion. To emphasize the unity of the province, the heroine sings a local folk song about Joan of Arc "saving the country of France."[15] Before the vogue for Revolutionary themes expired, Erlanger's *Kermaria* (1897), with a libretto by P. B. Gheusi, introduced yet another republican army hero, this time opposed by a brutish Chouan (Breton monarchist) villain.

The rich tableau of revolutionary history permitted more pointed political statements as well. *La Vivandière* and *La Femme de Claude* also defined for the opera public the acceptable heritage of the First

Republic by carefully condemning the ideas and practices of the Jacobins. There could have been little doubt, in the era of Clemenceau, that operatic denunciations of the Jacobins represented a repudiation of contemporary Radical republicanism as well. The Radical leader, who was a prominent devotee of the opera, incidentally, had made the moral character of Jacobin rule one of the touchstone historiographical issues that distinguished Belle Epoque Radicals from other republicans by declaring that the revolution had to be accepted "en bloc"--Robespierre and all. This view, well-known and often quoted as official Radical dogma, had been enunciated by the Tiger [Clemenceau] during a speech about another theater piece with a French Revolutionary theme. Victorien Sardou's *Thermidor* had been closed by the police in 1889 after causing riots in the streets; during the Chamber of Deputies debate that followed--described as the most intemperate debate of the whole Third Republic--Clemenceau's Radical defense of Robespierre almost caused a riot in the Chamber.[16]

At the Opéra-Comique, the librettists of *La Femme de Claude* attacked the Radicals by portraying the heroic republican general as a former victim of the Jacobins, who had unjustly imprisoned him on the strength of a false denunciation. Likewise, the her of *La Vivandière*, after participating in the triumphs of the republican armies, deplores the Jacobins' slaughter of their political opponents and endorses the Thermidoreans' attempts at reconciliation with defeated adversaries of the Republic. The opera ends happily with the amnesty for political prisoners that ended the Reign of Terror; among the captured Vendeens released by decree from the Convention is the hero's father, the misguided marquis. Thus, in denouncing the Jacobins of 1793-94 as false and impure representatives of the French republican tradition, the moderate republicans in power in 1893-94 contrived to exclude from the reflected glory of the First Republic the Third Republic leftists who were their vocal critics and chief rivals for power. At the same time, the moderates symbolically extended the hand of reconciliation to the heirs of the aristocratic tradition.

The potential audience for this kind of political drama was substantial. The most successful of the operas, *La Vivandière*, remained in the repertoire for four years, achieving a total of eighty-five performances before brief revivals in 1901, 1907 and 1914. A conservative estimate of 1,000 to 1,200 spectators per performance (from a full house of 1500), meant a total pre-war audience of about 100,000 spectators for this opera, a figure not including provincial performances in towns such as Rouen. *Kassya* may be described as moderately successful, having enjoyed one revival with a total of nineteen performances, the median number for new operas during the pre-war Third Republic. *La Femme de Claude* achieved the same total during its first year, while *La Jacquerie* dropped from sight after only thirteen.[17]

Did these librettos constitute a conscious attempt on the part of the moderate republican governments of the Third Republic to mobilize the Opéra-Comique for the propagation of their political ideology? French republicans had always recognized, usually from an envious distance, the pedagogic potential of the state theatres, including the opera. Once in power, they sought support from Republican politicians for substantial state subsidies for the Opéra and Opéra-Comique by portraying these elite institutions as a moralizing force:

> We would like the theatre to be a school. . . . The powerful influence of the theatre must come to our aid and second the efforts we make to instruct the people (*le peuple*), to fortify them, to make them worthy of exercising the power that the Republic puts in their hands in order to give France the moral grandeur appropriate to a democracy.[18]

On the other hand, in order to reassure the anti-republican right, highly influential in opera affairs, Republican governments publicly renounced any attempts to mobilize the opera for the advancement of partisan republican politics.[19] There is no evidence in the archives of the Ministry of Public Instruction20 that the state ever interfered in the opera repertoire for partisan political purposes. This negative evidence is not conclusive, since representatives of the government had frequent informal meetings with impresarios, in which the official viewpoint could have been communicated. But no revelations of any such clandestine activity appeared in the press, in the parliamentary debates, in the memoirs of state officials, or in those of the impresarios.

One possible explanation for the social and political content of the Revolutionary operas is merely anticipation by impressarios of the ideological preferences of their audiences. At the Opéra, which had exactly the same relationship to the state, but a very different clientele, there were no references to the Revolution at all. The Opéra impresario Gailhard acknowledged the strength of the aristocracy's intransigence in reacting to a proposed libretto based on a Revolutionary theme:

> The Revolution at the Opéra? *Tricoteuses* and *carmagnoles* on the
> stage? Why not the guillotine? Do you want to drive away the
> subscribers?[21]

The inadmissibility of this material at the Palais Garnier, while Opéra-
Comique librettos such as *La Vivandière* embraced the principles and
accomplishments of the Thermidorean Convention, strongly suggests
that differences in the social composition of the two audiences were
crucial to the formulation of Belle Epoque opera's ideological content.

But if audience preferences were decisive in the impresarios' choice
of librettos--if the state was not, in fact, meddling in the content of
opera's political messages--how did Opéra-Comique librettos come to
meet so precisely the needs of the politicians in power? The answer is
that government officials figured informally, but decisively, in the
impresarios' decision-making process as members of the audience ex
officio. In part because they controlled administrative decisions--and
patronage--of interest to other habitués, leaders of the government
regularly assumed the leadership of the "Tout-Paris of the opera" as
well.[22] They, in turn, introduced friendly critics and artists, and
prominent socialites attached to the appropriate parties. Thus the
composition of the Tout-Paris, and consequently its response to the
social and political content of the repertoire, varied according to
changes in political fortunes. This elite coterie decisively influenced
public reception of individual operas, and its judgments had extensive
repercussions in the subsequent calculations of directors and dramatists
as well. Its capacity for registering political change enabled it to bring
the ideology of the librettos into line with current political
developments.

Control of the Tout-Paris enabled supporters of the government to
exercise informal influence over the repertoire, which more than
compensated for the official restraint of the Ministry. As long as the
active influence of established politicians was unofficial, the opera was
able to maintain its reputation as a harmless, ideologically neutral
amusement, and therefore, I suggest, to propagate more effectively the
social and political program of the groups in power. The elites of the
Tout-Paris served their hegemonic interests without acknowledging--
perhaps even without recognizing--the social and political content of
the choices they were making; neither friends, nor enemies, nor
servants of the regime commented on the political messages implicit in
the French Revolution operas.

This self-serving self-deception could be maintained as long as the messages implicit in apparently uncontroversial, frivolous, or beautiful operas appeared to be simple common sense, rather than propaganda. As Arnold Hauser puts it,

> What most sharply distinguishes a propagandistic from an ideological presentation and interpretation of the facts is . . . that its falsification and manipulation of the truth is always conscious and intentional. Ideology, on the other hand, is mere deception--in essence self-deception--never simply lies and deceit. It obscures truth in order not so much to mislead others as to maintain and increase the self-confidence of those who express and benefit from such deception.[23]

Since overt government interference would have changed opera's function from a hegemonic one to a less effective propagandistic one, government officials' ability to manipulate the ideological content of the repertoire informally, through the Tout-Paris of the opera, was crucial. With implications for contemporary politics, the Opéra-Comique conveyed an ideologically biased interpretation of the Revolution to tens of thousands of receptive, unreflecting patrons.

NOTES

The librettos referred to in the text have all been published. There is a complete collection in the Bibliothèque Nationale in Paris.

1. Edouard Nöel and Edmund Stoullig, *Annales du Théâtre et de la Musique* 40 vols. (Paris, 1875-1914), 8:122.

2. Paul Farmer, *France Reviews Its Revolutionary Origins: Social Politics and Historical Opinion in the Third Republic* (Morningside Heights, N.Y., 1944), 2.

3. Emile Zola, *Le Naturalisme au Théâtre* (Paris, 1881), 63 f. For a sound discussion of Zola's attitude towards the opera, see Jean-Max Guieu, "Le Théâtre Lyrique d'Emile Zola," Doctoral Dissertation, University of Maryland, 1976, 91 f. and passim.

4. Alfred Bruneau, *Musiques de Russie et Musiciens de France* (Paris, 1903), 124 f. Camille de Saint-Saëns, "Lettre de Las Palmas," *La Nouvelle Revue* 30 (March 1897).

5. For a complete explanation of the concept of local color and its significance for French opera, see Heinz Becker, ed., *Die "Couleur locale" in der Oper des 19. Jahrhunderts* (Regensburg, 1976).

6. Jane Fulcher, *The Nation's Image* (New York: Cambridge University Press, 1987).

7. There is a collection of *cahiers des charges in France. Archives Nationales.* Dossier AJ XIII (1187). Article 78 of the *Cahiers des Charges* of the Opéra-Comique for 1911, available in Bibliothèque de l'Opéra, Dossier P.A. 1900-1927, P.A. 1/24 May 1911, states that "The Commissaire du Gouvernement . . . will send the Minister reports on all new works, revivals, debuts; on the manner in which business is conducted, on infractions of the *cahiers des charges* which might have been committed, and in general on all incidents which he feels should be noted."

8. Stephan Stompor in "Ein Opernhaus und seine Gattung," *Muskibühne* (1974), 141, quotes German critics from the period who called the Opéra-Comique "the foremost opera house in the world." In defence of the Opera, it had just begun (1891) introducing the works of Wagner to France, and continued to do so until 1914, when it staged the first production of *Parzifal* outside Bayreuth. See Andre Spies, "Lohengrin Takes on the Third Republic," *Nineteenth-Century Studies* 3 (1989):31-36.

9. Act 2, sc. 6.

10. Act 2, sc. 7.

11. Act 3, sc. 3.

12. Act 5, sc. 2

13. Act 2, sc. 2.

14. See Sanford Elwitt, *The Making of the Third French Republic: Class and Politics in France, 1868-1884* (Baton Rouge, 1975), passim.

15. Act 2, sc. 1.

16. For an account of this episode, see for instance David Robin Watson, *Georges Clemenceau* (N.Y., N.Y., 1974), 118 f.

17. Statistics on frequency of performance have been compiled from the yearly totals in Noel and Stoullig, Annales. For Rouen, Henri Geispitz, *Histoire du Théâtre-des-Arts de Rouen 1882-1913* (Rouen, 1913).

18. "Circulaire de M. le Sous-Secrétaire d'Etat des Beaux-Arts a MM. les Inspecteurs de theatre, 2/26/1879," reprinted in Société des Auteurs et Compositeurs Dramatiques: Annuaire, 7 vols. (Paris, 1887-1915), 1:139. Cf. "Rapport fait au nom de la Commission de finance," Sénat No. 111, Année 1910, in Bibliothèque de l'Opéra, Dossier P.A. 1900-1927. For the opinions of Victor Hugo, for instance, see Pierre Bossuet, *Histoire des Théâtres Nationaux: Les Théâtres et l'Etat* (Paris, n.d.), 19 f.

19. Chambre des Députés, Seance du 1/29/1891, *Journal Officiel*, 146-49, passim.

20. *France. Archives Nationales.* Series Series AJ[13], F[17], F[21].

21. Quoted in Adolphe Brisson, *Portraits intîmes*, Serie III (Paris, 1897), 41.

22. Albert Carré, *Souvenirs de Théâtre* (Paris, 1950), 256, 259. Cf. "Subventions theatrales," *l'Autorité*, 7/11/1900.

23. Arnold Hauser quoted in Thomas L. Haskell, "Capitalism and the Origins of the Humanitarian Sensibility, Part I," *American Historical Review* 90 no. 2 (April 1988):339-61, in the context of an extended, illuminating discussion of the concept of self-deception as it relates to cultural hegemony theory.

THE CONCEPT OF NATION IN THE DRAMATIC WORKS OF STANISLAW WYSPIANSKI

BARBARA A. NIEMEZYK

In Poland, as elsewhere in Europe, the last decade of the nineteenth century was characterized by an artistic revolt against the established order in the arts. Painting, architecture, music, literature and the applied arts were all affected by the new ideas on the form and function of art. The generation of artists and writers coming of age in the 1880s and 1890s shared a dislike for the Positivist literature they had been brought up on, with its emphasis on a naturalistic depiction of reality, its objective value system, and its social and often utilitarian orientation. By the end of the nineteenth century a full-scale artistic revolution was in effect, which continued until the end of World War I.

Poland's political situation at the turn of the century differed from that of other European nations, however. As a result of the partitions of 1792, 1793 and 1795, Poland had lost its independence. It had been carved up and divided among three major powers: the Russian, Prussian, and Austro-Hungarian Empires. Political, social, and cultural conditions varied considerably in the three sectors. In the Russian and Prussian sectors the population was forced to learn Russian and German respectively; these were the languages of instruction in schools and universities. Polish intellectual and cultural life naturally suffered as a result of the repressive linguistic policies of the Russian and Prussian Empires. Suppression was particularly severe in the areas under Russian rule. There had been two major insurrections in Poland against the Tsarist regime in 1830-31 and in 1863, and the government was particularly sensitive to stirrings of Polish national sentiment. All scholarly and artistic works had to be submitted to the official censorship board in St. Petersburg, whose standards were very strict. The political and cultural situtation was freest in Austrian-controlled Galicia, which was ruled from Vienna, where a somewhat more relaxed atmosphere prevailed.   Polish delegates sat in the Austrian Parliament, and several Poles from Galicia (including Alfred Potocki and Kaximierz Badeni), occupied important cabinet positions in Vienna.   An influential group of Kraków historians and politicians advocated retention of the *status quo* and loyalty to Austria-Hungary as the wisest political program for the future for Poles. By the 1880s and 1890s, however, the first stirrings of populist and socialist movements were making their presence felt, and the ethnic and religious minorities within Polish Galicia were beginning to express their own national concerns.   In 1869 a language decree had been passed which established Polish as the official language of the administrative, judicial and educational systems, so that Polish cultural life was relatively autonomous, and not subject to severe scrutiny from Vienna.   Vienna was enjoying its own revolution in science and the arts by the 1890s, and an atmosphere of considerable tolerance toward new ideas prevailed there.   The censorship board was also relatively relaxed.

It is against this background that the theoreticians, writers and artists of "Young Poland" (*Mloda Polska*) appeared and flourished.   In Poland, adherents of the new artistic philosophy, which had its roots in the Symbolist movement in literature and art, most often referred to themselves as the "Young Poland" generation.   The movement itself was referred to variously as "Modernism," "Neo-Romanticism" and "Decadence" by critics although the term "Young Poland" became the most popular label for the new movement after a series of theoretical articles about the new movement entitled "Mloda Polska" ("Young Poland") by Artur Gorski appeared in 1898 in the influential Kraków periodical *Zycie* (*life*).   Symbolist aesthetic theory stressed the autonomy of art; art should be separate from any extra-artistic concerns.   It also sought a synthesis of the spiritual and physical spheres of existence.   In Poland, however, the artistic revolution rapidly changed from advocating "art for art's sake" to reflecting a yearning for social transformation and national liberation.   By the eve of World War I, poets and artists of the "Young Poland" movement were making quite different demands on art than those envisaged by their French and Belgian forebears.   Symbolism evolved in Poland along distinctly national lines, passionately concerned with historical and contemporary political issues.   Emphasis in individual works of art shifted from an individual to a collective consciousness.

The literature of "Young Poland" centered on Promethean heroes

who were based on Romantic models that evolved to national Messiahs.
The poet's role clearly shifted from ennui, melancholy and pessimism
to active leaderhip of the nation's rebirth and a new order. The precise
nature of this new order was not clearly defined, however. The
inability of the artist to exist in isolation from his community became
the dominant theme in the literature of "Young Poland." The artist's
consciousness and conscience became the reflection of the collective
awareness and conscience of his community, expressed in purely Polish
historical and cultural terms. Polish national and literary myths
became the means of forging a new myth, that of national liberation.

The symbolic union of the poet and the people and the synthesis of
opposing social and artistic tendencies were most often to be brought
about through the celebration of a religious/theatrical rite that led to a
lively experimentation with theatrical forms. This most often involved
a return to primitive sources as well as a reliance on religious ritual as
the means by which individual and national consciousness could best be
united. It was in the drama that the writers and theoreticians of
"Young Poland" made perhaps their most significant and enduring
contributions. Symbolism as a style of art and literature enjoyed a
relatively short period of barely two decades of popularity before it
fragmented into diverse, often opposing, tendencies. Its impact on
theatre was, however, long-lasting and is evident in contemporary
theatrical experiments.

Stanislaw Wyspianski, one of the most talented and perhaps the best
known of the "Young Poland" artists and writers, best combined the
aesthetic ideas of "Young Poland" with the national theme in his work.
Born in Kraków in 1869, he was educated at Jagiellonian University,
one of the oldest and most distinguished in Europe, and at the Kraków
School of Fine Arts, where he studied under Jan Matejko, whose
monumental paintings on Polish historical themes were well known.
Wyspianski also studied in Paris from 1890 to 1894, where he became
acquainted with the current artistic trends blossoming in France. He
traveled to Italy and Germany and became acquainted with Richard
Wagner and his work.

Both an accomplished painter and writer, Wyspianski is perhaps
best known for his dramas, whose structure and detail were influenced
by techniques of painting. Strongly influenced by such diverse
elements as classical Greek theater, Shakespeare, Maeterlinck,
Nietzsche and Wagner, Wyspianski created highly original, dynamic
works based on these sources, but drawing heavily on Polish history

and tradition for themes and central concepts. Wyspianski felt very strongly that "the essence of tragedy lay in its power to arouse feelings of pity and terror" and that "human will was the most important component of tragedy."[1] His ideas about drama were greatly influenced by the great Polish Romantic poet and national bard Adam Mickiewicz. In his Sixteenth Lecture on Slavic Literature at the Collège de France, Mickiewicz stated that "in drama poetry is transformed into action before the audience..."[2] Slavic drama was to combine all the elements of national poetry--lyricism, a discussion of current problems historical images--into a harmonious unity "thanks to a typically Slavic gift for grasping the supernatural ... and bringing to life the solemn figures of saints and heroes."[3] In many respects Wyspianski continued the Romantic tradition and developed it. To a large extent he was a precursor of twentieth-century "experimental" and *avant-garde* theater in Poland and elsewhere in Europe. The noted Polish theater director Leon Schiller said of Wyspianski: "On the stage he solved the most personal problems, and they were always the nation's problems.... He created the idea of 'pure theater,' an autonomous theater which possesses its own aesthetics and its own craft, on which literature has no more claim than the actor, while the actor is as much a component of theatrical art as the decor."[4]

Wyspianski sought to create a "temple of the Spirit," a "Church militant" in the theater, which would be contemporary Poland. His theater was to be a "tribunal of national conscience,"[5] where Poland's fate would be linked to that of the "new theater." It would be a "temple where the people pass judgment on themselves, where they search for their own truth, where they gaze at the countenance of their own souls in the magic mirror of the poet."[6] The problem of Poland's future as a nation is ever present in Wyspianski's works, whether in the cycle based on Greek myths (*Archilleis, Powrot Odysa (The Return of Odysseus), Protesilas i Laodamia, Meleager and Akropolis*) or in those plays which drew on Polish myths and legends for their inspiration (*Legenda, Boleslaw Smialy (Boleslaw the Bold)* and *Skalka [The Cliff,* about the martydom of St. Stanislaus]. Several of Wyspianski's plays (*Noc listopadowa (November Night), Warszawianka, Lelewel and Legion*) deal directly with Poland's uprisings and national martyrdom, while others (*Wyzwolenie [Liberation], Klatwa [The Curse], Sedziowie [The Judges]* and *Wesele [The Wedding]*) deal with contemporary Polish life. Regardless of chronological setting, the theme of Wyspianski's drama is inevitably the nation and the individual's place

in it and responsibility to it. Past, present and future converge, and
often compress into one day in his plays. Contemporary life, even
when the play is sent in the distant past, intrudes into the action of the
play. Reality is always present as a reference point to events. A
complex system of visual and aural images is an integral part of the
action used to make or emphasize particularly important points.

One of Wyspianski's key geographical locations is that of Wawel,
the hill in Kraków on which the royal castle and cathedral stand. It is
the scene of dramatic action in several of Wyspianski's plays. As the
site of both temporal and spiritual power as well as the tombs of
Poland's kings, poets and heroes, Wawel functions as a multilevel
symbol. As "castle, church and grave ... it governs the Polish
conscience."[7] It is a Polish Acropolis. Wawel stands as a visual
reminder of past glory and as a reproach to the current age of weakness
and complacency.

One important theme of Wyspianski is class and social divisions
among Poles and the historical role of these divisions and tensions. For
Wyspianski, the common people, the peasantry, deprived for centuries
of any active participation in the political life of the nation, are the
unconscious creators of the only real art; "only the common people,
living and believing in their art" have not become estranged from their
ancient sources. In their plastic, theatrical, mimetic, musical and
poetic creations they preserved in ritualistic art their ancient Slavic
roots. Wyspianski believed that the Polish village retained
characteristics of ancient Slavic settlements in its structure and rituals.
The religious customs and festivals of the peasants retained elements of
pre-Christian rituals and pageants and were to provide the seed for
Polish art and theater of the future.

Szopka is another important feature in Wyspianski's plays.
Originally a Christmas custom of going from house to house with a
creche (which often contained Polish national features, such as Wawel
Castle and Cathedral, and which today even include Pope John Paul II
and Lech Walesa in the traditional manger scene), singing religious
and secular Chirstmas carols and sampling the hospitality of their
hosts, *szopka* eventually evolved into a theatrical form. Combining
mythical creatures (a *turon*, a shaggy, horned creature resembling a
wolf or a bear) with historical and allegorical figures (King Herod,
Satan), it was a mixture of *commedia dell'arte*, puppet show and
morality play all in one.[8] Wyspianski used the techniques of *szopka*--
the mixing of levels and time spans, the combining of mythological,

historical and contemporary characters, the rapid scene shifts--in his dramas. Not only did this provide a certain liveliness and link to folk culture which he wanted to maintain, but the looseness of structure and the freedom from classical theatrical conventions provided him with the flexibility he needed to express his complex ideas.

One of Wyspianski's indisputable masterpieces is *The Wedding*. It is, in many respects, the ultimate Symbolist drama. It is based on an actual event: the wedding of Lucjan Rydel, a young poet, and Jadwiga Mikolajczykówna, a peasant girl, which was in itself meant to be symbolic and consciously theatrical. In *The Wedding* Wyspianski deals with the issue of national liberation as a holy national myth. As in most of his dramas, the action occurs in one day, that of the wedding. The myth is based on the premise that at the right moment the people will rise and fight to free their homeland in a long-awaited alliance of peasantry and gentry. "The poet realizes the awaited moment and arranges a fantastic act of insurrection in order to test the validity of the myth in a contemporary literary model. The result is shattering, as revealed in the drama."[9]

Wyspianski was himself a guest at the wedding and a direct participant in the proceedings described in the play. *The Wedding* is self-conscious art--the writer observing the event and then writing about his observations. In a style similar to traditional *szopka*, Wyspianski combines living characters representing figures or classes in contemporary Polish society with visions of Polish historical and legendary figures, projections of the real characters' thoughts and emotions. Characters appear, disappear, reappear, uttering a few lines or engaging in conservation with each other. The action occurs in three acts, each consisting of several short scenes. The main setting is a small room of a peasant cottage in the village of Bronowice, outside of Kraków. Two obvious focal points of visual interest in the room are two paintings by Jan Matejko: *Wernyhora*, a portrait of the legendary bard who foretold Poland's resurrection, and *Kósciuszko on the Outskirts of Raclawice*, which commemorates Tadeusz Kósciuszko's insurrection in the late eighteenth century, in which the peasantry played an important role in the struggle against Tsarist authorities. The wedding festivities unfold in a room off-stage. There is no traditional plot development but scenes of interaction between different sets of characters. The action of *The Wedding* occurs on two levels: the realistic and the visionary. There are also two types of characters: the "real" characters, modeled after the actual wedding guests (which caused a scandal in Kraków society after the premier of the play in March, 1901), and the visions, or specters, with definite correspondences between the two sets of characters.

The actual wedding was held on November 20, 1900, in the home of Wlodzimierz Tetmajer, the brother of the poet Kazimierz Tetmajer and a member of one of the most distinguished Kraków families. Ten years earlier Wlodzimierz Tetmajer had married Anna, the older sister of Rydel's bride and had been living in the village of Bronowice, among the peasants since then. The marriage represented an earlier attempt at a union of social classes, although the earlier wedding was without any of the fanfare and publicity that accompanied Lucjan Rydel's wedding to Jadwiga Mikolajczykówna. The social divisions among the wedding guests (and within Polish society as a whole) constitute a major theme in Wyspianski's play. Wyspianski satirizes the attitudes of the townspeople toward the peasants, whether it be young society girls intoxicated by the music and color of the folk costumes or the groom himself, who has ostentatiously adapted what he imagines to be thre free, natural lifestyle of the peasants, which for him in Act I consists of dispensing with shoes and underwear:[10]

> for a month I've been walking barefoot, at once I feel healthy, I walk barefoot, bareheaded, I don't wear anything undernearth anymore at once I feel better[11]

The contrast between the Bride and Groom is striking. He obviously romanticizes and idealizes her naivete and simplicity. At one point, when she complains about her tight shoes, he urges her to "dance barefoot," as he imagines peasants do, dancing with wild abandon, free of the strictures and codes of behavior dictated by "polite" society. The Bride has her own standards of propriety and decorum, however, and tells him, "You have to wear shoes at a wedding."[12] The Groom does not really understand the peasants; he is infatuated with what he imagines to be the carefree, colorful customs and manners of the people. Poetically the Groom rhapsodizes his bewildered bride, oblivious to the fact that she has no idea about what he is talking.

In the first scene of Act I, the Journalist and Czepiec, the wedding master-of-ceremonies, discuss world events. The Journalist of course from an urbane, sophisticated circle of people implies that the peasant's world is self-contained, that he does not desire to know what lies beyond his village:

> But here the village is quiet -
> Let there be war all over the world,
> as long as the Polish village is quiet,[13]
> as long as the Polish village is calm.

Czepiec himself a peasant assures the Journalist that the peasant is concerned with national affairs and reminds him of the role peasants have played in Poland's history, particularly in national uprisings. He implies that the people would be ready to fight again for Poland's independence, but that the problem lies with the nobility "who don't want to want."[14] This reveals a sharp distinction between the national vision espoused by the two social classes. The peasants have a primitive vitality and strength, but their traditional leaders from the nobility lack the will to provide leadership for any struggle for national independence.

The stratification of Polish society and the conflict between social classes are ever-present elements in the play. Although the wedding is supposed to symbolize the union of nobility and peasantry, in reality this is not possible. The disturbing specter of Jakub Szela, the leader of a bloody peasant uprising in Galicia in 1846, haunts the wedding festivities. The ancestors of several wedding guests perished in the bloody incidents, among them members of the Tetmajer and Rydel families. It has been scarcely two generations since the uprising, and it is obvious that old resentments and hostility cannot be extinguished by an event as ephemeral as a wedding. As the Host says, "That which was can come again."[15]

The Groom himself states:

> We have forgotten everything;
> They cut up my grandfather with a saw...[16]
> We have forgotten everything...
> about the misery, the poverty, the filth;[17]
> we dress up in peacock feathers.

One of the most interesting characters in the play is Rachel, the daughter of the Jewish innkeeper. As a Jewess, she is outside the social circles of the other two groups but has affinities with both. She is a "modern" young woman and is associated with certain bohemian artistic circles in Kraków. With her mannered, studied gestures and affected, literary speech, she is somewhat of a caricature, but she is also direct, sensitive, and honest. She admits that she is attracted to the peasants, because for her they represent a return to nature. She has organic connections to nature, for it is she who summons the Mulch, the first phantom to appear and the only non-human specter. Rachel invites not only the Mulch but all of nature ("all wondrous things, flowers, bushes, lightning bolts, humming noises, songs")[18] to the wedding. She is the Muse who brings inanimate nature to life; once he has been summoned, the Mulch takes over the action of the play and summons the other phantoms, according to

> Whatever is playing in one's soul,
> Whatever one sees in his dreams:
> if a sin, if a grin, if a lout, if a lord,
> will come to dance at the Wedding.[19]

The specters begin to appear at the wedding guests. The Journalist represents Rudolf Starzewski, the editor of the conservative Kraków newspaper *Czas* (*Time*) who was also a member of the *Teka Stanczyka*, the conservative politial group in Kraków which advocated loyalty to Austria-Hungary. He has a vision of Stancyzk, the legendary court jester of Zygumnt I and Zygumnt August, rulers during Poland's Golden Age of political and cultural enlightenment and flowering. The historical Stancyzk was noted for his wisdom and patriotism. His appearance to the Journalist is a reproach to the political group which bears his name but not his ideals. When the Journalist laments Poland's lost glory and the present dismal state of affairs, Stanczyk berates him for his own passivity and paralysis of will. When Stanczyk sarcastically urges him to accept the *kaduceus* (Hermes' staff of office) the Journalist is unable to do so. He is blinded by the past; he is too complacent, too passive, all too willing to blame Fate for Poland's troubles. He lacks the energy to accept Stanczyk's challenge to rule. Confronted by Stanczyk, his nominal patron, he is tormented by self-doubt and inner conflict. He returns to the wedding celebration--to the dancing and the music--in order to forget about the challenge and to bury himself in illusion. The Journalist realizes that he is being lulled to inactivity by poetry and art, and he acknowledges this to the Poet:

Poetry! you are a quiet siesta;
you want to inebriate, to anaesthetize, to
hold me captive.
Oh, don't hide - don't pretend,
you yourself are in the fire - this is a mask
this apparent calm - this is a lie.
Ah! that music drones on so,
like the buzzing of bees from a hive -
and we are like hornets:
this great national mirth, it flies at my throat,
it expands my head with noise, murmuring, giddiness
and even pain is repellent to me.[20]

The Journalist is incapable of helping himself, however. He lacks the will to act and pull himself out of the stupor into which he has fallen. He who is an influential member of society and in a position to provide moral and political leadership proves to be merely a buffoon.

Hetman Branicki, one of the notorious magnates who acquiesced in the infamous Targowica Confederation which resulted in the paritions of Poland, appears to the Groom. Although he is tormented by demons and must pay for his past treachery, Branicki's specter is unrepentant. He reproaches the Groom for marrying a peasant girl (he himself married the daughter of Catherine the Great of Russia), and reminds him that he is a nobleman and should be mindful of his heritage. However, the Groom dispels the apparition as the specter of Jakub Szela, the laeder of the 1846 peasant uprising, again appears to haunt the festivities.

The last vision to appear is the most important. It is Wernyhora, a legendeary Cossack-augur who foretold the resurrection of Poland and the union of the people of Poland and the Ukraine. He was a popular figure among Romantic poets and among the writers and artists of "Young Poland." Wernyhora serves as the symbol of an earlier faith and belief that in some future struggle for Poland's freedom all social classes would be united. The peasantry would join with the nobility and would play a decisive role in the struggle due to its strength and vitality and the sheer force of its numbers. Wernyhora appears to the Host, the representative of a generation obsessed by peasantmania of a particularly superficial nature. Wernyhora gives the Host a commission to act, to lead in the struggle for Poland's freedom. As a token of this mission he gives him a golden horn. The Host in turn gives the golden horn to a peasant boy named Jasiek to summon the people to action, as in the Kósciuszko Insurrection. The Host is delirious:

> The world is drunk, the world is drunk,
> the whole world is bewitched –
> Release me, I have to go,
> I must, I swore by my soul.[21]

His wife and the wedding guests consider his delirium to be merely
drunken raving since most of the guests already have been reduced to
lethargy or drunkenness. One of the guests, the Nose (a caricature of
the contemporary painter Stanislaw Noskowski better known for the
escapades of the beohemian circle of friends with whom he associated
than for his art) expresses the sentiments of a significant segment of
his society:

> I drink, I drink, because I must
> for when I drink, I feel something;
> then I feel my heart in my chest,
> I intuit a great deal...
> If Chopin were still alive,
> he would drink...[22]

Wyspianski is thus critical of his contemporaries who felt it necessary
to drown their problems, concerns and often their talent as well in
alcohol or opiates.

If the final scenes of the play the realistic and visionary levels are
synthesized.   Jasiek returns but without the golden horn.   Taking
greater care of the peacock feathers in his cap than of his sacred
mission, he has lost it.   Only the cord remains as evidence of
Wernyhora's sacred mission. The Host recalls his vision of Wernyhora
as he and the guests fall under a spell. At the conclusion of the play,
the enchanted wedding guests form a "charmed circle" of dancers under
the direction of the Mulch. These scenes present a disturbing picture of
Polish national life on the eve of independence.   Incapable of action
themselves, the intelligentsia lose themselves in music, dance, and art.
The spell of Wernyhora is replaced by that of the Mulch and his
hypnotic music. Physcial nature has triumphed over the Spirit.   The
peasantry   also   is   incapable   of   fulfilling   the   national   mission.
Wyspianski's peasants in *The Wedding* represent simple brute force
without a plan or leadership. It is, after all, through the carelessness of
a peasant boy that Wernyhora's golden horn has been lost.   The
peasants are lulled into immobility by the same spell that has paralyzed
the nobles.

In Wyspianski's play the time for liberation has not yet come. There are no solutions to the national dilemma. Wyspianski is a poet, not a politician and does not suggest any specific political program. He, nevertheless, explodes the national myth and all Romantic illusions and reveals the "bankruptcy of Zygmunt Krasinski's famous dictum: 'The Polish people with the Polish nobility'."[23]   He exposes the hypocrisy and futile posturing of the intelligentsia who long for some sort of mystic union with the peasantry in the glorious mission of liberating Poland. He shows them to be out of contact with reality and with their own past. Wyspianski implies that Polish social classes have always been incomprehensible and inimical to each other and no symbolic union can draw them together. The liberation of Poland requires a will to act that is sadly lacking in the people best qualified to lead. The peasants have the will to act but cannot without leadership. The result is lethargy and stagnation on all levels--an "enchanted circle," endlessly turning, seeking refuge in its illusions.

Another of Wyspianski's most interesting plays, *Liberation*, deals with many of the same issues, but with even more complex and dazzling poetics. As in *The Wedding*, realistic and fantastic figures interact on many levels on the stage. Literary, political and personal allusions occur throughout the text. The variety of devices is truly extraordinary, including *szopka*, morality play, theater within theater and the introduction of journalistic prose into poetic drama.

Once again, the sequence of scenes in the play does not follow any logical order. The protagonist, Konrad, is a clear reference to two of Adam Mickiewicz's Romantic heroes, the Konrad of *Konrad Wallenrod* and the Gustaw-Konrad of *Forefathers' Eve*, both of whom undergo terrible ordeals in their struggle to save their fatherland. The action of *Liberation* takes place on the stage of a Kraków theater in the early evening, "when the Church has finished vespers."[24] The link between religion and what transpires in the theater is made clear from the very beginning; few writers emphasize the sacral nature of theater as strongly as Wyspianski. In the descriptive passage which introduces the play, the question is raised:

> The huge platform
> The Church of God or the Devil
> What will this temple of art become?[25]

Konrad, as he enters the scene, evokes the hero of <u>Forefathers' Eve</u>: dressed in a black coat, in shackles, presnting a contrasting picture of

passion and melancholy at one and the same time. His first words: "I
come from afar; I don't know whether from heaven or from hell,"[26] are
the exact words spoken by Gustaw-Konrad in Forefathers' Eve. He
identifies himself as a victin of the gods and fates, a "fallen star," who
became man, a Lucifer-Christ figure. (This last image wa a very
popular one in the literature of "Young Poland.") Konrad stresses his
universality, his universal mission: "I am in every man, I live in every
heart."[27]   In his iniital dialogue with the chorus, Konrad further
establishes his identity as a Christ and/or a Promethean figure:

> ... a church, a castle, a grave.
> I will build these and destroy them.[28]

This statement has much broader significance, however, for, in the
course of the play, Konrad will literally and figuratively create and
destroy Wawel Castle and Cathedral on the stage of the Kraków
theater. He will also create a new art.
    The chorus identifies itself as "peasants, rabble," who are awaiting
the hour of vengeance for all of the historial and social wrongs which
have been done to them. Konard enlists the aid of the workers in
presenting his play: "you are going to build and destory."[29]   The
Director and the Muse enter. In response to Muse's question "What do
you want?" Konrad replies: "*Liberation*."[30] The Muse questions him
further: "Liberation from what? of what? the soul? the mind? the
heart? Konrad replies: "The will!"
    The set for Konrad's play is to be Wawel Cathedral, with its tombs
of Polish kings, knights, bishops and bards. The set is also to represent
the parliament hall on Wawel, with a card table and a game of dice in
progress. Both spiritual and temporal levels of national existence are,
therefore, to be represented. Poland is to be recreated on the stage; her
national tragedy is to be played out:

> A theater of the nation,
> a play, a Polish play! We want to decorate it, we want to paint it,
> We want to build Poland in this theater![31]

The title of the play will be *Contemporary Poland*, and the beginning
of the play will be signalled by a gong representing Zygumnt's bell on
Wawel (a treasured national symbol dating from the "Golden Age" of
the sixteenth century). The theme of resurrection is stressed over and
over again in the play. Many of the decorative elements of the set are
to represent Christ's resurrection, and elements of the Roman Catholic

Easter liturgy are to be included in the play. The nation itself is to be
brought to life on the stage in the course of the play, which is to be a
tragedy:

> Our acting will be tragic:
> an accusation, a flogging and a confession.
> He will see the day of liberation
> Who is freed by his own will![32]

The action of *Liberation* begins with tableau-like scenes of groups
of characters representing different Polish social classes, as well as
various historical and allegorical figures.   Scenes 2 and 3, although
very brief, are particularly striking.   Scene 2 consists of a dialogue
between the Chorus and the President, widely interpreted to be
Stanislaw Tarnowski, a literary historian and professor at Jagiellonian
University, who belonged to a group advocating loyalty to Austria-
Hungary as the best political course for Galicia.   The President
advocates calm and quiet: the *status quo* must, after all, be preserved
for future generations.   There is only one condition: that the word
"Poland" never be mentioned. In striking contrast to this scene is the
following one in which a satirical picture of the opposing political
camp--the *tromtadraci*, the old fashioned democrats who loudly voiced
patriotic slogans, without any concrete, realistic political programs--is
presented. The refrain "Poland, Poland!" echoes throughout the scene,
in contrast to the preceding one in which the very word was forbidden.
The leader of this group bids everyone join hands and shout in unison,
and not look beyond their immediate surroundings: "Let's not look
beyond our table, let's not look.   Let's just join hands and shout:
Poland!"[33] Thus, Wyspianski satirizes both the advocates of political
compromise and pragmatism, as well as the emotional patriots, whose
enthusiasm was limited to issuing empty manifestos on national
holidays.   Various other ideas are bandied about in the remaining
scenes: the revival of Poland on a spiritual, metaphysical plane, the
role of the Church in Polish national life, the importance of love
between individuals in a family and in society in general. The primary
dispute Wyspianski presents, however, is that with the Romantic,
Messianic ethos embodied in the figure of the Genius (Adam
Mickiewicz). Wyspianski viewed Mickiewicz's brand of Romanticism
as a hollow and even dangerous philosophy, which nutured false hopes
and encouraged dreams which could only prove to be self-deluding and
self-defeating. The remainder of *Liberation* deals with this struggle of

the philosophy of action against the philosophy of empty dreams and false hopes.

Act II consists entirely of Konrad's dialogue with twenty-two Masks, representing the different attitudes and viewpoints of Wyspianski's contemporaries. Konrad begins with a severe indictment of the "trouble-makers, rabble, lackeys and flunkies" whose ultimate fate will be abject subjugation and oblivion, and attempts to assert his individuality and strength throughout the act. In his conversation with Mask Five, Konrad is very critical of the tendency to conceive of Poland in poetic, metaphysical terms, ignoring political reality. He discusses the future of the nation with Mask Six, who designates him spiritual leader of his people: "And wherever you go, your people will follow you."[34] Konrad will lead them by the strength of the WORD to the temple, which resembles Wawel Cathedral, a "Church of the dead," because Poland's history and past lie buried in it. As Konrad says: "On the day of the great holiday, which will be a national holiday, we will go down to the royal tombs."[35] Liberation is thus equated with death. As Konrad describes his scenario for national liberation, Mask Six cries to him: "You will die!" Konrad replies: "Liberated!" In his succeeding conversations with the Masks, Konrad discusses the role of art--the only constant, the only imperishable entity in a finite and chaotic world and the importance of action. In his conversation with Mask Eleven he argues that Poland--the land, the country, the people-- exists; only the sense of nation is lost. Poles themselves are to blame for the lack of a nation, however, in that they tend to over-philosophize, to argue endlessly, rather than actually doing anything concrete and constructive. For the people represented by Mask Eleven Poland is a myth, a dream, an ideal; it does not and never will exist. According to Wyspianski, it is these national charlatans who steal the soul of a nation. In his conversation with Mask Fifteen, Konrad rails against those who preach Messianism and salvation through pain and suffering. Why, he asks, are we to be the Christ of Nations (a concept advocated by Mickiewicz)--to suffer torture and crucifixion--for someone else's benefit? "A nation has only one right--to exist as a state."[36]

The third and final act takes place in Wawel Cathedral. The Genius--the Mickiewicz figure--enters and walks from group to group. Characters from Act I reappear, and the Genius wanders among them, directing their actions. The Genius finally begins to lead those assembled on stage to the crypt of the cathedral, to the tombs of the kings of Poland. He assures them that liberation will come through death, for death will lead to the eternal life of the spirit. He holds a golden horn (an obvious reference to *The Wedding*) in one hand and a golden chalice, filled with the mead of forgetfulness, in the other. As the sound of a bell tolling is heard, Konrad suddenly appears on stage, torch in hand, calling for blood and the consecration of knives. He has come not for peace, but to arouse the masses to hatred and revenge. Konrad condemns Messianism and the idea of salvation through suffering; he forcibly shuts the gates to the tombs, knocking the golden chalice from the Genius' hand. Konrad concludes his tirade with the command: "POETRY BE GONE!!! YOU ARE A TYRANT!!!"[37] This constitutes Wyspianski's severe condemnation of the entire Romantic tradition, which in Poland had lulled people into peaceful, complacent forgetfulness and political paralysis.

After his victory over the Genius, Konrad awakens as from a trance, and the scene of Wyspianski's play shifts back to the realistic level, to the contemporary Kraków theater. All of the actors have stepped out of their roles, except for Konrad. He becomes agitated as the actors strike the set of Wawel, but the rest of the cast pay no attention to him. The cast and stage crew realize that it has only been a play; only Konrad has taken everything that has transpired that night seriously. As the Director leaves, Konrad is left alone to deliver his final soliloquy, and to resolve his problem: "How will I get out of the circle of the spell of Art?"[38] As he speaks, the Erinyes[39] appear. They rise on the spot where the golden horn spilled and shattered. They place a wreath of serpents on Konrad's head, which burns and blinds him, and arm him with a sword. All frantically try to leave the stage, but in vain. The doors are bolted; they are trapped for the night, and must await the dawn and someone who can unlock the gate, enabling Konrad to burst his bonds.

There are three levels of "liberation" in Wyspianski's play: 1) the liberation of Poland as a nation from political captivity and subjugation; 2) the liberation of the Polish people from inertia of spirit and will; 3) the liberation of art from confining, outdated models and restrictions. Konrad undertakes the mission of salvation--it is he who must wage a battle for the hearts and minds of his countrymen. He aims to do this by means of truth and art. Since art is held captive by a falsely-soothing poetry, however, it is not taken seriously and has lost its credibility among the masses. The issue of art thus emerges as the most important one. It becomes the key issue of the drama, from which the other levels of spiritual, national and individual liberation are to proceed. "The thread of art is the organizing principle of the entire work. The success of Konrad's mission depends on whether or not he wins the battle for art."[40] Konrad is a representation of a Mickiewiczian romantic hero and, at the same time, an alter-ego of Wyspianski. The play is structured in such a way that Konrad speaks directly to his audience, sometimes as dramatis persona and sometimes as author. The function of the chorus is to question or contradict what was just spoken. The Masks of Act II represent the attitudes and opinions of Wyspianski's contemporaries, and are not intended to be literal representations of actual historical figures. If art can be liberated, it can then become action. Konrad wins the battle with the Genius, the battle for thought, for ideology. He is internally free, aware of his own strength and will, and seeks to lead his countrymen to the same state of freedom. They are not ready for it, however. They are too lethargic, too apathetic, too caught up in their daily routines and mundane cares to concern themselves with anything as lofty, noble and abstract as liberation, national or otherwise. Konrad did not betray his mission, nor did art betray him; rather, both were themselves betrayed. The poet attempted to lead the crowd, but they were not ready to follow him.

Neither Konrad nor Wyspianski had any concrete political program, however. Wyspianski's generation had lost patience with old-fashioned, traditional credos and beliefs. The younger generation of intellectuals were more inclined to action, to dream and talk less about abstract concepts of "nationhood" and "fatherland" and more inclined to take concrete measures to bring about the realization of this nation. Wypsianski presents a very negative picture of contemporary society in both *The Wedding* and Liberation. He had contempt for the so-called political leaders of Poland for their weakness and inability to establish Poland as a political entity, and for the ideological and spiritual leaders for their incompetence in awakening and maintaining national consciousness in the population. Wyspianski had no solutions, however. He did not believe in the possiblity of imminent rebellion; basically, he did not trust the masses. His program was emotional and intuitive and not strictly ideological or political.

After Liberation, which never achieved the popular or critical success of many of Wyspianski's other works, Wyspianski was no longer to deal with contemporary problems. In plays such as *Boleslaw the Bold* (1903), *Achilleis* (1903), *Akropolis* (1904) *Skalka* (1907) and

The Return of Odysseus (1907), he dealt with more general problems of philosophy and life. His last, unfinished work, *Zygmunt August*, was a new attempt to redefine his ideology, and to develop a new synthesis of philosophical and national political thought.

Regardless of time period, "artistic myths--of poetry, painting, sculpture, architecture, music and 'mythological' myths, historical and ideological myths all coexist in Wyspianski's works. The Symbolists' faith in symbolic art as a myth-creating art, possessing its own ability to create myths, finds its realization in the works of Stanislaw Wyspianski."[41] Wyspianski attempted to intergrate all of the different types of myth, however. Although he was concerned with universal problems of good and evil and greatly influenced by contemporary philosophical trends, Wyspianski nevertheless sought to deal with Poland's "national problem." Virtually all of his dramas are set in Poland, "where history takes up so much space; where the dead past lives, and the living resemble the dead."[42] He first showed the emptiness and shallowness of contemporary life in *The Wedding*, and went on to further develop another positive, creative ideology in Liberation.

The continuing popularity of Wyspianski's plays has attested to the fact that they are neither historical set-pieces nor dazzling examples of early twentieth-century theatrical experimentation. Such renowned theatrical directors as Andrzej Wajda, Jerzy Grotowski, Adam Hanuszkiewicz, and Konrad Swinarski have all staged versions of Wyspianski's works. Andrzej Wajda also directed a much acclaimed film version of *The Wedding*. Wyspianski's message has been as relevant for audiences in the post-war Polish Peoples' Republic as for his contemporaries at the turn of the century. Wyspianski's works have become increasingly popular in Poland since the 1960s, when censorship restrictions were eased. Since many of his plays--especially *November Night* and Liberation--contain very specific anti-Tsarist and hence anti-Russian sentiments, these plays have been especially popular during periods of turmoil and unrest in the late 1970s and 1980s, when anti-Soviet sentiment was openly expressed. Moreover, the problem of social stratification has not disappeared in socialist Poland, nor has the tendency to revert to Romantic models and ideals in dealing with *Realpolitik*. The current wave of unrest and many of the issues confronting the leaders of Solidarity today reflect many of the problems confronted by earlier generations and touched on by the writers of the "Young Poland" movement. The rebirth of Poland as an independent political state has become as vital an issue at the end of the twentieth century as it was at the beginning. The issues which concerned Wyspianski and his contemporaries are just as important today: the conflict between generations, between the *status quo* and the forces of change and reform within the society, and the best means for national self-expression and self-determination. In many respects Wyspianski's "enchanted circle" continues to revolve in contemporary Poland.

NOTES

1. Czeslaw Milosz, *A History of Polish Literature* (New York: Macmillan, 1969, 353.

2. Ibid.

3. Ibid., 354.

4. Quoted in Milosz, 354.

5. Leon Schiller, "Nowy teatr w Polsce: Stanislaw Wyspianksi," *Mysl teatralna Mlodej Polski* (Warszawa: Wydawnictwo Artystyczne i Filmowe, 1966), 220.

6. Ibid., 212.

7. Ibid., 233.

8. *Szopki* were very popular at the turn of the century and continue to be performed at Christmas time, both as folk rituals and theatrical pageants.

9. Aniela Lempicka, "Stanislaw Wyspianksi," *Obraz literatury polskiej* (Warsaw: Panstwowe Wydawnictwo Naukowe, 1968-77), 70.

10. All quotes from *The Wedding* are from: Stanislaw Wyspianski, *Wesele* (Wroclaw: Ossolineum, 1973), 258 pp. All translations of the Polish text into English are by the author of the paper.

11. Act 1, sc. 19, lines 584-88,

12. Act 1, sc. 12, line 333.

13. Act 1, sc. 1, lines 22-25

14. Ibid., line 33.

15. Act 1, sc. 30, line 1097.

16. Ibid., lines 1098-1100.

17. Ibid., lines 1109-10.

18. Act 1, sc. 36, lines 1282-83.

19. Act 2, sc. 3, lines 37-42.

20. Act 2, sc. 8, lines 513-26.

21. Act 2, sc. 29, lines 1449-52.

22. Act 3, sc. 2, lines 58-66.

23. Wilhelm Feldman, "O zloty Róg," Krytyka, III, (1901): 6:341.

24. All quotes from *Liberation* are from: Stanislaw Wyspianski, *Wyzwolenie* (Wroclaw: Ossolineum, 1970), 372 pp. All translations of the Polish text into English are by the author.

25. Act 1, lines 13-15.

26. Ibid., line 34.

27. Ibid., line 56.

28. Ibid., lines 84-85.

29. Ibid., line   115.

30. Ibid., line   195.

31. Ibid., lines 268-70.

32. Ibid., lines 400-03.

33. Act 1, sc. 3, lines 530-31.

34. Act 2, line   251.

35. Ibid., lines 280-81.

36. Ibid., lines 788-89.

37. Act 3, line   453.

38. Ibid., line   671.

39. The Erinyes were infernal deities in Greek mythology whose special mission was to punish parricides and those who had violated oaths. Their hair was plaited with serpents, and they usually carried whips and torches. They are sometimes referred to as "the dogs of Hades" or "the children of Eternal Night."

40. Aniela Lempicka, introduction to Stanislaw Wyspianski, *Wyzwolenie*, iv.

41. Jan Nowakowski, "Symbolizm i dramaturgia Wyspianskiego," *Pamietnik Literacki*, 53 (1962), no. 4: 446.

42. Aniela Lempicka, *Wyspianski, pisarz dramatyczny.   Idee i formy* (Kraków: Wydawnictwo Literackie, 1973), 118.

The John L. Snell Prize Seminar Paper

BURY ST. EDMUNDS: A REASSESSMENT OF TOWN-ABBEY RELATIONS

MICHAEL GRAHAM

Because of a wealth of surviving records, many of them published, the East Anglian town of Bury St. Edmunds has received a great deal of attention from historians interested in the high and late middle ages.[1] But despite all the ink spilled, our understanding of the relationship between the town and its abbey is still overly simplistic. No one has yet attempted a major study of the monastery's economic history, and Robert Gottfried, in his recent social and economic survey of the town, seems hasty to force valuable new statistical research onto the procrustean bed of old preconceptions.

Put simply, the standard interpretation is that from at least the twelfth century, the town's history was dominated by a struggle for control between the citizens of the town and their monastic overlords. This struggle has been presumed to have been common to all monastic towns. Norman Trenholme wrote: "the burgesses of the monastic towns...were in a constant state of political unrest from the close of the twelfth century to the dissolution of the monasteries," because their ecclesiastical overlords failed to "recognize the growing corporate spirit of the townsmen and to concede to them rights of self government and commercial control."[2] Gottfried seems generally to agree, maintaining that "the dominant activity [in late medieval Bury] was the struggle of the town's burghal elite to assert their independence."[3] Elsewhere, he writes of the abbey as "the common enemy" of the townspeople.[4]

This "struggle" interpretation relies heavily on the evidence of violent outbreaks in Bury in 1264, 1327, and 1381. Historians have assumed that the violence was a manifestation of militant opposition by Bury's residents to abbey rule. Again, Gottfried does nothing to change this view: "Riots and rebellions in other English towns often matched violent outbreaks in Bury in 1264, 1327, and 1381. Historians have assumed that the violence was a manifestation of militant opposition by Bury's residents to abbey rule. Again, Gottfried does nothing to change this view: "Riots and rebellions in other English towns often matched one stratum of town society against another. In Bury, this was never the case; frustration against St. Edmund's was always enough to overcome 'class' conflicts."[5]   Gottfried does change slightly the foundation of the old edifice. He sees the battle after 1381 as economic rather than political, with the townsmen more successful in the financial arena: "Violence was unnecessary in fifteenth-century resistance because the townsfolk were in an increasingly strong position."[6] Yet his argument that the abbey was in serious economic trouble during its last century rests on flimsy evidence, leaving him unable to explain why the town became more peaceful after 1381. He and the others have been too quick to see the attitudes of the townsmen and the monks throughout the late middle ages as monolithic. In fact, both citizens and monks may have been as contentious when dealing among themselves as they were in town-abbey relationships. A. F. Butcher has recently debunked the myth that Canterbury's residents fought in unity in 1381; perhaps Bury heeds a similar corrective.[7] First, some explanation of the town's origin and history is needed.

Origins of the Town and Liberty of Bury St. Edmunds Saint Edmund himself, king and martyr, was a half-legendary figure. As king of East Anglia, he supervised a Christian revival in the late 860s while England's Danish invaders were busy elsewhere. When the Danes returned in 870 they captured him probably in battle, and ordered him to renounce his faith and pay tribute to the Danes for his kingdom. For whatever reason--his hagiographers naturally held that he found the first requirement more odious than the second--he refused, and was killed.[8] His cult quickly developed, becoming a focal point for both Christianity and English resistance to the Danes. More than fifty Anglo-Saxon churches were dedicated to him, five of them surviving in Suffolk to this century.[9]

Remains reputed to be those of St. Edmund came to the town of Bedricswroth in 903, and sometime between then and 1086 the town became known as Bury St. Edmunds.[10] A college of secular canons watched over the sacred remains from the time of their arrival, but Bury St. Edmunds became a Benedictine colony in 1020, receiving a charter from (ironically) the Danish king Knut in 1026.[11] As the Benedictine house grew, so grew the reputation of the saint. More powerful in death than life, his curse was said to have killed Knut's father Swein, as well as (later) King Stephen's son Eustace. Naturally, the monastic chroniclers of the abbey made no attempt to diminish the saint's power. Jocelin of Brakelond used as an *exemplum* the story of Henry of Essex, apparently a minor baron, who defrauded the abbey of five shillings and attempted to curtail its legal jurisdiction. The saint threatened him in a vision; he repented, becoming a monk.[12] Later, royal officials seeking some of the monastery's jewels to help pay the ransom for Richard I were opposed by the formidable abbot Samson, who dared them to enter the church and take part of the feretory. They declined, noting: "St. Edmund strikes those remote and absent; much more will he strike those present who wish to carry away his tunic."[13] But the saint's powers were not all negative. He drew many pilgrims to Bury and performed numerous miracles. Active in the latter capacity as late as 1375, he was reputed to have saved one Simon Brown nearly lost at sea.[14]

While St. Edmund was doubtless a great friend to his monastery, it had some powerful living patrons as well. Edward the Confessor was particularly fond of the abbey, regarding St. Edmund as one of his greatest ancestors. In 1044 he gave the abbot full regalian rights over eight-and-a-half hundreds surrounding the monastery, roughly corresponding to West Suffolk today.[15] This area became known as the Liberty of St. Edmund.

The liberty was actually two liberties. Although royal itinerant justices could hear the cases of free men in the wider liberty of the eight-and-a-half hundreds, they could not enter the *banleuca* which stretched a mile out from the town in every direction. With control over this *banleuca* came the right to hear all cases arising within it save those involving the king's person. Even the wider liberty was in many ways a kingdom unto itself.[16] Naturally, the monopoly on justice held by the abbey brought it many profits. But the courts operated by the abbey were "popular" courts. While the abbey could reap the profits of justice, the assembled freemen declared the law, putting a curb on the arbitrary power of the abbey. The possession of regalian rights enabled the abbot to collect all revenues, such as Danegeld, which would otherwise have gone to the king, not only on abbey demesne land, but on all land within the liberty.[17] The liberty as a unit became so institutionalized that it outlasted the abbey by more than four centuries, serving as an administrative unit until the English counties were reorganized in 1974.[18]

Edward the Confessor also gave the monks at Bury the right to operate a mint that remained in operation until the early 1300s.[19] In 1065, he made his personal physician, Baldwin, formerly a monk of St. Denis, abbot.[20]

Domesday Book gives a good glimpse of both the abbey and the town of Bury St. Edmunds in 1086. The abbey was a tenant-in-chief in six counties and the largest landholder in Suffolk. It dominated the immediate area around Bury, holding thirty-two of the thirty-eight manors in Thingoe and Thedwastre hundreds. The abbot was the largest landholder in Suffolk, even surpassing the king.[21] In all, the abbey held over three hundred manors.[22] The town of Bury grew considerably between 1066 and 1086, doubling in annual value from ten pounds to twenty pounds. Since 1066, 342 houses had been built, expanding the town outside its old boundaries. There were 118 men of the abbot in the town, all able to give and sell their land. Under them were fifty-two bordars owing aid to the abbot. In addition, the town had fifty-four freemen and forty-three alsmen, each with one bordar. Outside of the abbey there were thirty priests, deacons or clerks, and seventy-five abbey employees involved in baking, brewing, tailoring, washing, shoemaking, ropemaking and cooking. Thirteen of the abbot's rural reeves lived in Bury, as well as thirty-four of his knights and twenty-two of their bordars.[23] With roughly 550 persons enumerated, the vast majority of them likely to have been heads of households, Bury in 1086 can conservatively be estimated to have had at least two thousand residents. The abbey was doubtless its major employer, and the shrine of its patron saint assured the town a steady stream of visitors. The relationship between town and abbey, despite the latter's extensive legal control, was symbiotic, and would remain that way into the early sixteenth century.

LATER DEVELOPMENTS

The "men" of the abbot in Bury, the town's burgesses, retained their right to sell and bequest land freely; this gave them more economic freedom than most burghs under lay or ecclesiastical control.[24] A charter of Henry I gave the town a market, and the burgh customs first appeared in charters of Abbot Anselm between 1121 and 1148.[25] Among them was the right of the burgesses to have their pleas heard in the town's portman-moot rather than in the hundred or liberty courts. The abbot did not preside in the portman-moot; the abbey's sacrist did, and he quickly became lord of the town, safeguarding the abbey's interests therein. The sacrist also appointed the town's bailiffs or *prepositi*.[26] Among the bailiffs' duties was the collection of forty pounds annually from the burghers for lights in the abbey church.[27] As the burghers were substantial men and able to spread the financial burden among their fellow townsmen, this was probably not an onerous burden. Norman Trenholme has argued that "on the whole, there cannot be said to have been heavy taxation in the monastic boroughs during the middle ages. There was no need of it, as abbots and convents were wealthy corporations and had ample revenues without oppressing their burgesses."[28] While the forty pounds was the main obligation faced by the townsmen, there were other smaller fees as well, and the fourteenth century considered a one hundred-mark fee customary upon the confirmation of a new abbot.

The town itself continued to expand and develop. The parish church of St. Mary's on the abbey grounds dated from Baldwin's abbacy, and Anselm founded the parish church of St. James also on the abbey grounds instead of making a pilgrimage to Santiago de Campostela.[29] There were several major mills just outside the town gates, but within its banleuca--perhaps through the influence of the physician-abbot Baldwin--Bury became a major medical center with six hospitals for lepers and others in the banleuca by the mid-thirteenth century.[30] St. Edmunds remained one of England's leading monasteries, ranking fifth in terms of knights' fees according to the *cartae baronum* returns of 1166.[31]

But despite the town's prosperity and the monastery's importance reinforced by numerous royal visits, the monks were not always on solid financial footing and were at times quite capable of spending more than they acquired. If it is true (and the case is not proven) that the abbey faced serious debts in the last century of its existence, as Gottfried maintains, then it was not the first time such a situation had arisen, and on previous occasions the fiscal illnesses had not been fatal. Jocelin reported that Abbot Hugh (died 1180) generated considerable red ink in the later years of his abbacy, adding between two hundred and four hundred pounds annually to the abbey's indebtedness.[32] His successor, Abbot Samson, discovered that the house owed over 3,050 pounds in debts but, apparently through shrewd fiscal reform and management was able to pay them off early in his abbacy.[33] Gottfried maintains the abbey received major loans from the Florentine Bardi in the mid-thirteenth century, and from Henry III in 1290, but the latter seems hard to believe, because Henry III died 18 years earlier.[34]

Jocelin provides rich evidence to undercut the argument that the power struggle at Bury was simply between the town and its monks. Samson's monks are often seen fighting among themselves or with their abbot. Samson himself often sided with the townsmen against his own sacrists or convent. Samson's sacrists appear to have been very careful to keep control of properties adjacent to the town's market.[35] While the sacrist may have thus been consolidating power, the cellarer, who had previously controlled much of the banleuca outside the town's gates, was losing it. In addition to breaking up the cellarer's monopoly on the collection of dung from the streets of the town, Samson united much of the cellarer's independent court into the portman-moot, thus eliminating the possibility that burghers might face trial by ordeal or trial by battle in disputes over property they owned in the banleuca.[36]

The men of the town held one carucate of land outside the town gates, and Samson ensured they held it on favorable terms, with a freehold (*libere tenent*) and a guarantee against any increases (*gersa*) in socage dues.[37] Such a guarantee appears unique among all the tenancies enumerated in the *Kalendar*. Samson gave the burgesses a charter whereby they could choose guards (who must then swear homage to the sacrist) for four of the town's gates, would never have to leave Bury to attend courts elsewhere in the liberty, and could freely sell tenancies among themselves.[38] Another charter gave the burghers the right to build a stone house in the marketplace and rent it out to themselves or others for twenty-four shillings a year.[39] This may have been the charter which Jocelin reported as being so unpopular with the convent monks, who argued that the forty pounds a year required of the burgesses was not enough, compared to what other town overlords received. But Samson sided with the burghers, and gave them the charter (admittedly, for sixty marks), "nobis autem murmurantibus et grunnientibus," according to Jocelin.[40] Samson also allowed the burghers to compound for repselver and sorpenny, two customary dues owed the cellarer (the former to pay for cutting corn, the latter for the privilege of grazing cattle on common land), for twenty shillings and four shillings a year respectively.[41] Indeed, Samson's grants to the men of the town so enraged his monks that at one point a plot to kill him was rumored.[42]

Through these actions, Samson appears to have recognized the common interest of the abbey and the town in having a healthy local economy. The "dead hand" of the church, so often vilified for strangling free enterprise, seems to have been interested in encouraging it at Bury. Samson battled with London merchants who claimed an exemption from all tolls throughout England including those at Bury on the basis of a charter from Henry II. Samson at first refused to recognize the royal charter as having any validity within the Liberty of St. Edmund, but the result was a two-year boycott of Bury's market by the London merchants. Recognizing the danger to the town's economy, Samson suggested a ruse whereby the Londoners paid the toll to keep up appearances but had it immediately refunded in secret. While on the one hand this lessened the exclusivity of the Bury burghers' market privileges, it ensured a crowded market healthy to the town in the long run despite what toll revenue the abbot might have lost. The Londoners agreed, and Bury's market rebounded from its temporary depression.[43]

Samson also increased the attractions of the town by granting property and income to the hospitals and providing free housing for clerks studying in the town's schools.[44] The townsmen seem to have responded favorably. Even before Samson was abbot, they gave him money to complete the tower at the west end of the convent, and St. John's Chapel inside the abbey gates was constructed by a townsman on application to Samson.[45]

UNREST BEFORE 1381

The abbey was no more united after Samson's death than it had been when he was alive, and after his death a three-year dispute arose over the next abbacy. In that struggle, the townsmen sided with Hugh of Northwold, the eventual choice, over the anti-papal candidate, sacrist Robert of Gravely. The monks themselves were almost evenly divided on the question.[46] This began two difficult centuries for the town. A large part of it accidentally burned down in June 1215, and it was attacked and despoiled by the French Prince Louis.[47] In the 1250s, the abbey's Benedictines battled attempts by Franciscans, supported by Henry III, to settle in the town, with the latter eventually choosing nearby Babwell instead.[48] While Gottfried views the Franciscans as champions of the townsmen against the abbey, relations between the two houses did improve significantly, and in 1412 the abbey permitted the Franciscans to convene their general chapter in Bury and contributed ten pounds.[49] In 1264 a group of town youths sympathetic to the Montfort party ("quidam Juniores et minus discreciores," according to one of the abbey's writers) formed themselves into a guild and attacked the sacrist's dominance of the town.[50] But the older burghers, fearing a loss of their not inconsiderable privileges, turned against the youths. A charter bought by the burgesses for forty pounds in the aftermath recognized the office of alderman and a town "communitas," which would seem to have been a step forward for them.[51] Yet Mary Lobel traces what she sees as the retarded growth of the town from this struggle, laying the blame on the abbey.[52]

In 1292-93, Abbot John of Northwold agreed that the burghers could nominate candidates to the office of alderman, and he would select from among them. He also reconfirmed the burghers' rights and duties concerning four of the five town gates.[53] Trenholme hailed this as a "considerable victory" for the townsmen, apparently not realizing that they already had the latter right, dating back to Samson's time.[54] A roll of pleadings from 1304 indicates that at that time burgher Nicholas Fulke and sixty-one other townsmen attempted to set up what sounds like a town corporation, collecting a tax called hansingsilver and trying to appoint their own bailiffs. They claimed that, as merchant guild of the town, this was their right. A jury found them innocent of most charges, but refused to recognize that a merchant guild existed and convicted Fulke of having hindered the abbot's bailiffs, levying taxes on the abbot's poor tenants against the abbot's will, having unlawfully made distraints of property and having attempted by force to take property held in distraint by the abbot. Damages were assessed at two hundred pounds.[55] There is real evidence of a battle here, but the charge that the burghers unlawfully taxed the abbot's poor tenants suggests that it might not have been entirely between the abbey and the town. Fulke was obviously a man of considerable means; he paid a fine of twenty pounds himself in order to avoid a jail term.[56] By this time, the burghers were holding feasts and meetings in a town guildhall, built by the townsmen on abbey property, and maintained at the burghers' expense.[57]

Bury suffered an even more violent outbreak in 1327, as did numerous other English towns that year. That turbulent chapter in the history of the monastic boroughs has been ably examined by Trenholme; it was clearly a manifestation of a political struggle between the burghers and abbey over certain issues.[58] But Trenholme does note the influence of national politics. Edward II had just been deposed, and rebels in Bury, St. Albans and elsewhere received encouragement from agents from London. There was little "class" strife involved, as there would be in 1381. Rather, the outbreak at Bury was a local manifestation of a national political struggle between two factions. The prior and several monks were held hostage in the Guildhall,[59] and London criminals kidnapped Abbot Richard de Draughton, taking him to Brabant where he remained until April 1329.[60] In the aftermath, thirty cartloads of prisoners were taken from Bury to Norwich for trial.[61]

During the struggle, the burghers extorted a charter from the monks, which was renounced when peace returned. Examination of this document gives a good indication of burgher goals at the time.[62] The merchant element was clearly behind the revolt; the charter called for a merchant guild whose freely elected alderman would also serve as town alderman. Under its terms, anyone owning property in Bury with an annual value over ten shillings had to pay hansingsilver to the merchant guild, and anyone wishing to participate in trade in the town had to join the guild. Non-Bury merchants were forbidden from setting up shops. Other clauses dealt with property: townsmen were forbidden from willing more than half their property outside their family, and relatives could redeem property sold by their relatives outside the family by paying the sale price to the buyer within the year. Thus the burghers were trying to restrict the freedom to buy and sell property, fostered in the town by successive abbots. Which was the more reactionary element, burghers or monks? Additionally, the burghers sought the elimination of possessory writs such as Mort d'Ancestor and Novel Disseisin from town courts, and they wanted the power to distrain goods without the intervention of the town's bailiffs.

The burgesses were clearly becoming a significant force, but the abbey retained a commanding economic position. A 1340 taxation roll for the town shows the burgher as controlling 941 acres, the sacrist 1,697.[63] The alderman, selected annually, was still subject to the abbot's final approval, as indicated by the recorded exemplification from the 1351 election, in which the burghers offered three candidates.[64] In 1352, Edward III confirmed the abbot's power to hear possessory writs within the liberty, as well as "certifications and attaints concerning tenants within the borough."[65]

The fourteenth century was certainly not the happiest in European history. A host of economic problems, the result of chronic bad weather, population straining at the bounds of the natural resources and agricultural technology available, as well as the demands of widespread warfare, may have been partly responsible for violent outbreaks such as those which occurred in 1327. In addition, the Black Death caused

massive mortality, dislocation and economic depression, although
offering a Malthusian solution to the long-term resource problem. The
urban losses in population were probably close to fifty percent,[66]
leading one to wonder how it may have changed the face of a town like
Bury. The straight line which historians have traditionally drawn
between the town's violent outbreaks in 1327 and 1381 is actually rent
through the middle by a catastrophe which must truly have made the
earlier date a distant and perhaps irrelevant memory to those alive at
the latter. The town, perhaps only two-thirds full, surrounded by fertile
fields, sheepfolds, and a rural labor shortage which existed in 1381 was
vastly different from the packed, seething mecca of dwindling
opportunity of 1327.

Charles Phythian-Adams and Susan Reynolds have argued that the
late middle ages were a time of dreary urban decline, but Gottfried sees
Bury bucking that trend, largely because of the tariff-induced wool
cloth industry that developed in East Anglia.[67] Further, he maintains
that "declining population contributed to the rise of the town by
seriously damaging the financial base of the abbey."[68] But the abbey,
with its extensive sheepfolds, was in a good position to profit from
expansion in the wool cloth industry, as East Anglian wool would have
been a convenient source for East Anglian weavers. And if population
shrinkage was hitting the rentier abbey particularly hard, why does the
complete town rental of 1295, including St. Peter's hospital, only list
307 tenancies, while the incomplete sacrist's rental of 1433 enumerates
582?[69] And what civic projects were the corporate-spirited burghers
undertaking with their new economic clout? Probably very few in the
fourteenth century: on February 24, 1378, Richard II had to order the
town's alderman to compel the inhabitants to repair the guildhall, as
"the said house has now become weak and ruinous, for neglect of
repair, so that part of it has fallen...."[70] If the guildhall was the focal
point of burghal pride and solidarity, neither was riding very high as
1381 approached. The burghers seem to have been ill-equipped for the
"struggle for municipal independence" in which Mary Lobel claimed
they were embroiled.[71]

Bury St. Edmunds and the "Peasants' Revolt"

Bury was again a seat of unrest in 1381, with one monk murdered
in the monastery, and the abbey's prior and the chief justice of the
King's Bench murdered in nearby villages. Because the town burghers
were short-term beneficiaries of the mayhem, and Bury was the only
town in England exempted from the general pardon issued by Richard

II in the aftermath, historians have not been hesitant to implicate retrospectively the town elite.   Again, despite the national issues involved in the 1381 revolt, such as serfdom and taxation, the Bury conflict has been seen as an intramural struggle between town and abbey.

This view certainly had contemporary origins; John Gosford, almoner of the monastery, claimed that "at that time, a war company of all the cruder sort in the county of Suffolk rose up, which, at the instigation of the men of Bury, was seeking to destroy the prior, convent and monastery of St. Edmund."[72]   Thomas of Walsingham, probably based on information supplied by a Bury monk, accused the burghers of cynically using the rioters to achieve their goals "while themselves remaining aloof from the mob so as to seem innocent of such scandalous behavior."[73] Even the dullest nose might smell a rat here, but more recent historians have taken essentially the same tack. Andre Réville averred in 1898 that, "les bourgeois de Bury furent les allies secrets de John Wrawe," the rebel captain who led his band through the town.[74]   Charles Oman wrote in 1906 that in Bury and five other towns, "the majority of the townsfolk had been implicated in the rising."[75]   Goodwin saw it as a simple delegation of responsibility: "Murder and pillage they delegated to their catspaws the country villeins and the riffraff that followed John Wrawe."[76]   Even contemporary historians, usually so eager to correct their pre-World War II counterparts, have followed in those monkish footsteps. According to Rodney Hilton, "the leading townsmen...although secretly encouraging the rebels from outside under Wrawe, pretended that the physical attack on the monastery and its inmates was none of their wish or doing."[77] Lobel agreed, and Gottfried hastily passes over the subject.

The main problem with this view is that there is little evidence linking any more than three members of the town elite with the depredations committed. For the rest, it has been guilt by association, despite the likelihood that the burghers implicated were on the political fringe, out of step with the rest of the leading townsmen. Gosford's case against the burghers was highly circumstantial, as we shall see. Moreover, the violence of 1381 intervened during another simmering dispute that had already divided the monastery--a battle over a 1379 abbatial election. So there were two factions within the abbey walls already, and, as they had been in the past, some of the townsmen became involved.

THE DISPUTED ELECTION

   Abbot John of Brinkeley died in late 1378, and on January 6, 1379, King Richard gave the monastery leave to elect a new abbot.[78] The monks, after a lengthy dispute, chose John Tymworth.[79] Because of the war with France and papal schism, Richard was reluctant to allow him to go to Rome for confirmation, and ordered him on February 1 to send proxies instead.[80] In the meantime, Edmund Brounfeld, a Bury monk serving in Rome as proctor general of the English Benedictines, secured election to the abbacy from the pope himself--through bribery, according to the highly biased Gosford. When Tymworth's proxies arrived in April, Brounfeld refused to yield.

   The King warned the Bury monks that if Brounfeld landed in England he would be arrested under the 1364 Statue of Provisors. Nevertheless, he landed at Ipswich in October, and had the support of seventeen Bury monks, with roughly forty against.[81] After a chapter meeting, the brothers supporting Brounfeld rushed into the two parish churches, stirred up the populace in support of their cause "through false suggestions" and sent two of their allies to Ipswich to fetch the provisor.[82] Brounfeld arrived to wide acclaim, celebrated mass, and was soon summoned to appear in Westminster, as were burghers Thomas Halesworth, William Chapman and John Clakke, charged with having aided him.[83] On October 20, Brounfeld and eleven Bury monks were committed to the Tower of London for conspiring to violate the Statute of Provisors, and Brounfeld remained in various royal prisons until 1385.[84] Eventually, Halesworth, Robert Westbroun, James Marham, Hervy de Lacford and John de Beketon, all of Bury, were bonded for various sums up to two hundred pounds not to press Brounfeld's claims.[85]

   Why did the townsmen embrace Brounfeld so enthusiastically? One clue appears in Gosford's description of the events of 1381, where he implied that Brounfeld had a relative among the wealthy burghers.[86] When Brounfeld's installation became a rebel demand in 1381, Halesworth, a former Bury alderman, was to act as custodian for abbatial properties pending Brounfeld's release from prison, suggesting that he was that relative.[87] Might the "false suggestions" made to the townsmen by monks supporting Brounfeld included promises of additional freedom? In any case, Brounfeld was a Bury monk, and a legitimate candidate for the abbacy with significant convent support. Town support for him should not necessarily be viewed as opposition to the monastery per se, but rather as an attempt to install a sympathetic abbot.

OTHER CAUSES OF UNREST

In addition to the possibility of installing a popular abbot, Bury residents and their rural neighbors had other reasons to be restive in 1381, reasons common to most Englishmen. The unpopular war in France dragged on, and the men of Bury had to help finance it in numerous ways, including the provision of a ship, ordered in February, 1379.[88] In the previous year, the crown attempted a crackdown on East Anglian wool manufacturers who sold cloth without the requisite royal seal.[89] Feudal labor obligations were tightly maintained on the rural properties of the abbey and its neighbors.[90] And, of course there was the repeated Poll Tax, which even Gosford recognized as a "taxa onerosa."[91] The poll tax return for Bury in 1377 reported 2,445 adults (making it the largest town in Suffolk), while that of 1381 reported only 1,507.[92] Obviously the tax was meeting resistance, but not any more so than in Ipswich where returns fell from 1,507 to 963. As Réville noted, any unrest was liable to spread quickly in a relatively dense, manufacturing population like that of East Anglia.[93]

Once the unrest of June 1381, broke out it did spread quickly, but not outward from Bury. Rather, the unrest overwhelmed Bury from the outside.

CHRONOLOGY

On June 13, 1381, as the Kent and Essex rebels were gathered at Mile End near London, seeking concessions from the boy-King Richard, a band of insurgents under John Wrawe, liberally estimated by the author of the *Anonimalle Chronicle* at ten thousand,[94] stormed into Bury St. Edmunds. On the following day, they journeyed to nearby Lackenheath where after an impromptu trial, they beheaded Sir John Cavendish, chief justice of the King's Bench. Prior John de Cambridge of the Bury monastery became nervous and fled from Bury. Another group (Gosford charges that this one included men of Bury) captured him on the morning of June 15 near Mildenhall, from which he had tried to flee to the Isle of Ely. De Cambridge suffered the same fate as Cavendish, and the prior's head was carried in procession back into Bury, where it was mounted next to that of Cavendish, one turned so as to whisper into the other's ear.[95]

Subsequently, the members of "illa maledicta comitava" broke into the monastery itself, claiming that they were seeking Brother Walter Totyngton, according to a marginal note in Gosford's text. As Walter was unavailable, they seized Brother John Lackenheath, custodian of the barony of Bury St. Edmunds and killed him.[96] The mob left the monastery, only to return on June 16 and demand all the charters relating to the town, a demand which seems to implicate the burghers circumstantially. The monks complied with the demand, because, "if they did not do this hastily, the whole ill-spoken company said again, they would kill the monks and extirpate the monastery."[97] The charters were taken to the guildhall, where they were given to the "majoribus villae"--the leading men of the town. The mob also wanted Brounfeld made abbot, so that the abbey "would concede to them not only their ancient liberties, but new ones as well,"[98] and demanded some jewels as surety. The monks, represented by the sacrist and the subprior, agreed to the terms since the king had already promised the Essex rebels in London that Brounfeld would be made abbot of Bury.[99]

But Wrawe's band departed by June 16 or 17, probably reinforced by a few Bury men, and on the 23d, Earl William Ufford of Suffolk arrived in town with five hundred lancers and peace was restored. By Christmas, all the jewels and charters had found their way back to the monastery. As a group the burghers were certainly punished for the violence in the town; they had to pay two thousand marks for a royal pardon, as will be explained below. But the question remains; were they really instigators or even participants in the insurrection?

ANALYSIS OF BURY'S ROLE IN THE UPRISING

Oman certainly believed the burghers of Bury were very active in the uprising. Based on no apparent evidence, he made two extremely rash claims. First, Wrawe "knew that he was eagerly expected" in Bury, because the townsmen "sent messages to Wrawe and his horde, inviting them to come to Bury and set matters right;" and, second, de Cambridge had been Brounfeld's chief opponent and was hated as a result.[100] There is no evidence to confirm or deny the latter claim, but then why did the mob also seek Walter Totyngton, who eventually had to be pardoned by Richard II for having backed Brounfeld?[101] As for the charge that Wrawe was invited to Bury, then why even in Wrawe's deposition before the royal justices (an unsuccessful attempt to preserve his life by implicating as many others as possible) did he say he was invited into the town? What Wrawe actually said was that his band approached the south gate of the town from Sudbury and ordered the gatekeepers to open and cooperate with the rebels, "under the penalty of beheading to those who urge against doing this."[102]   England was unaccustomed to civil war, and particularly in the economic climate of the late 14th century, the fortifications of an inland town like Bury were probably fairly decrepit, unable to withstand an armed mob.

Wrawe himself was said to be "a Suffolk chaplain," and his band had formed in northern Essex before visiting Bury. Both Walsingham and the *Anonimalle Chronicle* held Wrawe's band responsible for the deaths of de Cambridge and Cavendish and for carrying their heads back to Bury on pikes.[103] Rebellion was widespread in East Anglia on June 13-16,[104] and the mob probably found willing allies at Mildenhall and Lackenheath. The only men of Bury charged by Wrawe with being his accomplices for the murders or any depredations committed in the town were Halesworth, Robert Westbroun, and Geoffrey Denham, all three of whom he said were present when the prior was killed. The two men he implicated for having taken part in the looting of Cavendish's Bury mansion were not from Bury, and a 1383 pardon was issued to William Bennington of Bumsted, Essex, "a ringleader in the disturbances at Bury."[105]

Just as few Bury men were directly implicated in outrages committed there, the victims selected by the mob seem unlikely burghal enemies. As explained above, Totyngton had been a Brounfeld supporter. Why was the sacrist relatively unmolested, if he was, indeed, the hated lord of the town? Aside from having had to negotiate with an unruly mob, his largest loss seems to have been some goods he was holding in pawn, taken by the wife of Henry Lacford of Bury."[106] Cavendish had little to do with the Bury monastery although Gosford was sure he was killed because "he was a most true friend of the prior and church of St. Edmund."[107] The only problem with that view is that it makes the murder of Cavendish seem like an afterthought, killed after his friend, public enemy number one, whereas Cavendish was the first victim. The crowd's jest of placing one victims mouth in the other's ear suggests that the two were seen as allies, but Cavendish was undoubtedly the more important. One of the peasant grievances in 1381 was the hated Statute of Labourers, and he had been in charge of its enforcement in Suffolk and Essex.[108] The term "proditor" (traitor), the epithet which the Latin chroniclers put in the mouths of the crowd when attacking Cavendish and de Cambridge, was also that used to describe the enemies of the commoners in other districts. Walsingham opined that the fact that de Cambridge and Lackenheath were specifically chosen by the mob indicated that the burghers were egging the rebels on.[109] But this makes no sense; why would they select Lackenheath, custodian of the feudal barony, who had nothing to do with the town? More likely, as the man responsible for making sure the abbey's rural tenants fulfilled their feudal obligations, he was killed at the behest of the same rural laborers who would have hated Cavendish. Even the prior may have been victimized for "rural" reasons. According to Walsingham, who did not quite digest all of Gosford's slanders on the burghers, de Cambridge "was condemned to death not by the villeins of the said town of Bury...but by the decision and judgement of his own serfs and villeins."[110] The Bury area murders were not so unique in the annals of 1381.

It should also be remembered that the Church was victimized by rebels all over England that year, and confiscation of church property was one of Wat Tyler's demands.[111] In Petit-Dutaillis' words, "in nearly every county, it was the monasteries above all which suffered from the insurrection."[112] Rebels attacked the abbot of Peterborough, and three prominent residents of St. Albans were executed for attacks in the abbey there.[113] Those executed were prominent citizens, whereas all the Bury burghers escaped with their lives. Dunstable priory was likewise attacked. So attacks on the monastery of Bury St. Edmunds in 1381 should not surprise us to the degree that we seek a particular cause in poor town-abbey relations.

R. B. Dobson, in the introduction to his excellent sourcebook on the 1381 rising, has suggested that "the alliance between peasants and townsmen so ubiquitous throughout much of southern and eastern England in the summer of 1381 may often have been based on very fragile foundations."[114] This suggestion can be applied to Bury, and one might even ask if there was much of an alliance at all. Wrawe's band did, according to Walsingham, demand that the charters be handed over on the burghers' behalf. The burghers, he claimed, "pretended to be said about these matters as though what was being done displeased them"[115] The town elite was thus held to be guilty simply because it was a potential beneficiary of the crowd's action. The articles of complaint against the townsmen prepared by the monks charged that the alderman and other "valentes" of Bury entered the abbey grounds on 16 June (after the murder of Lackenheath) with the "magna multitudine rebellium," seeking "certas personas de conventu."[116] Historians have placed great significance in the fact that the crowd became angry when a particular charter it expected was not produced, and threatened to ransack the monastery.[117] "In the outburst of their passion, they naively betrayed the men of the town."[118] For Réville, the question was, why would a bunch of country bumpkins have been seeking a particular charter unless they were being advised by the alderman and burghers? This is the most damning evidence that exists against the town elite, and it is somewhat flimsy. First of all, it comes from a monk who was manifestly biased against the townsmen (Gosford). Second, looting was quite common in the 1381 insurrection, and a rich abbey like St. Edmunds was a ripe plum for those so inclined; the supposed absence of a charter, whether true or only rumored by agitators, would have provided a pretext for pillage. Third, it would not have required more than one townsman with a reputation for local knowledge to convince the rioters that the monks were holding something back.

Thomas Halesworth may have been such a person. As we have seen, he was probably related to Brounfeld, and it may have been at his instigation that the rebels included a demand that Brounfeld be made abbot. It would not even have been a large mistake for Gosford to call him "aldermannus," as he had been alderman in 1377. As stated above, Halesworth, Geoffrey Denham and Robert Westbroun were the only Bury burghers accused by Wrawe of] having participated in any of the murders, and those three, plus three town artisans, were the only Bury residents specifically outlawed by Parliament in the aftermath.[119] Denham was charged with having taken de Cambridge's account-book after his murder, and then attempted to collect the debts himself, claiming to be the late prior's executor. In addition, he was said to have taken two of his horses.[120] Such a crime seems to have been motivated more by greed than any struggle for municipal independence.

What were the real alderman and the rest of the burghers doing at this time? That is a difficult question, but none of them appear in any of the available records as having been specifically accused of anything. They were even sometimes at the other side of the bench, as when John Osbern, the alderman, charged George de Donnesby of Lincoln before royal justices with having been an outside agitator at Bury. Osbern was believed and Donnesby was beheaded.[121] There is no record of Donnesby claiming his accusor was an inside agitator. In 1383, with Bury still exempted from the general pardon, the alderman (by then Roger Rose) and twenty-three burghers petitioned Parliament that they "not be blamed or undone for the evil deeds of others, particularly since the said evildoers had been indicted by the good men of the said town."[122] The jewels and charters were all returned to the monastery although it did take six months. But, considering the fact that they were carried away by a rebellious mob, perhaps we should simply be impressed that they were all returned safely. Gosford wrote that the burghers "understanding their error, and fearing the hand of the king," returned the charters and jewels, but that seems rather simplistic.[123] It is more likely that Osbern and company were embarrassed by the action of Halesworth's faction, fearing it would bring ruin on them all, as it did, in a way. The return of the charters undamaged is particularly significant in light of what Réville called "cette guerre acharnee au parchemin" that was going on in East Anglia at the time, with numerous records put to the torch by rebels. Only one record belonging to the Bury monastery was burned, and that was a sacrists' register for a rural manor; and it was set aflame by a rebel from Bradfield, not Bury.[124]

BURGHAL POLITICS, 1377-86

Through examination of the Patent Rolls, Close Rolls, and Fine Rolls, it is possible to identify the twenty-five to thirty leading burghers of Bury at this time and suggest the development of a minority faction led by Halesworth. When the first Poll Tax was levied in the last year of Edward III's reign (1377), Halesworth, James Marham and Walter Bennet were appointed to oversee the collection of Bury's contribution.[125] Those three escaped the odious assignment two years later when Hervy and Thomas Lacford, Edmund Lucas, John de Bury, Richard Charman, Roger Potter and Adam Waterward were chosen.[126] Their successors in December, 1380, appointed to collect the most unpopular of all the Poll Taxes were de Bury, Thomas Lacford, Osbern, Geoffrey Wolman and Thomas Bernyngham.[127] As the Poll Tax was a major grievance of 1381, and evidence indicates it me strong resistance in Bury and elsewhere, as stated above, the members of the last group-- including Alderman Osbern--are unlikely to have been rebel champions when violence broke out. On the other hand, Halesworth and the other 1377 collectors, having fulfilled their public duty four years earlier, before the tax became annual, may have been more popular. Interestingly, Halesworth and Marham were among those charged by the government with having supported Brounfeld in 1379, while none of the others listed above, except Hervy Lacford of the middle group, shared the same distinction.[128]

In the aftermath of 1381, Bury was the only town exempted from the general pardon issued by the king, and the burghers ended up having to pay a two thousand-mark fine, partially payable to the monastery, to redeem themselves. In December, 1382, the king commissioned a group of twenty named burghers, including Osbern, Marham, Thomas Lacford, Bernyngham, Wolman and new alderman Roger Rose, but not Halesworth, to collect the fine. They were instructed to assess "every man accord to his estate, possessions and means," with no mention made of culpability in the events of June, 1381. They were to make payments by four semi-annual installments.[129]

A year later, since one thousand marks had been paid on time, the same group was given a delay in payment of the next installment.[130] However, one of the group, Thomas Fornham, also a Brounfeld supporter in 1379, had prove uncooperative, and "hindered by threats and otherwise" the collection of the fine. His arrest was ordered by the king in January, 1383.[131] Collection of the fine was becoming problematic, and in February 1384, the above group was given an indefinite reprieve in the collection of the next installment.[132] On September 1, 1384, on the grounds that "certain of the king's lieges of mean estate of Bury assemble unlawfully by night and day," doing damage to the king's subjects, especially the convent of Bury, "against whom they have a grudge," Richard ordered twenty-five named burghers,including Osbern, Marham, Thomas Lacford, John de Bury, Bernyngham and Fornham (back in the fold?) to arrest evildoers and ensure that the peace was kept.[133] Early the following February, Alderman Rose and twenty-three others, most of whom were included in the previous order, were ordered to collect the remainder of the two thousand marks by Easter.[134]

But, just as they had trouble collecting the 1381 Poll Tax, these town elites were encountering heavy resistance from the poorer segments of the population. "Les povrez gentz de la ville de seint Esmond de Bury" complained to the king that same month that the rich collectors were underassessing themselves and pillaging the houses of the poor to collect the remaining sum. They asked Richard to commission an investigation and appoint "un bone homme de survier les rolles de lour agistement."[135] Were these petitioners "the king's lieges of mean estate" referred to above? It is likely that they were. In March, the king appointed Thomas Ikworth and William Hoore of

Bury, neither of whom had appeared in any of the previous orders, as
well as the two town bailiffs and the king's sergeant-at-arms, to
investigate the case.[136] The men of Bury apparently sought to hinder
the investigation by arranging for John de Overton, one of the bailiffs,
to be sued for debt in London.[137] But Halesworth and Hervy Lacford,
the old Brounfeld partisan, came to Overton's aid, and by October,
Overton had appointed Halesworth, John Berard (who had previously
appeared on only one order, that of February 1385), and four other
burghers--who thereby made their first appearance in the records--to
collect the remainder of the fine.[138] They apparently failed, and in
January, 1386, the king gave up and empowered the abbot to collect the
rest.[139] On December 1, 1386, Halesworth was formally pardoned.[140]
Robert Westbroun received the same grace in April, 1385, and Geoffrey
Denham in January, 1388, "at the supplication of the abbot and convent
of Bury St. Edmunds.[141]

Thus Halesworth appears as the leader of a small faction of
burghers, many of them associated with the Brounfeld candidacy, who
opposed the rest of the town elite on behalf of its poorer residents. The
elite--Osbern, Rose and company--may have levied the fine more
heavily on the poor because they felt that the poor were primarily
responsible for the violence of 1381, in which Halesworth, Westbroun
and Denham clearly played a part as well. In any case, historians of
Bury and of the 1381 revolt have certainly been too quick to lump all of
the burgesses together--like the abbey, the town was often rent by
factional dispute. As for Halesworth, he was an unquiet spirit; he and
Marham were again in trouble with the law in 1401, this time for
having unlawfully broken into houses and distrained goods.[142] A
Thomas Halesworth appears in town records as alderman in 1408,
although, given the typical life span of the period, this may have been
the first Halesworth's son or nephew.[143]

BURY ST. EDMUNDS AND THE ROYAL PARDON

Any attempt, like that above, to exonerate posthumously most of the
Bury town elite for participation in the 1381 rebellion must also address
the fact that, of all the towns in England, many of which suffered
extremely violent outbreaks, Bury was the only one not included in
Richard II's general pardon. In fact, as the pardon was originally
conceived in late 1381, Canterbury, Beverly, Cambridge, Bridgewater
and Scarborough were also excluded.[144] When the Commons asked
that the towns be pardoned too, Richard agreed in every case "saving

expressly the town of Bury St. Edmunds, which the king does not want to forgive, on account of their outrageous and horrible misdeeds so long continued."[145] It appears that Richard considered the leading crimes of the revolt to be the murders of de Cambridge, Cavendish, Archbishop Simon Sudbury and Lord Treasurer Thomas Hales. Repeatedly, when discussing the revolt in official correspondence, he mentioned those deeds, and they became formulaic in pardons that generally specified that any misdeeds the person in question may have committed were forgiven unless he was found to have participated in any of those four acts.[146] The latter two crimes occurred in London, the former in the vicinity of Bury. It was at the pillory in Bury that the heads of de Cambridge and Cavendish were displayed in ridicule; it was the burghers of Bury who had tolerated such behavior. London was too powerful to alienate, but Bury was not. It appears that the men of Bury became scapegoats because of their proximity to the crimes and so that he king could feel he was taking a stand, however arbitrary or inconsistent.

In 1382, the king was again petitioned to pardon Bury, but refused to do so until "those of Bury offer sufficient surety of their good behavior in the future."[147] In 1384, the abbot suggested a solution: the men of the town would be made to offer recognizance for their good behavior and swear their property as bond.[148] Rather than enumerating specific properties, a found (and huge) figure of ten thousand pounds was selected. The townsmen would swear to behave, and the fine would not be collected unless the broke the pledge. In theory, any insurrection could be punished by wholesale dispossession of the entire town. But, perhaps in recognizance that the burghers alone could not be held responsible for the behavior of all their neighbors, 722 people, including twenty-two women, were made to take the pledge administered at Bury by representatives of the king and the abbot.[149] Given that the Poll Tax return of 1377 listed Bury as having 2,445 adult residents, the 722 people who swore oaths in 1384-85 must have included virtually every household head in the town. There is no record of any resistance to the oath, and, for whatever reason, Bury did not experience any significant unrest between 1381 and the dissolution of the monasteries in 1539.

BURY'S ECONOMIC STRUCTURE, 1385-1539
    Prosperity may have played a role in Bury's peacefulness after 1381.

At times the town might have even been too successful for its own good. A cryptic 1406 charter from Henry IV gave the abbot the right to extend the length of the annual fair held at Bury on the Feast of St. Matthew and move it out of town if need be--apparently the large crowds in attendance were "very harmful to the said town."[150] Despite the economic difficulties common to most English towns in the late fourteenth century, Bury in 1385 possessed a wide variety of trades. Many of the residents who swore recognizances in 1385 also listed their occupation. The listing below cannot pretend to be a scientific survey of the town's employment breakdown (clearly chaplains always listed their occupations while merchants--many of them the town elite-- almost never did), but it does give some idea of the types of trades practiced in the town, based on the 1384-85 recognizance rolls. Those with trade-related surnames such as Weaver or Tailor were not included since possibly only an ancestor plied the trade in question.

SOME BURY OCCUPATIONS, 1384-85

Chaplains	41	Fishers	2
Bakers	6	Shearmen	2
Weavers	4	Spicers	2
Servants	4	Cutlers	2
Candlemakers	3	Fullers	2
Skinners	3	Cooks	2
Butchers	3	Glovers	2
Tailors	3	Tanners	2

The following occupations had one each: Goldsmith, Shoemaker, Brewer, Mason, "Woolman," Wright, Blacksmith, Draper, Tavernkeeper, Currier, Cordwainer, Clerk, Laborer, "Corceour."

Even in so haphazard a survey, the importance of weaving and related activities such as shearing and fulling is noticeable. Gottfried, based on the evidence of wills, argues that the weaving industry in Bury took off after 1440, as he found ten weavers' wills for the period 1354-1440, and forty for 1441-1530.[151] Such a jump is more apparent than real, however--wills in general were much more common after 1440. What Bury's weavers did do was move from a ranking of third (behind corvisers, fullers and chandlers) in number of wills 1354-1440 to a ranking of first, (followed by tailors and mercers) for 1441-1530. Clearly, the importance of raw wool (fullers) was declining while pliers of the cloth manufacturing trades were becoming certainly more prosperous (more likely to leave wills) and probably more numerous.

But Gottfried is rash to suggest a "collapse" in the Bury fishing industry after 1440.[152] The score of wills is close (nine for 1354-1440, eight for 1441-1530) and fisherman seem unlikely to have left many wills in any case. Perhaps he posits such a collapse because--as controller of many of the fish ponds in the area--the abbey profited from fishing, and Gottfried's overriding thesis is that the abbey was in serious financial decline in the fifteenth century.

GUILDS AND FRATERNITIES: A CHALLENGE TO THE MONASTERY?

Much information about guilds and fraternities in Bury can be gathered from the Suffolk guild certificates prepared in 1389 at behest of the crown.[153] A total of eighteen guilds made returns. Interestingly, eleven of them reported that they were founded in the fourteenth century, indicating that there was considerable corporate activity afoot at that time, despite the decrepit condition of the guildhall (see above, p. 14). One of these guilds, "The Passion of St. Edmund," dedicated to providing lights for his shrine in the abbey church, was founded in 1385--an odd foundation if we are to accept the conventional wisdom that the town's attitude toward the monastery at that time was one of simmering resentment. The only guild besides the above eleven that reported a foundation date was the Guild of St. Nicholas, often referred to in wills and other evidence as the "Douze" or "Dusse" Guild, founded in 1282.[154] Its *Ordinaciones* survive, and there is little in them that indicates much of a political character to the guild, set up to celebrate the feast of St. Nicholas and to offer masses and pray for the souls of departed brothers and sisters.[155]

So it would seem that Gottfried makes a somewhat dubious argument when he concludes that because only 30 percent of those writing wills 1440-1530 left bequests to the monastery, while 27 percent left bequests to the guilds, the latter were rivals to the former in the affections of the populace, used as an avenue to get free of abbey control.[156] First of all, many of the 27 percent who contributed to guilds also contributed to the abbey. For example, Lady Ela Shardelowe (will written in 1457) left spread among three guilds a total of 5 pounds, 13 shillings and 4 pence plus a fur hood, while the monastery and its monks were to receive 6 pounds and a gold figurine.[157] The wealthy John Baret (1463) left "my lord abbot" 6 shillings and 8 pence and a gallon of wine per year. The prior was promised a purse as well as an annual gallon of wine. The sexton received that same wine bequest, convertable to a shilling a year if desired. Every monk in the convent (probably fifty-seven) was to receive a shilling and the shrine of St. Edmund 20. In addition, Baret set up an annuity of 3 shillings and 4 pence, payable to the abbey, for his soul and his parents' souls. Baret had been a member of the St. Nicholas Guild, and he left it one mark plus one gallon of wine annually to the Alderman's, or Candlemas Guild and 8 pence a year to the Resurrection guild. Baret also made arrangements for a banquet after his burial to be attended by the alderman and burghers, town priests and his tenants.[158] Doctor Henry Rudde (1506) left 10 pounds to the monastery, 5 marks to the St. Nicholas Guild.[159] The dyer William Honeyboorn (1493) left nothing to the monastery, but only 1 shilling to a guild.[160] Both William Baret (1502) and his wife Anne (1504), on the other hand, left money to the monastery (10 shillings and 5 marks) plus 40 shillings and amber beads to the abbot, respectively and nothing to any guild.[161]

In addition to the fact that contributions to both monastery and guilds were common, it should be noted that six of the eighteen guilds reporting in 1389 were dedicated to providing lights for or maintaining various shrines within the abbey church, so that contributions to these guilds were indirect contributions to the abbey. Further, eleven others were dedicated to shrines in the parish churches of St. Mary's and St. James, both on the abbey grounds. What is more, virtually every published will in Bury for the period 1381-1539 includes a bequest to one of these parish churches, though admittedly, they were the only churches available in Bury. John Baret, for example, made large bequests for the restoration of St. Mary's. But even if it is assumed that a contribution to maintain a parish church was not seen as supporting the abbey in any way, it should be noted that of 367 people who made bequests to guilds between 1440-1530, at least 274 bequests went to guilds associated with the abbey church while only sixty-one went to the Alderman's Guild, that crusader for burghal independence.[162]

The Alderman's Guild did have one very significant benefactor though, and it was primarily through his endowment that it was able to remain a force, despite relatively little public support. John Smith (died 1481), former alderman and probably the richest burgher of his day, left most of his substantial estate, including rural lands, to the alderman and burgesses to be administered by them as feofees in perpetuity.[163] By naming twenty-four individual feofees, Smith got around the disability of the burghers to hold property in common since they were not a recognized corporation. The profits from the land were to help maintain the guildhall (it received a new roof and major renovation in the late fifteenth century), to pay off the 100 marks due to the abbot each time a new abbot was installed and for other civic projects.[164] Smith was praised in an anonymous Bury poem:

> The which John aforerhersyd to this toun hath be full kynde, CCC
> marc for this toun hath payd, no peny onpayd behynde, Now we
> have informyd yow off John Smythis wyll in wrytyng as it is,And of
> the greet gyfts that he hath govyn, God bryng his soule to blys.
> Amen[165]

But even Smith, for all his support for the burghal cause, left gifts to the monastery as well, and left to the prior the advowson to the chantries he set up at St. Mary's and on the rural manor of Hepworth, with the stipulation that the advowson pass to the college of priests at Bury once it attained corporate status. In strict financial terms he was more generous with the Franciscans at Babwell, leaving them 12 pounds. The Babwell friars were more popular in terms of bequests 1441-1530 than the Bury monastery, 56.8 percent to 30 percent, but again, the overlap among testators should be noted, and the average contribution to the friars was 11 pence while the average for the Bury monks was 12 shillings.[166] Chances are, those with less to give may have given only to the friars. J.J. Scarisbrick has found that in the last years of the Catholic Church in England one out of five testators left bequests to the mendicant orders, and one out of six to monks or nuns.[167] In that case, Bury St. Edmunds was above average on both fronts. Of the twelve published wills of Bury residents for 1500-35 (admittedly a small sample), the Bury monastery received bequests in six, or one half, while the Babwell friars did in four, or one third. While the monastery was dissolved in 1539, that did not help the cause of the Alderman's guild. Although it was still in existence as late as 1558, it is not mentioned in any published Bury will after 1504.

So despite its efforts on behalf of the burghers, the Alderman's Guild ranked well behind the Benedictine Monastery in the affections of Bury's residents. The abbey brought civic benefits, visitors and prestige to Bury. In its heyday, the monastery probably employed around two hundred servants.[168] Late in its existence, the abbey distributed 398 pounds a year in alms.[169] The abbey library (rebuilt in 1430) was open to the leading townsfolk.[170] Several Parliaments were held at Bury, including the one convened in 1446 to try Humphrey, duke of Gloucester, who died of apoplexy on the outskirts of town.[171]

Abbot William Curteys and the town alderman cooperated in planning for the reception of Henry VI in his four-month Christmas visit, 1433-34, and five hundred townsmen turned out for the feast. Several nobles of the king's household became honorary members of the monastery thereby adding to its fame[172]. Even as late as 1520, Bury's last abbot, John Reeve, was a royal privy councilor. In 1531, he was made a commissioner of the peace for Suffolk.[173]

One might ask, if the burghers were as desperate for urban independence as Lobel and Gottfried would have us believe, why did they not seek a charter of incorporation in 1539, when they were finally rid of their monastic overlord? In fact, the alderman and burghers did not receive a charter of incorporation from the crown until April, 1606,[174] although earlier attempts were made in 1562 and 1601 that failed due to the resistance of area gentry, many of whom were descended from the leading burgher families of the fifteenth century.[175] Other former monastic boroughs became incorporated much sooner--Abingdon in 1555, Reading in 1542, Leominster in 1554, and St. Albans in 1553.[176]

THE FINANCIAL HEALTH OF THE MONASTERY

As stated above, Gottfried maintains that violence against the monastery was rare after 1381 because it was no longer necessary; the monks, out of step with the growingly capitalistic times, were doing little to improve their income and were saddled with debt. He sees the burghers, on the other hand, as becoming increasingly wealthy through the wool trade. But there is little evidence to support this contention and some to refute it. First of all, as stated above, the decline in raw wool exports after the high tariffs of Edward III were instituted did not mean English raw wool producers lost money. Rather, they began selling at home to wool cloth producers, many of whom were located in the Bury vicinity, particularly the weaving towns of the Stour Valley. As owner of most of the sheepfolds of West Suffolk, the monastery of Bury St. Edmunds, was in a good position to profit from this. In addition, the monks took steps to ensure that they profited from the weaving that took place in the town of Bury through, for example, the enforcement of the weaving ordinances of June 1477.[177]

These ordinances provide evidence of the monastery working in cooperation with the town weavers and their Corpus Christi Guild to the financial benefit of all three. In their preamble, the ordinances were said to have been drawn up at the request of twenty-nine named weavers, who complained that "be the deceyvable and untrewe werkyng and wewyng of some persons usyng the seyd crafte [it] ys greateley discresyd, apeyred and decayed...to the greate displesure of Almyghty God, and greate hurte henderyng and loss of alle the inhabitants of the seyd toune and cuntrie." All weavers, including journeymen and apprentices, were to meet annually at the guildhall and elect four craft wardens, who would then be confirmed by the abbot's bailiffs. Anyone who wished to weave in Bury had to swear to uphold the regulations and pay the wardens annual dues of four pence. Most of the fines for non-compliance with the regulations were 1 mark (13s 4d), of which half always went to the sacrist, half to either the wardens or the Corpus Christi Guild. Thus the abbey was in a good position to profit from enforcement of the regulations. The bylaws specified that all apprenticeships were to be for seven years, and that masters were not to steal employees from each other. Masters were required to compensate journeymen for layoffs, and the simultaneous operation of more than four looms was prohibited. All "foreyne" weavers were to hire local apprentices and pay a mark to set up shop.

So the abbey, far from being irrelevant to the strong area wool trade, was a prime supplier of raw materials and took an active role in regulating production. Nor does it appear that the abbey was out of touch with the times in terms of estate management. Comparisons of abbey income over time are difficult to make, owing to the difficulty of knowing what was included in particular figures. The *Victoria County History of Suffolk* proposed that the abbey's 1291 income was one thousand pounds, based on returns for a papal tax, while a fifteenth-century pittancer's register shows an annual income of 2,030 pounds.[178] The earlier figure seems too low, considering the speed with which Samson had been able to pay off over three thousand in debts. Perhaps the 1291 figure was only conventual income, not including the abbot's share, or was artificially low because alms, etc., had already been deducted.

The gross income of the abbey in 1535, according to the *Valor Ecclesiasticus*, was 2,336 pounds.[179] The *Valor* tended to undervalue incomes by 10-25 percent,[180] so the real figure was probably higher, indicating an increase in revenue over the previous century, if the figures are comparable. Of those 2,336 pounds, the Bury monks were spending 130 a year on the salaries of lay officials such as bailiffs and rent collectors,[181] or roughly 6 percent. As the national average of all monasteries was 5 percent.[182] Bury St. Edmunds does not appear to have been particularly inefficient in terms of administrative costs. In November, 1539, Royal Commissioner Sir Richard Rich estimated the annual income of the monastery at four thousand marks, suggesting a five hundred-mark pension for abbot Reeve.[183] That would put the actual income at over 2,500 pounds.

Gottfried argues that the debt-ridden abbot was selling off abbey property to people like Thomas Kytson, Nicholas and Thomas Bacon and Anthony Rous in order to make ends meet in the 1520s and 1530s, based on evidence from what he calls the "1539 Dissolution Rental."[184] It seems a careless conclusion: the document in question is actually the 1540 Court of Augentations account for the year 1539-40.[185] It records Kytson's purchase from the crown as having been made on March 5, 1540; Nicholas Bacon's on March 22; Rous' on March 29; and Thomas Bacon's on May 12.[186] Despite the facts that twenty manors were missing (all sold off in the previous year), that no profits were reported from the abbey gardens, orchards and fisheries because they were in the king's hands, and that no hadgovel rent was included because it was to be reported separately by someone named John Holt, the gross return on rents, court perquisites, fair tolls, and numerous other sources was 2,337 pounds.[187] Admittedly, the report lists numerous tenements as being in a state of disrepair or vacant, but the four previous years of monastic despoilment across England would not have encouraged the abbot to maintain his properties.

In fact, there is some indication that Reeve had adopted some of the principles of capitalistic estate management. His income from demesne land in 1535 had been only 25 pounds, 13 shillings and 4 pence,[188] but during his abbacy, he converted numerous customary leases into fixed-term leases.[189] Among the few charges John ap Rice, investigator for Vicar General Thomas Cromwell, could make against him in 1535 was that he spent a lot of time at his granges and "that he converted divers fermes into copie holdes, wherof poore men doth complayne."[190] The previous century had also seen considerable construction at the monastery, another indication of economic health. The southern part of the abbey bell tower had fallen down in 1430, but Abbot William Curteys raised 60,000 ducats to replace it and also restore the east and west fronts of the abbey.[191] Likewise, he rebuilt the abbey church after it accidentally burned down in 1465.[192] Both parish churches were rebuilt in the late 1400s, and the abbey church got a new western spire in 1506.[193]

The steady population of monks is also an indication that the monastery was healthy in the last years of its existence, or at least until 1535. While it had comprised roughly eight brethren in Samson's day, it had never completely recovered after the Black Death--recall the 42-17 split over the Tymworth-Brounfeld election in 1379. Only forty-four monks were in attendance at the final surrender on November 4, 1539, but ap Rice had found sixty-two at his visit four years earlier.[194] The other eighteen had probably seen the writing on the wall.

CONCLUSION

Trenholme wrote that "the monastic boroughs constituted a peculiar class."[195] His view was the traditional one, that monastic overlords smothered town liberties and economic development. While incorporated towns developed, the monastic boroughs struggled in a remedial medieval backwater permanently stunted in their growth. Lobel found such a model appropriate for Bury, as does Gottfried, although he argues that the burghers were able to develop successfully their own institutions through free enterprise while the monastery went to seed. But it was government policy that destroyed the monastery of Bury St. Edmunds, not financial management. When it was gone, so was much of the reason for Bury's success and much of its attraction for visiting consumers. Like an Appalachian mining town after the coal is gone, the town fell into decay, its relative position in East Anglia falling, never to recover. This decay was a two-edged sword though-- with it came a better integration into the larger Suffolk community. After 1539 the county quarter-sessions were able to meet inside the town gates for the first time ever, no longer banished to a heath a mile away.[196] Bury was now simply an oversized East Anglian weaving town.

But it still had to contend with semi-feudal overlords, gentry who, having bought various properties of the abbey, attempted to reassert some of its legal authority. In 1546, William Clifton of London held the farm for all the tithes formerly due the abbey's almoner, and in 1620, Nicholas Bacon the younger was making the same kinds of complaints abbots had made three centuries before--the alderman and burghers were levying unauthorized fines and taxes.[197] Like the abbey before them, these overlords were attempting to exercise the sort of control that offends the sensibilities of modern historians, products of liberal democracy. Certainly, the abbots of Bury St. Edmunds placed serious restrictions on the political rights of their burghers both before and after 1381.[198] But most of the latter recognized the benefits the abbey brought to the town, and those benefits disappeared with the abbey. As a crown chantry commissioner reported in 1546: "The town of Bury has 3,000 houseling people and a great number of youth. It has no school or other lyke devise in the town or within 20 miles; nor hospital for the poor except those above named, whose revenues the people petition may be formed into a foundation for the relief of the poor and for education."[199] But all three hospitals--St. Nicholas', St. Parnell's and St. Peter's--were given by the crown to laymen, regardless of the needs of the poor or illiterate. If the abbey was an overwhelming cancer on the local body politic, its removal may have killed the patient as well.

NOTES

1. The leading works on the town and its abbey are Robert S. Gottfried, *Bury St. Edmund's and the Urban Crisis: 1290-1539*, (Princeton: Princeton University Press, 1982), Mary D. Lobel, *The Borough of Bury St. Edmunds*, (Oxford: Clarendon Press, 1935), and A. Goodwin, *The Abbey of St. Edmundsbury*, (Oxford: Oxford University Press, 1931). The last is a short, primarily narrative, essay, but the other two are more ambitious, analytical works. Also useful for town geography and the abbey's architectural history is the government pamphlet by A.B. Whittingham, *Bury St. Edmunds Abbey*, (London: Her Majesty's Stationery Office, 1971), taken from an essay in vol. 108 of the *Archaeological Journal*. For relations between the abbey and the surrounding countryside, see the *Victoria County History, Suffolk*, 2 Vols., (hereafter referred to as VCH) (London: Constable, 1907-11).

2. Norman M. Trenholme, *The English Monastic Boroughs*, (Columbia: University of Missouri Press, 1927), 1.

3. Gottfried, 215.

4. Ibid., appendix F, 290.

5. Ibid., 251.

6. Ibid., 235.

7. A.F. Butcher, "English Urban Society and the Revolt of 1381," in R.H. Hilton and T.H. Ashton, eds., *The English Rising of 1381*, (Cambridge: Cambride University Press, 1984), 84-111.

8. VCH, 2:5.

9. Assignton, Bromeswell, Fritton, Kessingland and Southwold. Ibid., 7.

10. Lobel, 1.

11. Trenholme, 3.

12. *Cronica Jocelini de Brakelonda*, edited and trans. H.E. Butler, (London: T. Nelson, 1949(, (referred to hereafter as JB) 69-71.

13. Ibid., 97: "In remotos et absentes seuit Sanctus Aedmundus; multo magis in presentes seuit, qui tunicam suam ei auferre uoluerint."

14. VCH, 2:64.

15. The confessor's charter granting the eight-an-a-half hundreds is printed in David Douglas and G.W. Greenaway, eds., *English Historical Documents, Volume II: 1042-1189*, (New York: Oxford University Press, 1953), 429.

16. Lobel, 113. In her article, "The Ecclesiastical Banleuca In England," from *Oxford Essays In Medieval History Presented to Herbert Edward Salter*, (Oxford: Clarendon Press, 1934), Lobel classifies the liberty of Bury St. Edmunds behind only the first tier of the palatinates of Durham, Chester and

17. *The Kalendar of Abbot Samson* is an account book for these regalian revenues in the late twelfth century. See R.H.C. Davis, ed., *The Kalendar of Abbot Samson of Bury St. Edmunds and Related Documents*, (London: Royal Historical Society, 1954). For a discussion of the "popular" court issue, see Davis' introduction, xxxi.

18. Diarmaid MacCullouch, *Suffolk and the Tudors: Politics and Religion In an English County 1500-1600*, (Oxford: Clarendon Press, 1986), 20.

19. Antonia Gransden, "The Legends and Traditions Concerning the Origins of the Abbey of Bury St. Edmunds," *English Historical Review*, 100 (January 1985), 12.

20. Gottfried, 26.

21. VCH, 1:391 and map between pp. 356-57. In the "Little Domesday" for Suffolk, the lands of the abbot fill sixteen folios. See the Domesday Book translation in VCH (1), the abbot's lands on 491-509.

22. VCH, 2:9.

23. Little Domesday, Suffolk, printed in translation in VCH, 2:508-09.

24. Lobel, 108.

25. Ibid, 10. For market chapter, see D.C. Douglas, ed., *Feudal Documents From the Abbey of Bury St. Edmunds*, (London: Oxford University Press, 1932), 73. For burgh customs, see p. 114 of the same volume.

26. Lobel, 17, 32-33.

27. JB, 73.

28. Trenholme, 87.

29. Whittingham, 9, 27.

30. Gottfried, 18.

31. Returns listed in David Knowles, *The Monastic Order In England*, (Cambridge: Cambridge University Press, 1940), appendix, 702.

32. JB, 1.

33. Ibid., 30.

34. Gottfried, 240-41. Gottfried offers little evidence for financial trouble after that time.

35. See charters 3, 5, and 6 printed in the appendix to *Kalendar*, 77-78.

36. JB, 100-01, 104.

37. *Kalendar*, 27: "Isti omnes predicti libere tenent et nihil amplius faciunt pro ista carucata neque ad auxilium vicecomitis neque ad commune auxilium domini abbatis."

38. Charter printed in appendix to *Kalendar*, 75-76.

39. Ibid., 76.

40. JB, 77-79.

41. Ibid., 99-100.

42. Ibid., 119.
43. Ibid., 76.
44. Ibid., 45, charters 24-26 in appendix to *Kalendar*, 88-90.
45. JB, 9, charter 29 in appendix to *Kalendar*, 91.
46. See R.M. Thomson, ed. and trans., *The Chronicle of the Election of Hugh, Abbot of Bury St. Edmunds and Later Bishop of Ely*, (Oxford: Clarendon Press, 1974).
47. Lobel, 125.
48. Ibid., 125, Gottfried, 221.
49. VCH, 2:125.
50. *The Pinchbeck Register*, ed. Lord Francis Hervey, (Oxford: Clarendon Press, 1925), 1:55.
51. Ibid., 57-58.
52. Lobel, 126-28.
53. *Manuscripts of the Corporation of Bury St. Edmunds*, Historical Mansucripts Commission, Fourteenth Report, Appendix, Part 8 (hereafter referred to as HMC), (London: Her Majesty's Stationery Office, 1895), 130.
54. Trenholme, 23-24.
55. HMC, 126-27.
56. Lobel, 142.
57. Margaret Statham, "The Guildhall, Bury St. Edmunds," *Proceedings of the Suffolk Institute of Archaeology*, 31 (1968), Ipswich, 1969, 117, 137-38.
58. Trenholme, 31-38.
59. Statham, 119.
60. Gottfried, 230.
61. Goodwin, 54.
62. The charter is printed in T. Arnold, ed., *Memorials of St. Edmunds Abbey*, (hereater referred to as *Memorials*), (London: Her Majesty's Stationery Office, 1890-96), 3:302-17.
63. HMC, 157.
64. *Memorials*, 3:177-78.
65. *Calendar of Charter Rolls* (hereafter Chart. Rolls), 5 (15 Edward III - 5 Henry V), (London: Public Record Office, 1920), 125.
66. Butcher, 86.
67. Gottfried, 7-10.
68. Ibid., 71.
69. Numbers of holdings, without revenue figures, given in ibid, appendix C, 272-75.
70. *Calendar of Close Rolls*, (hereafter CCR), Richard II, 1 (1377-1381), (London: Public Record Office, 1920), 57.

71. Lobel, 118-70.

72. *Electio Johannis Tymworth*, from *Memorials*, 3:126: "Eodem tempore in comitatu Suffolchiae surrexit comitiva omni belua crudelior, quae, instigata per homines de Bury, priorem, conventum, et monasterium sancti Edmundi destruere proponebant."

73. Walsingham, *Historia Anglicana*, excerpted and translated by R.B. Dobson in *The Peasants' Revolt of 1381*, (London: Macmillan, 1983), 246.

74. Andre Réville and Charles Petit-Dutaillis, *Le Soulevement des Travailleurs d'Angleterre en 1381*, (Paris: A. Picard et Fils, 1898), 67.

75. Charles Oman, *The Great Revolt of 1381*, (Oxford: Clarendon Press, 1906), 88.

76. Goodwin, 60.

77. Rodney Hilton, *Bond Men Made Free: Medieval Peasant Movements and the English Rising of 1381*, (London: Temple Smith, 1973), 201.

78. *Calendar of Patent Rolls* (hereafter CPR), Richard II, 1377-81, (London: Public Record Office, 1895), 296.

79. *Electio Johannis Tymworth*, in *Memorials*, 3:113: "altercationem diutinam inter confratres de via scrutinii et compromissi."

80. CCR, Rich. II, 1377-81, 176.

81. *Electio*, 115-18.

82. Ibid., 118: "per falsam suggestionem."

83. CCR, Rich. II, 1379-81, 269.

84. Ibid., 276, CPR, Rich. II, 1381-85, 583.

85. CPR, Rich. II, 1381-85, 13-14.

86. *Electio*, 131, states that "frater vero provisoris" was among the rich men of the town.

87. *Articuli sive punctus...*, *Memorials*, 2:139.

88. CCR, Rich. II, 1377-81, 182.

89. Ibid., 140.

90. Petit-Dutaillis' intro. to Réville, xxvii-xxviii.

91. *Electio*, 125.

92. Poll Tax data printed in Oman, appendix II, 162-66.

93. Réville, 55.

94. *Anonimalle Chronicle*, trans. Sir Charles Oman, excerpted in Dobson, 236.

95. *Electio*, 127-28.

96. Ibid., 129.

97. Ibid., 130: "Nisi hoc facerent festinater, tota maledicta comitiva rediret, monachos occideret et monasterium extirparet."

98. Ibid., 131: "...concederent eis non solum libertates antiquas, sed etiam

rediret, monachos occideret et monasterium extirparet."

98. Ibid., 131: "...concederent eis non solum libertates antiquas, sed etiam novas."

99. Ibid.

100. Oman, 105-06.

101. CPR, Rich. II, 1385-89, 100, *Rotuli Parliamentorum* (hereafter RP), (London, 1767-77), 3:178.

102. Wrawe's deposition, printed in the appendix to Réville, 177: "sub pena decapitacionis ipsorum qui hoc facere contradixerunt."

103. *Anonimalle Chronicle*, from Dobson, 236, Walsingham, ibid., 244-45.

104. Réville, 82-83.

105. Wrawe's deposition, ibid., 177-78. On the following page, Wrawe did charge several Bury men with having participated in the looting of a church at Cavendish, but none of them appear to be burghers, and teh attack seems unrelated to any town-abbey struggle. For Bennington's pardon, see CPR, Rich. II, 1381-85, 297-98.

106. *Articuli*, from *Memorials*, 3:141.

107. *Electio*, ibid, 128: "Fuit praedicto priori et ecclesiae sancti Edmundi amicus fidelissimus."

108. Réville, 69.

109. Walsingham, from Dobson, 247.

110. Ibid., 245.

111. *Anonimalle Chronicle*, ibid, 164-65.

112. Petit-Dutaillis, in his intro. to Réville, li: "Dans presque tous les comtes, ce furent surtout les monasteres qui souffrirent de l'insurrection."

113. J.R. Lumby, ed., *Chronicon Henrici Knighton*, (London: Her Majesty's Stationery Office, 1895), 2:140, Oman, 93-97.

114. Dobson, intro., xxxi-xxxii.

115. Walsingham in ibid., 246.

116. *Articuli*, in *Memorials*, 3:137.

117. Ibid., 138.

118. Réville, 72-83: "dans l'emportement de leur passion, ils trahissent naivement les gens de la ville..."

119. RP, 3:111.

120. *Articuli, Memorials*, 3:141.

121. from *Ancient Indictments*, given in Dobson, 255-56.

122. RP, 3:175: "ne soient pas gastez ne desers pur les malefaitz d'autres, desicome les ditz meffesours sont enditez par les bones gentz de la dite ville."

123. *Electio, Memorials*, 3:131.

124. Réville, 113.

125. *Calendar of Fine Rolls* (hereafter CFR), Edward III, 1368-77, (London: Public Record Office, 1926), 390.

126. CFR, Rich. II, 1377-83, 150, 152.

127. Ibid., 232, 234.

128. CPR, Rich. II, 1377-81, 420.

129. CCR, Rich. II, 1381-85, 190.

130. Ibid., 346.

131. CPR, Rich. II, 1381-85, 250.

132. CCR, Rich. II, 1381-85, 429.

133. CPR, Rich. II, 1381-85, 501.

134. Ibid., 586.

135. Public Record Office, Ancient Petitions, 14953, given by Lobel in appendix, 178-79.

136. CPR, Rich. II, 1381-85, 592.

137. CCR, Rich. II, 1381-85, 631.

138. CCR, Rich. II, 1385-89, 10-11.

139. Ibid., 38-9.

140. CPR, Rich. II, 1385-89, 244.

141. CPR, Rich. II, 1381-85, 547, Rich. II, 1385-89, 383.

142. C.U.L. MS. Gg. 4.4, folios 341-42, given in Lobel, appendix, 179-81. See also Lobel, 158.

143HMC, 132.

144. R. P, 3:103.

145. Ibid., 118: "Horspris par expres la ville de Bury Seint Esmon, quele le Roi ne voet mie, a cause de leur outrageouse et horrible meffait de long temps continuez."

146. See, for example, CCR, Rich. II, 1381-85, 175, 194.

147. RP, 3:147: "...ceux de Bury troeffent seuretee suffisante de lour bon port en temps a venir."

148. Ibid., 170-71.

149. Richard's commission to his officers, July 24, 1384, can be found in CPR, Rich. II, 1381-85, 498. The recognizances themselves are listed, names and all, in CCR, Rich. II, 1381-85, 580-86.

150. Chart. Rolls, 15 Edward III - 5 Henry V, 431.

151.Gottfried, 111.

152. Ibid., 114.

153. A calendar, with some details, of these returns was prepared by V.B. Redstone, and published in the *Proceedings of the Suffolk Institute of Archaeology*, 12 (1906):24-29.

154. For Wills, see the collection edited by Samuel Tymms, *Wills and*

Inventories from the Registers of the Commissary of Bury St. Edmunds and the Archdeacon of Sudbury, (hereafter referred to as *Bury Wills*,) (London: Camden Society, 1850).

155. *Ordinaciones* given, with translation, by Redstone, op. cit., 14-23.

156. Gottfried, 181-84. Elsewhere, he refers to "the corporate guilds, which struggled to free themselves from abbey control."

157. *Bury Wills*, 13-14.

158. Ibid., 15-44.

159. Ibid., 106-08.

160. Ibid., 81-83.

161. Ibid., 93-99.

162. Figures arrived at by a comparison of charts in Gottfired, 183, 189, 191.

163. *Bury Wills*, 55-73.

164. Statham, 120-21, 141.

165. Bury and West Suffolk Record Office, H1/2/1, given in ibid., 140.

166. Gottfried, 183, total number of wills in sample: 1358.

167. J.J. Scarisbrick, *The Reformation and the English People*, (Oxford: Blackwell, 1984), 6.

168. Gottfried, 83.

169. VCH, 2:69.

170. Gottfried, 212, Whittingham, 23.

171. John S. Davis, ed., *An English Chronicle Written Before the Year 1471*, (London: Camden Society, 1856), 62-63, 116-17.

172. Arnold's introduction to *Memorials*, 3:xxxi-ii.

173. VCH, 2:66.

174. HMC, 140.

175. MacCulloch, 329-30.

176. Trenholme, 70-74.

177. Ordinances published in HMC, 133-37.

178. VCH, 2:68.

179. *Valor Ecclesiasticus*, (facsimile copy), (London: Record Commission, 1810-34), 465.

180. Alexander Savine, *English Monasteries on the Eve of the Dissolution* (Oxford Studies in Social and Legal History), (Oxford: Clarendon Press, 1909): 72-75.

181. Ibid., 249.

182. Ibid., 250.

183. *Letters and Papers, Foreign and Domestic, Henry VIII*, (Vaduz: Kraus Reprint of 1920 London ed., 1965), 14 (pt. 2):170-71.

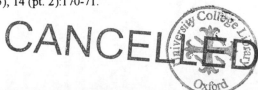

the Suffolk Institute of Archaeology, 15 (1911):311-66.

186. Ibid., 329, 361-63. Sales to others were recorded as well, but all within the previous year.

187. My calculation--the total is for money owed, not all of which had necessarily been paid, and no deductions were made for repairs, tenements empty for part of the year, etc.

188. Savine, 146.

189. See for instance, Court of Augmentations Roll, 334-34, 350-51, 365-66.

190. Ap Rice to Cromwell, from Thomas Wright, ed., *Letters Relating to the Supression of the Monasteries*, (London: Camden Society, 1843), 85.

191. Arnold, intro. to *Memorials*, 3:xxix-xxx.

192. Ibid., xxxiv.

193. VCH, 2:25, Whittingham, 11.

194. ap Rice to Cromwell, 86.

195. Trenholme, 94.

196. MacCulloch, 122-23.

197. HMC, 138-39, 143.

198. See, for instance, the documents relating to an early sixteenth-century dispute printed by Trenholme, appendix, 98-102.

199. Chantry Certificates of 1546, calendared by V.B. Redstone, *Proceedings of the Suffolk Institute of Archaeology*, 12 (1906):40.

Part II. The 1989 Annual Meeting
Lexington, Kentucky

The Joseph J. Matthews Address

REFLECTIONS ON AUSTRIAN ANTI-SEMITISM

BRUCE F. PAULEY

Since 1945 the Jews of Austria have been almost as forgotten as the Austrian Nazis. The government of occupied Austria, struggling to regain the country's full sovereignty, had every incentive to dissociate itself as completely as possible from the Third Reich. Hence the role of the Austrian Nazis in the Anschluss of March 1938 and the partly spontaneous, partly organized persecution of Austria's more than 200,000 Jewish citizens following the Anschluss, became taboo subjects in Austria for politicians, the general public, and to a lesser extent even scholars. Only the revelations about Kurt Waldheim's war record made by the Austrian magazine, *Profil*, during the presidential campaign in 1986 finally broke the silence.

Ironically, the United States played an important and usually overlooked role in this cover-up. As one of the signatories of the "Moscow Declaration" of November 1943, it helped create the half-truth that Austria was the "first victim" of Nazi aggression, although the Declaration also stipulated that Austria was expected to contribute to its own liberation. Secondly, neither the United States, nor the other postwar Western Powers, wished to destabilize or alienate the Austrian government by pressing the unpopular issue of compensations for Jewish victims of the Anschluss. Therefore differences between the American and Austrian governments over the reparations issues were kept out of the press.[1]

Anyone even superficially aware of the history of Austrian anti-Semitism knows that it was hardly an imported item first brought into Austria by German Nazis in 1938. Although Austrian anti-Semitism cannot be divorced from its European context, it had native origins stretching back to the Middle Ages. For centuries it was nourished by the Catholic clergy who taught the faithful that Jews were collectively and hereditarily responsible for the murder of Jesus. Religious intolerance and envy of Jewish wealth led to the expulsion of the Jews of Vienna in 1421 and again in 1669-70. The medieval and early modern history of Austria shows that when the Jews enjoyed the protection of the emperor they flourished, but when that protection was removed they perished. The vulnerability of Austria's Jews to popular persecution was never more apparent than in 1938 when the new Nazi authorities, far from protecting the Jews, actually encouraged their persecution.

The early modern history of Austria as well as the history of the Second Republic also demonstrates that anti-Semitism does not require the presence of Jews to survive. The violent anti-Jewish diatribes of the court preacher, Abraham a Sancta Clara, came *after* their expulsion in 1670.[2] And a public opinion poll conducted early in 1989 revealed that approximately 10 percent of the Austrian people were still hard core anti-Semites and another 27 percent held at least some anti-Semitic opinions[3] despite Austria having a minuscule Jewish population of only about 6,000 people.

Nevertheless, it would be misleading to deny any relationship between Austrian anti-Semitism and the size of the country's Jewish population. After the annexation of Galicia in the late eighteenth century the number of Austrian Jews was second only to that of the Russian Empire. As for Vienna, its Jewish population rose from about 4,000 in 1846 to over 200,000 in 1923, making its growth rate by far the fastest for Jews anywhere in Europe[4]. Whereas the percentage of Jews living in such cities as Berlin, Frankfurt, Prague, and Cracow actually declined between about 1870 and the 1930s, in some cases by nearly 50 percent, the percentage of Viennese Jews rose from less than one percent in the mid-nineteenth century to 10.8 percent in 1923 and was still 9.4 percent in 1934. By that time only 3.8 percent of Berlin's population was Jewish and 4.7 percent of Frankfurt's.[5]

In the meantime, the character of Vienna's Jewish population had also changed. Prior to 1860 nearly all of Vienna's Jews had been German-speaking immigrants from the Bohemian crownland, but by 1920 at least 20 percent of the Jews consisted of much less easily assimilated Eastern Jews or *Ostjuden*, who usually spoke Yiddish, sometimes practiced Orthodox Judaism, and provided many recruits for Zionism. Only Berlin experienced a somewhat similar influx of *Ostjuden* before, during, and immediately after the First World War.[6]

The huge migration of *Ostjuden* to Vienna was made possible by the gradual emancipation of Austria's Jews between 1848 and 1867 and the country's rapid industrialization. These two phenomena helped lead to the impoverishment of the Jewish artisans and peddlers of Galicia at the very time the building of railroads facilitated the large movement of population. The already acculturated Jews in Vienna played a prominent role in financing Austria's industrial growth as well as in founding industries. Non-Jewish Viennese artisans now faced competition from mass-produced factory goods and small shopkeepers were being undersold by the newly-arrived Jewish peddlers.[7]

It was to these "little people" that Karl Lueger, the mayor of Vienna between 1897 and 1910, made his most successful appeal. His Catholic and conservative Christian Social party (or CSP) became the most successful political movement based on anti-Semitism in nineteenth-Century Europe. His depiction of Jews as a single monolithic enemy with international connections against which Christians had to unite made a profound impression on none other than the young Hitler. For Lueger, however, anti-Semitism was primarily a means of gaining power, not a philosophy of government.[8] Anti-Semitism, therefore, actually abated after Lueger's appointment as mayor, aided also by rising prosperity.

This hopeful trend was suddenly and catastrophically ended in 1914. The Russian invasion of the Austrian crownland of Galicia and Bucovina inaugurated one of the greatest mass migration of Jews in modern European history. By 1915, 125,000 Jewish war refugees had fled to the Austrian capital, bringing with them little more than the clothes on their backs. Within a matter of months Vienna's Jewish population had been increased by almost 75 percent thus contributing to the already severe prewar shortage of housing and wartime shortages of fuel and food. Although all but 34,000 of these Jewish refugees had left Vienna by April 1918, anti-Semites continued to blame them for all of Austria's many postwar social, economic, and political ills.[9]

War and revolution helped to produce a radicalized Right in Central and Eastern Europe in contrast to Western Europe which experienced neither defeat nor revolutions. There were no real pogroms in Austria, but the Bolshevik revolutions in Russia, as well as in the bordering states of Hungary and Bavaria, revolutions in which Jews played conspicuous roles, alarmed Austrian conservatives. At the same time the rapid growth of the Marxist Social Democratic Workers' party (or SDAP) in which Jews were also prominent, especially in leadership positions, and the widespread acceptance of the *Protocols of the Elders of Zion*, both added to the anti-Marxist and anti-Jewish hysteria of the early postwar years.

Although Judeophobia was especially acute in Austria between 1918 and 1923, it would probably not be an exaggeration to suggest that alleged "Jewish predominance" remained the single most pervasive issue in Austrian politics in the six decades preceding the Anschluss. To be sure, the Treaty of St. Germain was uppermost in the minds of most Austrians in 1919 and the Anschluss question and anti-Marxism also enjoyed widespread support. However, between about 1878 and 1938 probably no other idea was denounced more frequently and by so many political parties and private organizations. The Anschluss issue was pursued by only a tiny minority of Austrians before 1918 and was rejected by something like two-thirds of the population after 1933. Anti-Semitism, on the other hand, enjoyed at least some support from every social class and every major political party both before and after the First World War.

Anti-Semitism was far more than a mere private prejudice in Austria. It was a political weapon which every party adapted to its philosophy in order to embarrass its enemies and more fully integrate its own followers into its organization. The need to use anti-Semitism as a device to integrate party members was less essential for the SDAP and the much smaller Communist party because there was little direct competition between industrial workers and the Jewish population of Austria. Nevertheless, the SDAP's leadership, and ironically, especially those leaders who had Jewish backgrounds, found it helpful to reinforce their denunciations of hated capitalists by frequently referring to them as "Jewish." Although the party never espoused or practiced religious or racial anti-Semitism, it likewise had no unified program to combat anti-Semitism.[10] Its repeated depiction of Jews as ultra-rich, exploiting industrialists and bankers, could only reinforce already existing prejudices. In reality, there were far more impoverished and lower-middle class Jews in Austria than wealthy ones. However, the stereotype of the fat, swarthy, cigar-chewing capitalist was utilized not just by Marxists, but also by Catholic Christian Socials and pan-German· racists in the Greater German People's party, and finally by the National Socialist German Workers' party.

For Roman Catholics in the Christian Social party, religious issues were still important, although by no means the only areas of conflict with Jews. To be more exact, however, it was not so much the Jewish religion which bothered Christian Socials as it was their apparent lack of it. Relations between the CSP and Orthodox Jews and Zionists remained reasonably "correct," thus encouraging both Jewish groups to imagine that their philosophies of self-defense would save them against all anti-Semites in the future.

The indignation of Christian Socials was aimed not at those Jews who wished to withdraw at least partially from the Christian community, but at secularized Jews who wanted to play an active role in Austrian politics and culture, particularly those who had joined the Socialist party, and most of all the Jewish leaders of the SDAP. The complete separation of Church and State, including the removal of most religious influences from public schools, which was advocated by the Austrian Socialists, seemed to threaten the very foundations of Catholicism and the traditional values of the bourgeoisie. The high profile of Jews in the SDAP as well as in many areas of Austrian cultural life, including the cinema, theater, journalism, and book publishing industry, convinced Catholic traditionalists that the whole modern trend toward secularism and liberalism in popular culture could be halted if only Jewish influence were removed or ar least drastically reduced through a *numerous clausus* or cap on Jewish representation in the liberal professions and fine arts. Catholic anti-Semites were incapable of viewing modernist trends in Austria as simply part of an international movement in which gentiles were even more involved than Jews.

Pan-Germans in the Greater German People's party, the paramilitary Front Fighters' Association, part of the Austrian Heimwehr, and the Nazi party also rejected Jewish secularism. For them, however, the ultimate source of Jewish wickedness lay not in any free-will decision Jews might make, but in their "racial characteristics." Marxists could easily accept Jews who renounced capitalism. Catholics always claimed to reject racial anti-Semitism and in theory would welcome any Jew who converted to Catholicism. But a true-believing racial anti-Semite would never accept someone who had the wrong number of Jewish grandparents or even great-grandparents.

The difference between pan-German nationalists and Catholics on the question of race should not be exaggerated, however. It is true that Catholic moderates like Chancellor Ignaz Seipel and Theodor Cardinal Innitzer, or for that matter a not-so-moderate Catholic like Friedrich Funder, the editor of the CSP's official organ, *Reichspost*, had little difficulty accepting Jewish converts into the fold. The same could not be said, however, for extreme anti-Semites like Leopold Kunschak, the leader of the Christian Social "Workers' Association," or Anton Orel, a Catholic youth leader, who would at most tolerate converted Jews only after several generations.

As a political weapon anti-Semitism had a wide variety of uses. Marxists employed it to point out the hypocrisy of Christian Socials who denounced Jews and demandedanti-Semitic legislation, but who accepted baptized Jews into the party and did not enact anti-Semitic laws. Christian Socials and pan-Germans tried to create dissension between Socialist workers and their leadership by saying that the proletariat was being led by alien and unpatriotic Jews.

Anti-Semitism was also unsurpassed as an integrating device, not only in Austria, but in Germany, Poland and no doubt other countries as well.[11] In Austria the need for an ideological glue was particularly important for the Christian Socials and pan-Germans. For both Georg von Schonerer, the pan-German rabble rouser of the 1880s, and the Nazis, anti-Semitism gave some coherence to their otherwise contradictory anti-Socialist and anti-capitalist slogans. Members of the Christian Social party and NSDAP in particular came from a wide variety of social and economic backgrounds. Their dislike, envy, and even fear of Jews were among the few things they had in common. However, because these rank-and-file members had different reasons for disliking Jews, and different ideas about how the "Jewish problem" ought to be solved, the leadership of the CSP and even the NSDAP avoided making specific proposals which might alienate either their moderate or their radical followers. The same was true of the Nazi leadership in Germany. The Greater German People's party was more socially cohesive than the Christian Socials or Nazis, but it was ideologically fragmented except for its anti-Semitism and desire for an Anschluss with Germany.[12]

Anti-Semitism was not only an important integrating device *within* the Christian Social and pan-German parties, but also *between* them; it even facilitated cooperation at the international level among right-wing elements in Germany, Austria, and Hungary. Ultra-conservatives in all the bourgeois parties of Austria, including the Nazis, associated Jews with the hated ideologies of liberalism, Marxism, pacifism, internationalism, and even modern art. They all found it easier to equate these trends with Jews and the "Jewish spirit" than to criticize them on their own merits. They could all simply be dismissed as "Jewish" or *verjudet*. Right-wing and even left-wing anti-Semites also used some of the same terminology to denounce Jews. Conservatives of various kinds described the Jews as "parasitic," "cancerous," "usurious," "disintegrating," "materialistic," and "alien," whereas Marxists frequently referred to wealthy Jews as "bank" or "stock market" Jews.

Anti-Semitism was the most important issue enabling Catholic and nationalistic students to join forces in the Deutsche Studentenschaft, a student organization which existed in Germany, Danzig, and the Sudetenland as well as in Austria. Many of these students then became a vital element in the Austrian Nazi party. Likewise, anti-Semitism was the only thing that enabled Catholics and nationalists to cooperate in the umbrella organization known as the Antisemitenbund or League of Anti-Semites. Anti-Semitism was also a perfect vehicle of antidemocrats wishing to embarrass the government because there was always some "Jewish problem" which the government could not possibly solve by democratic means or whose solution would be unacceptable to the international community.[13]

Nevertheless it would be wrong to suggest that any of Austria's political parties was utterly dependent on anti-Semitism for its very existence, at least in the interwar period. For Marxists, anti-Semitism was primarily a propaganda tool used to defend themselves against the anti-Semitic attacks of other parties, especially the CSP. There is no reason to doubt that the Socialists could have survived without such propaganda, as indeed they have in the Second Republic.

To a lesser extent anti-Semitism was also a mere propaganda tool of the CSP which it used when pan-German anti-Semitism threatened to become too popular in the early 1920s and again a decade later. At those times the party was anxious to prove that it had been anti-Semitic long before the pan-Germans had even thought of the idea. When the competition of pan-German anti-Semitism faded in the late 1920s, so too did the anti-Semitism of the Christian Socials. When hostility toward Jews declined as an issue for the CSP it suffered no substantial loss of popular support.

Even most Nazis did not cite anti-Semitism as a major reason for their joining the party, at least not in Germany.[14] Anti-Semitism had been part of the Austrian Nazi ideology since 1913 and a very important part since 1918; yet it was not until the Great Depression hit Austria, and the NSDAP began enjoying an astonishing series of electoral successes in Germany, that the Austrian NSDAP began its rapid ascent. In explaining the party's success in the local elections in

April 1932, Walter Riehl, one of the party's early leaders, did mention anti-Semitism, but he also said it was "above all our anti-Marxist positions . . ." which accounted for the victory.[15] Even more important for the Nazis after 1933 was their near-monopoly of the Anschluss issue after the CSP and SDAP decided to reject a union with the anticlerical and anti-Marxist Third Reich.

Although political anti-Semitism in Austria was primarily a weapon used to attack one's enemies and was not crucial to any party's ideology, this does not mean that it was nothing more than pure demagoguery. Minutes of the Greater German People's party's so-called Committee of Experts on the Jewish question provide us with chilling evidence to the contrary.[16] However, even the demagogic character of political anti-Semitism had its disastrous consequences for Jews because it meant that there was never a realistic possibility of their eliminating anti-Semitism or escaping its consequences by changing their professions, political affiliations, religious beliefs, or desire to assimilate with Christians. To a certain extent the post-World War II phenomenon of "anti-Semitism without Jews" already existed before the war. The anti-Semites did not require real live Jews to hate; the mythical Jew sufficed, or even the "Jewish spirit."

However, it was also this highly abstract nature of anti-Semitism which enabled most Austrian Jews to lead normal lives during the First Republic, unless they happened to live in the heavily Jewish district of Leopoldstadt in Vienna or attend the University of Vienna where anti-Semitic violence was endemic.[17] Anti-Semitism was almost entirely a war of words fought between the anti-Semites themselves. Each party wanted to prove that its anti-Semitism was superior to all the others. Only rarely did anti-Semitism involve direct confrontations between Jews and gentiles.

None of this meant to imply that anti-Semitism had no practical consequences for Austrian Jews. On the contrary, the six decades of political and private anti-Semitism and all the propaganda which accompanied it made the anti-Semitism of Austrian (and also German) Nazis seem neither novel nor particularly radical. Indeed, the depressing fact is that prior to the Anschluss the Austrian Nazis had not proposed, and the Nazi government in Germany had not enacted, any legislation which had not already been demanded by the Antisemitenbund, Leopold Kunschak's Christian Social Workers' Association, the Greater German People's party, and in some cases even the Christian Social party and Social Democratic party. The Austrian

Nazis simply combined all the earlier forms of religious, economic, and racial anti-Semitism. They could now also legitimately claim that their brethren in Germany had the courage actually to do what Austrian anti-Semites merely talked about. In fact, when non-Nazi/Austrian Judeophobes commented on Nazi anti-Semitism in Germany at all it was mostly to complain about its moderation, not its severity.[18]

The Austrian government also facilitated the transition to Nazi rule by quietly implementing some of the Nazis' anti-Semitic program. To be sure, such measures were made without the flamboyance associated with German anti-Semitism in order to avoid alienating the government's wealthy Jewish supporters and the international Jewish community as well as the western democracies in general. Consequently, there were no ostentatious burnings of Jewish books, no government-organized boycotts, and no loudly-proclaimed dismissals of Jewish civil servants. There were, however, quiet dismissals of Jewish physicians and teachers and a toleration of vicious anti-Semitic newspaper articles and public speeches.[19]

After the Anschluss the Nazis quickly enacted the anti-Semitic legislation that Austrian anti-Semites themselves had long demanded. The handful of Jews who held civil service jobs or were the managers of banks and large industries were dismissed in a matter of days. Jewish pupils were segregated into separate schools, and Jewish university students were reduced to their percentage of Austria's population and finally expelled altogether. Some Austrians were offended by the violence perpetrated against Jews, especially during Kristallnacht, but not enough to make the kinds of united protests which the Christian wives of Berlin Jews made in 1943 to stop their husbands from being deported to death camps, or which the Catholic Church successfully made to reinstate crucifixes in public classrooms in Bavaria.[20] When the deportation of Austrian Jews began in 1941, it too simply fulfilled a demand that such politicians as Leopold Kunschak and Walter Riehl had made more than twenty years earlier, although neither man probably envisioned the extermination of the deportees.

Even though it is impossible to prove in any empirical way, it is also highly probable that six decades of anti-Semitic propaganda had left Austrian Jews so isolated socially that few Christians were willing to help them in their hour of mortal danger. To argue otherwise is to suggest that propaganda has absolutely no influence on the public no matter how often it is repeated over no matter how long a time. This is not a thesis which the advertising industry would gladly accept.

While the war of words was raging between anti-Semites, a curiously parallel verbal battle was taking place between Austrian Jews. If anti-Semites vehemently denounced their opponents as being soft on Jews and promoted themselves as the best anti-Semites, Austrian Jews likewise accused each other of playing into the hands of anti-Semites while they themselves represented the best of Jewry. This is not to imply a kind of moral equivalency between Jews and anti-Semites. The Jewish "civil war," as it could almost be called, was to some extent a war for survival dictated by the rise of modern political anti-Semitism.

The Jewish war of words in interwar Austria, like the domestic politics of contemporary Israel, was so intense for the simple reason that it involved absolutely fundamental philosophical issues which might very well determine whether the Jews would survive as an identifiable group. Each Jewish faction was profoundly convinced that in the long run--and all Jews were ultimately more concerned about the distant future than the present--only their philosophy would insure survival. By contrast, the philosophy of their opponents would allegedly guarantee either the end of Jewry as a separate religion or as a separate community--the argument of the Zionists--or a permanent status of legal and social inferiority, which was the position of the assimilationists organized in the Union of Austrian Jews. More crucial issues can hardly be imagined. Unfortunately, none of the philosophies of the various Jewish factions would have assured the survival of the Austrian Jews. Not only did they badly divide the Jewish community at a time when unity was desperately needed, but they also encouraged illusions about the future and weakened the urge for self defense.

The assimilationists, clinging to their liberal belief in the goodness and rationality of mankind, were sure that the revival of anti-Semitism after 1914 had been caused merely by temporary military, political, and economic circumstances which in time would disappear. In a sense they were correct, but 65,000 Austrians did not live to witness the partial remission of anti-Semitism after World War II. In the meantime, the assimilationists' long-held desire to blend into the local population contradicted the need to defend themselves as Jews.

The Zionists' belief that anti-Semitism was permanent implied that any effort to combat it was essentially futile. Theodor Herzl, the founder of modern political Zionism, had even suggested that the intensification of anti-Semitism would benefit the Zionist movement by attracting new members.[21] Moreover, occasional positive comments from Catholics and even pan-Germans about Zionism encouraged them to feel that Nazis would also leave them alone if only they voluntarily withdrew from the gentile community. Orthodox Jews were convinced that anti-Semitism was God's punishment for those Jews who had abandoned the traditional faith. The anti-Semitic threat could therefore be overcome simply by returning to Orthodoxy.

Jewish hopes for survival also rested to a very large extent on their ability to survive so many apparently similar dangers in the past. Six decades of anti-Semitic agitation, accompanied by next to nothing in the way of concrete anti-Semitic legislation, played a central role in giving Austrian Jews a false sense of security. Adolf Hitler himself recognized this fact in *Mein Kampf* when he cynically observed that "the Jew is so accustomed to this type of anti-Semitism [meaning Christian Social anti-Semitism] that he would have missed its disappearance more than its presence inconvenienced him."[22] *Judische Front*, the mouthpiece of the veterans' organization called the League of Jewish Front Fighters, was virtually alone when in April 1937 it debunked the idea that Jews would survive Hitler because they had survived so many hardships in the past. This was a dangerous error, the paper warned, which only made the Jews passive. In the past Jews had been able to escape persecution by simply emigrating to another country where there was no hostility towards Jews. This option no longer existed for the Jewish masses because all countries had, in the paper's only slightly exaggerated words, "hermetically sealed their borders."[23]

> Ignoring these ominous words, most Austrian Jews as well as gentiles had come to take anti-Semitism for granted by 1938. Neither group found anything particularly unusual about the anti-Semitism of the German or Austrian Nazis. Gentiles saw no need to oppose the Anschluss simply because of the Nazis' anti-Semitism; and Jews, though obviously concerned enough to oppose the Anschluss, assumed that the new Nazi threat was no more serious than the many they had survived in the past, most recently in the time of Karl Lueger.[24]

NOTES

1. *Ich bin dafür, die Sache in die Länge zu ziehen: Wortprotokolle der österreichischen Bundesregierung von 1945-52 über die Entschädigung der Juden* (Frankfurt am Main, 1988), 50, 54.

2. Robert Kann, *A Study in Austrian Intellectual History: From the Late Baroque to Romanticism* (New York, 1960), 79.

3. Christian Haerpfer, "Anti-Semitic Attitudes in Austrian Society, 1973-1989: A Study for the Liga der Freunde des Judentums, Vienna" (Vienna: Institute for Conflict Research, July 1989).

4. Robert S. Wistrich, *The Jews of Vienna in the Age of Franz Joseph* (Oxford, 1989), 42.

3. Georg Glockemeier, *Zur Wiener Jüdenfrage* (Leipzig Vienna, 1936), 9; Günter Fellner, "Der Novemberpogrom 1938: Bemerkungen zur Forschung," *Zeit Geschichte* (November 1988), 40.

6. For the immigration of *Ostjüden* into Germany see Jack Wertheimer, *Unwelcome Strangers: East European Jews in Imperial Germany* (New York, 1987) and Trude Maurer, *Ostjuden in Deutschland 1918-1933* (Hamburg, 1986).

7. John W. Boyer, *Political Radicalism in Late Imperial Vienna: Origins of the Christian Social Movement, 1848-1897* (Chicago, 1981), 64.

8. Wistrich, *Jews of Vienna*, 205, 208; Kann, *Austrian Intellectual History*, 112 n.

9. Beatrix Holter, "Die ostjüdischen Kriegsflüchtlinge in Wien (1914-1923)," (University of Salzburg, Hausarbeit aus Geschichte), 14-19, 56.

10. John Bunzl, "Arbeiterbewegung und Antisemitismus in Österreich vor und nach dem Ersten Weltkrieg," *Zeit Geschichte* (1976-77), 170.

11. Hugo Valentin, *Antisemitism: Historically and Critically Examined* (Vienna, 1937), 120; Celia S. Heller, *On the Edge of Destruction: Jews of Poland between the Two World Wars* (New York, 1977), 77.

12. Evan B. Bukey, *Hitler's Home Town: Linz, Austria, 1908-1945* (Bloomington, 1986), 54-55; Gunter Fellner, *Antisemitismus in Salzburg 1918-1938* (Salsburg, 1979), 166.

13. Oskar Karbach, "Die politische Grundlagen des deutsch-österreichischen Antisemitismus," *Zeitschrift für die Geschichte der Juden* (1964), 8.

14. Sarah Gordon, *Hitler, Germans, and the "Jewish Question"* (Princeton, 1984), 53-55; Donald L. Niewyk, *The Jews of Weimar Germany* (Baton Rouge,

1980), 80.

15. Letter of Walter Riehl (Vienna) to Alfred Proksch (Linz), 26 April 1932, Bundesarchiv in Koblenz, Sammlung Schumacher, Carton 305 folder 2, p. 1.

16. Allgemeines Verwaltungsarchiv (Vienna), Bundeskanzleramt, Grossdeutsche Volkspartei, Carton VI-36 (Judenausschuss).

17. John Haag, "Blood on the Ringstrasse: Vienna's Students 1918-33," *The Wiener Library Bulletin* (1976), 29-34.

18. Such complaints were commonplace in the Catholic weekly periodical, *Schönere Zukunft* (Vienna).

19. Sylvia Maderegger, *Die Judem im österrreichischen Städestaat 1934-1938* (Vienna and Salzburg, 1973).

20. Ian Kershaw, *Popular Opinion and Political Dissent in the Third Reich* (Oxford, 1983), 347.

21. Wistrich, *Jews of Vienna*, 189.

22. Translated by Ralph Manheim (Boston, 1943; originally published in 1927), 121.

23. 15 Apr. 1937, 1.

24. See, for example, *Die Wahrheit* (Vienna), 24 Apr. 1931, 1; 10 Feb. 1933 1; 12 July 1935, 1; *Judische Arbeiter* (Vienna), 2 Feb. 1934, 1; *Die Stimme* (Vienna), 2 June 1932, 2.

Selected Papers

SCHWARZENBERG, THE BALLPLATZ, AND THE BALKANS: THE CASE OF THE DANUBIAN PRINCIPALITIES, 1848-1852

KENNETH W. ROCK

By the early eighteenth century the growing weakness of the Ottoman Empire and the growing strength of the Russian Empire had become one of Europe's great diplomatic dramas which historians have termed the Eastern Question. In the competition for influence in southeastern Europe, geography alone, underscored by historical, political, and economic interests, mandated that the Habsburg Monarchy, which shared a common border with Ottoman domains from the Adriatic seacoast to Transylvania's Carpathian passes, concern itself about continued Ottoman decline and continued Russian expansion.[1] After Austria's extensive territorial gains ratified by the 1699 Treaty of Karlowitz and the 1718 Treaty of Passarowitz, Empress Maria Theresa and Chancellor Clemens von Metternich advised against additional Balkan territorial aquisitions.[2] Oriented toward central and western Europe, Habsburg foreign policy sought to prevent instability in the Balkan peninsula and to preserve Ottoman suzerainty south of its borders. But Austria could not overlook the Orient, for the French Revolution and the Romantic movement precipitated a national awakening of the East Central European and Balkan peoples which reverberated across the continent and into the Balkans.

The 1848 Revolutions shattered Habsburg disregard for nationalism and, as Enno Kraehe has written, "almost completely inverted the premises on which Austrian policy had been based for two generations."[3] Since 1848 proved nationalism to be an interrelated internal and external problem which everywhere challenged imperial Austria's existence, the Ballhausplatz could ignore the Balkan peoples and governments no more than Habsburg statesmen could disregard the

German, Italian, and Magyar insurgents. Henceforth nationalism became "at every critical juncture the main determinant of Austrian diplomacy."[4] This situation implies that Austrian foreign policy must be viewed in its wider European context, for Austria, like the proverbial Achilles, possessed vulnerable heels everywhere! Mid-century conditions mandated a more resolute assertion of Habsburg imperial prerogatives and prestige within and beyond the empire's frontiers.

Seven months after Metternich resigned from office Prince Feliz zu Schwarzenberg in October 1848 assumed control of Austrian policy. A "military diplomat" (Armée Diplomat), Schwarzenberg presided over Habsburg policy as Minister President of a "responsible government" vigorously determined to defeat "the revolution," to guarantee dynastic rule, to maintain imperial unity and great power status, and to "rejuvenate" the entire Habsburg state (Gesammtmonarchie).[5] Acting with vigor and confidence, Schwarzenberg hoped that a Mitteleuropa, politically and economically unified under resolute Habsburg leadership, would outweigh national aspirations for dissolution. Henceforth the Habsburg Monarchy would comprise a Central European great power possessing equal status with tsarist Russia, Great Britain, and France.[6] Acclaimed as the saviour of the monarchy after 1848, Schwarzenberg's German, Italian, and domestic policies remain controversial.[7] Less attention has been devoted to his Eastern program.

This essay focuses on the Austrian Empire's relations with the eastern Balkans, with the Danubian principalities and the Ottoman Empire, in order to clarify how post-1848 Habsburg policymakers under Schwarzenberg's direction, sought to contain political instability, to counter foreign "intrigues", to bolster local princely and Ottoman authority, and to safeguard Habsburg security, political, and commercial influence within and along the Monarchy's southeastern frontiers. Space prevents an analysis of Austrian policies throughout the entire Balkan peninsula where long-suffering peasant resentment of feudal overlordship and incipient ethnic nationalism exploded in March 1848 when word of the revolutionary events in Paris, Vienna, and Budapest reached the Austro-Turkish borderlands. The Habsburg-Ottoman frontier temporarily dissolved as Serbian, Croatian, and Magyar activists crisscrossed the Sava and Danube Rivers calling for the establishment of national homelands. Slavic disunity, Magyar intransigence, and Habsburg determination ultimately enabled Vienna to enlist Croatians and conservative Serbs against the Hungarian revolution while Russian and Turkish diplomatic pressure in Belgrade and Constantinople assisted Habsburg agents in persuading the government of the Serbian principality to remain "loyally" neutral. Suffice it to say that by late 1849 Schwarzenberg's Ballhausplatz, albeit with difficulty, had managed to maintain Habsburg authority within Dalmatia, Croatia-Slavonia, and the Vojvodina region of southern Hungary as well as its "good neighborly" role in the principality of Serbia and in Ottoman Bosnia-Hercegovina, where in 1849 Vienna began to expand its consular network.[8]

In contrast to the western Balkans, however, the Hungarian "disorders" severed Vienna's regular communication routes with Habsburg civil and military authorities in Transylvania, forced Habsburg military units to seek temporary refuge on Wallachian soil, and thereby seriously reduced Austrian prestige and influence in the Danubian principalities of Wallachia and Moldavia. Despite the mid-century rise in Danubian shipping and the growing commercial importance of the Levantine grain trade, Austria under Metternich had generally viewed the Danubian principalities with benign indifference. Desiring tranquility along the the lower Danube, Vienna had bolstered Ottoman Turkish and Romanian boyar authorities, had acquiesced to the virtual protectorate Russia had established in 1829 over both Moldavia and Wallachia, and periodically had sought accommodations with Turkey, Russia, and Britain for favorable regulation of Danubian trade. The revolutionary events of 1848 and 1849 aroused Austria from its Pre-March lethargy and forced the Habsburg government to acknowledge the strategic and commercial importance of the Romanian lands.

With their government preoccupied by the Hungarian revolution and deprived of instructions because of erratic communications, throughout 1848 and early 1849 Habsburg consuls August von Eisenbach in Iasi, Moldavia and Franz von Timoni in Bucharest, Wallachia nervously witnessed indigenous nationalist demonstrations, de facto Russian preponderance, de jure Turkish presence, French ideological inspiration and British practical manipulation of rising Romanian nationalism. The May 1848 petitions in Iasi and the more portentous June 1848 public demonstrations in Bucharest, which unexpectedly toppled the Wallachian regime of Prince George Bibescu and resulted in a provisonal government of youthful enthusiasts, climaxed two decades of conspiracy against Russia's protectorate and its native boyar officials.[9] Alarmed that the revolutionary "contagion" had inspired Paris-educated Romanians to stage Russophobic demonstrations, Tsar Nicholas I pressured Constantinople to undertake a joint military occupation of the principalities. Despite British diplomatic resistance and Turkish governmental reluctance, by September 1848 25,000 tsarist troops under General A. N. Lueders and Commissioner General Alexander Duhamel, plus 16,000 Turkish soldiers commanded by Omer Pasha and Commissioner Fuad Efendi occupied Wallachia, while an additional 40,000 Russianspatrolled Moldavia. Tsarist and Ottoman public camaraderie could not mask the fact that Turkish officials resented Russia's tightened protectorate nor the indigenous populace's Russophobia and yearning for liberation from foreign repression that rippled across both lands.[10] Romanov Russia's manifest strength highlighted Habsburg Austria's demonstrated weakness. This perception only increased when Hungarian insurgents, inspired by the nationalist euphoria of Louis Kossuth and commanded by the veteran Polish Russophobe József Bem, seized control of much of eastern Hungary and central Transylvania between December 1848 and early January 1849.

With Russian troops poised on Transylvania's Moldavian and Wallachian frontiers, tsarist officers in January 1849 declared their willingness to cross the Habsburg border at Austria's request. When Habsburg consul Timoni appealed for instructions, Schwarzenberg discounted Austria's need for Russian "armed assistance in response to Hungarian rebels' threat to the Saxon cities of Transylvania." Martial aid was "not now desirable." The Ballhausplatz did, however, request that "Hungarian rebels" in the principalities be arrested and extradited. The Russians agreed immediately, but Ottoman Commissioner Fuad referred the matter to Constantinople.[11]

Events superseded diplomacy. When on 2 February 1849 General Anton von Puchner, harassed Habsburg commander in Transylvania, requested aid at Rothenturm Pass to defend Hermannstadt (Sibiu, Nagyszeben), against the Hungarian insurgents, some 6,000 Russian troops on 4 February promptly crossed the frontier passes to Hermannstadt and Kronstadt (Brasov, Brassó). Alarmed that the situation in Transylvania would arouse the "inhabitants on this side of the border" since, as Timoni reported, "neither officers nor men here are reliable"; Russians, Turks, and Austrians closed ranks against Romanian, Polish, and Magyar activities on both sides of the Carpathians.[12] In contrast Britain's veteran Bucharest consul general Robert J. Colquhoun, who had staunchly opposed Russia's occupation of the Danubian principalities, protested Romanov martial intervention

on Habsburg soil and dispatched his deputy, Effingham Grant, to
confer with General Józef Bem, commander of the Magyar-Polish
forces in southern Transylvania.[13] When Bem's troops at Hermannstadt
on 11 March unexpectedly routed and expelled both Habsburg and
Romanov imperial armies from Transylvania by 20 March, Russian and
Austrian officials angrily blamed the British and French consuls for the
Russophobia rampant in Bucharest. A bitter Timoni noted that while
Austrian soldiers begged for hospitality in Wallachia, he took solace
that Ottoman Commissioner Fuad refused to correspond with "rebels"
as he termed the "current Transylvanian government."[14] The 1 May
1849 Russo-Turkish convention at Balta-Liman, by which Russia and
Turkey formally regulated their joint "pacification" of the principalities,
announced that they would install conservative boyars Prince Barbu
Stirbei and Prince Gregory Ghica as hospodars of Wallachia and
Moldavia, and stipulated that the Russian army would occupy the
principalities until 1851, caused "considerable stir" among the
Romanian populace, Timoni reported. An anxious Austrian consul
penned with approval, "only the certainty that the Principalities will
remain occupied by the Turks and the Russians guarantees public
order."[15]

Grateful   for   the   Russo-Turkish   imposed   stability   in   the
principalities and after May 1 buoyed by the knowledge that Habsburg
and Romanov armies were operating in unison against "the revolution"
in central Hungary   Schwarzenberg   in   June   sought   to   heighten
Habsburg visibility upon the lower Danube by pointedly expressing
Austria's appreciation to Fuad for his refusal to communicate with the
Hungarian insurgents, promised to reimburse Turkey for assisting
Austrian refugees, and bestowed inducements for further "loyalty" in
the form of decorations for the Turkish commissioner and other pliable
Russian   and   Wallachian   officials.[16]   On   22   June   Habsburg   and
Romanov troops re-entered Transylvania, quickly retook Hermannstadt
(Sibiu), and forced Bem onto the defensive. On the same day the
Russians and Turks installed princes Stirbei in Wallachia and Ghica in
Moldavia as hospodars. Politically conscious Romanians saw their
"dreams ... for future independence" broken while Magyars in
Bucharest became "fanatical" as the "bloody drama in Hungary and
Transylvania" ended with the victory of the imperial powers, Austria's
consuls noted with satisfaction.[17]

Emboldened by martial success in Hungary and eager to reassert
Austria's stance as a European great power, the Ballhausplatz pressed

Fuad to conduct himself as befitted a "friendly neighbor." The
Ottoman commissioner should punish Turkish and Wallachian officials
guilty of "inimical behavior" toward Habsburg soldiers regrouping on
Wallachian soil. More specifically, Schwarzenberg charged Timoni to
utilize Habsburg treaty rights "to demand the extradition of *all*
(saemtlichen) Magyar rebels who have crossed to Turkish soil, ... to
protest against the Turkish commissioner's intentions simply to intern
these refugees and to insist upon their extradition."[18] To strengthen
Austria's case, Schwarzenberg furnished his agents with documents
captured in Bem's coach indicating that Bem had intended to form a
Wallachian legion which would have endangered all legal authorities
on both sides of the Carpathians.[19]

As dispirited Hungarian soldiers crossed the Wallachian frontier
after their 13 August surrender at Vilàgos and while British consul
Colquhoun "openly" lauded Louis Kossuth and expressed "his sorrow at
the failure of the Hungarian insurrection," Timoni pressed for
extradition.[20] Fuad admitted the logic of Austria's arguments and did
not discount the danger to Turkey posed by the "concentration of such
elements" upon its soil, but insisted that "the matter could only be
resolve in Constantinople." Pending the Porte's decision the Turkish
commissioner would intern the refugees.[21]

Frustrated by Fuad, Timoni approached Hospodar Stirbei, who
requested Austrian support to maintain order in Wallachia once the
Turkish and Russian troops departed. Eager to consolidate stability
along the lower Danube, Schwarzenberg replied that "in accordance
with the well-known principles that guide the Austrian cabinet ... for
our part we shall cooperate in every way possible to attain a goal so
important for *both* neighboring states" and exhorted Wallachia's prince
to "carry on with firmness (*Festigkeit*)".[22] The Ballhausplatz sent an
analogous message promising neighborly benevolence to Moldavia's
prince Ghica.[23]

Having achieved military mastery in Hungary, Schwarzenberg
moved in late summer 1849 to safeguard Habsburg security by
eradicating potential future insurgency along the Monarchy's Balkan
borders. Austria's policy rested upon treaty rights, legality, and firm
executive authority. It was pointedly counter-revolutionary,
preoccupied with national agitation, eager to apprehend and to
extradite Hungarian exiles, suspicious of British and French intrigues,
and everywhere opposed to national insurrection. The Ballhausplatz
expected its southeastern neighbors to adopt a reciprocal good

neighborly attitude toward the Habsburg Empire. When Vienna found its will thwarted by local functionaries, it appealed directly to the Ottoman government at Constantinople.

After the Hungarian capitulation at Vilagos on 13 August 1849, some 3,600 Magyar and 800 Poles fled across the Turkish border near Orsova, among them Governor-President Louis Kossuth and Polish general Józef Bem. Ottoman officials initially interned the refugees at Vidin in northwestern Bulgaria. Although Austria's promise of amnesty for the lower ranks induced some 3,000 common soldiers to return home by late October, the status of the more prominent exiles quickly became a major issue of contention between the Habsburg and Romanov empires on one side and the Ottomans, the British, and the French on the other.[24]

When the Porte declined the 25 August 1849 Austro-Russian formal demand to extradite the leading Magyar and Polish refugees, Russian ambassador Vladimir Petrovich Titov and Austrian ambassador Bartholomaeus Count Stuermer, on 17 September 1849 jointly suspended diplomatic relations with Constantinople. British ambassador Stratford Canning, Lord Redcliffe, urged the Turks to reject the Austro-Russian demand as incompatible with Ottoman sovereignty.[25] By late October British and French naval squadrons sailed to Levantine watersto bolster the Porte's resistance. Even if the ambassadors at Istanbul and Admiral Sir William Parker exceeded their respective governments' explicit instructions, the specter of great power conflict in the Levant, following months of revolutionary tension, preoccupied Europe's chancelleries from October to December 1849. The preemptory nature of the extradition demands branded the Russian and Austrian rulers as despotic tyrants in the eyes of the western European and American public, among whom Austrophobia and Russophobia became widespread. Nicholas I himself took umbrage at Schwarzenberg's uncompromising stance toward the Magyar insurgent leaders. Austria's "firm" Hungarian, Balkan, and eastern policies thus acquired wider European dimensions.[26]

As rumors of an imminent Russo-Turkish clash spread through a tense Bucharest in September and October 1849, tsarist officers, who had recently toasted their Turkish colleagues, anticipated a trial of arms. To forestall armed conflict Istanbul urgently dispatched Commissioner Fuad to St. Petersburg to seek reconciliation with Nicholas I. In Bucharest Ottoman commander Omer Pasha explained Turkey's dilemma to Austrian consul Timoni. Many refugees feared the worst if they were extradited to Austria or to Russia; hence they had appealed to the Sultan for protection. To assure such protection some, including General Bem, had converted to Islam. Facing a possible military conflict with Russian, Turkey's general pressed Austria's consul to clarify Vienna' intentions.[27]

Although the Ballhausplatz never contemplated resorting to arms over the Hungarian refugees, Schwarzenberg insisted that Turkey honor Austria's treaty rights and defer to revitalized Habsburg authority. Behind such legal arguments lay Vienna's vulnerability to and therefor antagonism toward revolutionary and nationalist insurrection. Austria's "aggressive" stance was essentially a defensive tactic designed to eliminate -- perhaps exaggerated -- dangers from individuals who from Vienna's perspective were proven insurgents. There is also evidence that Schwarzenberg personally disliked the Magyar leaders and resented the wide-spread European perception that after Russia's 1849 intervention in Hungary, Habsburg Austria merely seconded Romanov Russian in European political affairs.[28] Austria, like other European great powers, might bully the Turks, but Schwarzenberg sought no war in the East. The Ballhausplatz welcomed a relaxation of tensions in the fall of 1849. Seen in the wider European context Schwarzenberg achieved such relaxation by the Interim agreement with Prussia, the peace of Milan with Piedmont, the surrender of the last Magyar insurgents at Komorn, and a resolution of the refugee crisis in the Orient.[29]

The Eastern war clouds dissipated as diplomats in St. Petersburg, Vienna, and Constantinople agreed in late October that the Ottoman government would intern the most illustrious Hungarian refugees far from Habsburg and Romanov borders at Kuetahya in Anatolia.[30] When Timoni reported in December that he had learned of a Kronstadt (Brasov), Transylvanian "journal in the Wallachian language" with "revolutionary tendencies" which the Russians feared would rouse Romanians on both sides of the border, Schwarzenberg directed Austria's Interior Ministry to investigate the "Wallachian newspaper." If it encouraged "the expansive aspirations of the entire Romanian nation (*die ganze romanische Nation)*" Schwarzenberg characteristically ordered it "countered with all possible determination."[31] By the spring of 1850, the Ballhausplatz again directed Austria's Balkan representatives to forestall additional apostasies to Islam and otherwise to render "harmless" any Ottoman-protected refugees from Hungary in their jurisdiction.[32] With the 1848-

49 revolution-spawned emergencies surmounted, a good neighborly stance rather than preemptory demands could prove more conducive to safeguarding the Monarchy's eastern interests.

As "rejuvenated" Austria consolidated its authority in the early 1850s, Habsburg policymakers consciously focused more attention upon the Balkans. Under Schwarzenberg's guidance the Ballhausplatz sought to augment Habsburg surveillance and political counsel in these restless areas. Austria's Ministry of Commerce, under the energetic Karl Ludwig Freiherr von Bruck, reorganized the Habsburg consular system in order to expand the Monarchy's share of Danubian and Levantine trade. New, better trained and salaried Habsburg consuls general established residence in 1850 in the Danubian and Serbian principalities. Austria's consular network expanded into Bosnia-Hercegovina, while vice consulates and agenci es (*Starostien*) multiplied from Moldavia to Albania. Although surveillance of political refugees and Roman Catholic patronage of religious activities initially overshadowed the promotion of commerce, Vienna encouraged Habsburg consuls to champion vigorously the legal and civil rights of Austrian shipping and commercial interests, of Austrian citizens abroad, and of Balkan Roman Catholics. In sum the Habsburg government in 1850 deliberately moved to enhance its eastern interests by promoting Austrian political, commercial, and cultural influence in the Balkans and indeed the Orient.[33]

Consul General Anton Ritter von Laurin's March 1850 arrival in Bucharest heralded a reinvigorated Austrian presence in the Danubian principalities. Schwarzenberg charged Laurin "to *increase* and *defend* our rights in Wallachia." He should particularly foster Austria's material interests as a means to enhance Habsburg political influence. Laurin was to conduct himself toward the Ottoman, Russian, and Wallachian authorities with "sagacity, moderation, and firmness" (*Klugheit, Maessigheit, und Festigkeit*) and in no case to display "weakness" (*Schwaeche*). He should treat British consul general Colquhoun cautiously.[34] Laurin's instructions epitomized Habsburg policy toward its Balkan borderlands in the 1850-1852 post-emergency phase of the Schwarzenberg ministry.

Laurin immediately noted that Bucharest's "so-called liberal party" as well as the British and French consuls were pleased with Ahmed Wefik Efendi, the new Turkish commissioner who had replaced Fuad. It boded well for Austrian interests that tsarist troops had commenced their withdrawal, although the "bottomless roads" and spring flooding delayed their movements.[35] Turkish general Omer Pasha's late April departure (for Bulgaria and subsequently Bosnia), however, was a mixed blessing. Omer's very career, Laurin believed, was a prime incentive for continued Hungarian refugee apostasies to Islam since Omer had been born a Croat and was himself a renegade from the Habsburg army. On the other hand the Turkish commander's strong sense of discipline and lavish spending in Wallachia had re-won some native support for Ottoman rule and thereby had lessened Russian influence. Austria's agent sensed that the indigenous populace preferred Turkish to Russian rule and that the place-hungary boyar oligarchy ruled Wallachia thanks only to tsarist bayonettes.[36]

Zealous to foster Austrian commerce and on behalf of some Austro-Jewish merchants at the Danubian port of Braila, Laurin protested Wallachian officials' "beatings, judicial murders, and arbitrary arrests of Austrian subjects." He implored Schwarzenberg "to show these people that Austrians are not helots!" When Laurin raised this matter with Prince Stirbei, he found the hospodar to be full of "fears and complaints" and in general he characterized "officials in the Principalities" to be of "miserabe caliber."[37]

The Ballhausplatz applauded Laurin's firmness against the "violent encroachments and infringements" of Habsburg subjects and lectured Wallachia's hospodar that such "brutalities" committed "in a country that aspires to march forward with other civilized European nations" had created in Vienna a "painful impression." Stirbei should discipline his officials:

> The Imperial Government is and always will be disposed to offer
> Wallachia proofs of its sincere desire for good neighborly relations,
> but it expects that the princely government will reciprocally
> undertake all efforts to prevent such attacks upon the rights and
> privileges that subjects of the Emperor enjoy in Wallachia according
> to the existing stipulations[38]

Schwarzenberg's missive to Stirbei, in accord with his instructions to Laurin, summarized Austria's Balkan policy. Vienna supported neighboring authorities but stipulated that they conduct themselves with firmness, with respect for the law, and that they honor Austria's prerogatives.

Austria's policy on the lower Danube must nonetheless be viewed within a wider European context. Habsburg commercial and political interests could advance within a pacified Balkans only if Austria could neutralize "intrigues" engineered by the British, French, Russian, and even Prussians. Sensitive to detrimental commercial competition and aware of 1850 Austro-Prussian political tensions in Central Europe, Laurin alerted Vienna that the Prussian consul, Baron von Meusebach, proposed to establish a Bucharest bank to be financed by Leipzig and Berlin capitalists. If this project succeeded, Vienna might cease to be the financial intermediary between the Danubian principalities and the Leipzig business community. The Ballhausplatz immediately launched diplomatic initiatives in Bucharest and in Constantinople to counter the Prussian proposal.[39]

Like his colleagues throughout the Balkans, Laurin repeatedly remarked on the misery of the local peasantry and with civilized Austrian superiority observed that injustice ruled the land. He wrote, "Mameluke rule in Egypt was probably more violent, but no less lawless than the rule of the boyars here. May Divine Providence spare this land from the punishment which would have happened to the *szlachta* of Galicia without the official intervention of our government."[40] Prince Stirbei discounted the "ill-feeling among the rural people," but when rumors of an uprising swept Bucharest in September 1850, he hastily rearranged his ministers. Aware of the sullenly hostile native population and attuned to the residue of 1848 on both Wallachian and Transylvanian soil, Laurin forwarded to Vienna an intercepted letter from exiled Bucharest forty-eighter Stephen Golescu outlining an émigré plan to create a "Daco-Romanian Empire" or a future "Romania" ("*Romanie*").[41] The Ballhausplatz took note of yet another proof of Romanian nationalism, but Schwarzenberg, preoccupied with the mounting Austro-Prussian confrontation in the Germanies, characteristically endorsed Stirbei's efforts to establish a Wallachian gendarmerie and border patrol.[42] Resolute governmental authority was Schwarzenberg's antidote to popular nationalism within and beyond Habsburg frontiers.

A like-minded Eisenbach confirmed from Iasi what Laurin relayed from Bucharest: frustrated nationalism after 1848 spawned a "popular malaise:"

Malicious self-interest and evil tendencies combined with native and foreign political agitators' blind and audacious impudence, together with similarly-motivated Romanian patriots of Hungary, Transylvania, and the Bukovina are seeking to excite national sentiment not only in the ... Austrian crownlands but especially in the Romanian Danubian Principalities.[43]

Moldavia's Prince Ghica, like his Wallachian colleague Stirbei, believed that a gendarmerie was the best way to guarantee tranquility. Vienna concurred, but until an effective Moldavian gendarmerie came into being, Schwarzenberg advised Eisenbach to seek Russian military assistance to seal escape routes and quietly to apprehend and extradite to Habsburg authorities Hungarian refugees discovered in Moldavia.[44]

By 31 May 1851 tsarist troops had withdrawn across the Pruth River to Bessarabia while the Turkish forces previously in Wallachia now patrolled the Bulgarian-Serbian frontier. Although the departing Russians announced that they would hold positions permitting them to "suppress any movement of the revolutionary party," Laurin noted that security in Wallachia currently consisted "merely" of a militia, a feeble gendarmerie, and the prince's household guards.[45] More positive was the fact that Hospodar Stirbei in October 1851 appointed his Viennese-educated son, George Stirbei, to be his state secretary and that Walachia's prince had "significantly altered" his earlier opposition to Austria's alleged "anti-Wallachian policy." Laurin clarified this statement by noting that Stirbei now honored "our prerogatives."[46] A pleased Schwarzenberg lauded Laurin for his achievements and indicated that Francis Joseph might decorate Stirbei if Wallachia officially acknowledged the grazing rights of Transylvanian shepherds and if Wallachian justice adopted a more benevolent attitude toward Habsburg subjects and their property rights in the principality.[47]

Quiet but persistent Austrian influence based upon ingratiation with the hospodar and the promotion of commercial expansion also characterized Moldavia. Schwarzenberg charged Heinrich Freiherr von Testa, Habsburg consul general in Iasi after June 1851, "to make our *political* interests felt in Moldavia by fostering our *material* interests." Since Hospodar Ghica seemed well-disposed towards Austrian counsel, Testa like Laurin, should conduct himself with "sagacity, moderation and display no weakness." He should foster Austrian commerce and Roman Catholic missions, cooperation with Russia's consul, be alert to any proposals from Prussia's consul or the *Zollverein*, and be circumspect with the French and British consuls.[48]

These instructions for Testa aptly summarized Schwarzenberg's policy toward the Danubian principalities in 1850-1852.

When Ghica confided to Testa his bitterness at Russia's demand for a twelve million piaster indemnity to reimburse "so-called wartime losses" during the 1848-1851 occupation, the Ballhausplatz, seizing its opportunity, bestowed the Order of the Iron Crown upon Ghica, an act which pleased Moldavia's hospodar as Vienna had intended.[49] Although the tsar's shadow loomed large over the Danubian principalities, Russian and Turkish troops had been withdrawn and order prevailed. Austria had reason to appreciate the enforced stability that contained restive nationalism and promoted the development of Habsburg commercial and political influence along the lower Danube.

By the spring of 1852 Schwarzenberg's Austria had outwardly recovered from the 1848 revolutions, had maintained its imperial frontiers intact, and had reasserted Habsburg prestige and counsel at the courts of the Balkan border princes in Bucharest, Iasi, and Belgrade and even with the Ottoman government at Constantinople. Although the Hungarian refugee issues still simmered, tranquility prevailed in the eastern Balkans and Austrian commerce and political counsel moderately spread down the lower Danube. Yet the fundamental issues underlying Austria's relationship to the Balkans and its peoples had not been resolved. A policy of governmental firmness, legality, and the acknowledgment of treaty rights in a climate of festering nationalism and social discontent could inspire deferential behavior from unsteady princes but could not generate popular allegiance nor genuine "good neighborly" respect.

Always imperial, often preemptory, quick to notice slights, energetic, arrogant, even condescending, Schwarzenberg's Balkan policy was not overtly expansive but essentially defensive, dynastic, and anti-revolutionary. Austria's vulnerability to nationalist revolution, its intertwined domestic and wider European crises, its scarcity of reliable soldiers, and the plethora of Austrophobic nationalist exiles after 1849 made the Habsburg government desire orderly, dependent, "good neighbors" along its southeastern borders to safeguard Austria's interests and security. Schwarzenberg's eastern policy gave the illusion of imperial confidence, but fear of revolution and injured dynastic patriotism motivated the Ballhausplatz's demands for firmness, legality, respect for treaty rights, and the maintenance of Austria's great power prestige.

Such considerations suggest not only diplomatic continuity but also a heightened assertiveness in mid-century Habsburg eastern policy. Both diplomat and soldier, Schwarzenberg instinctively recognized that legal arguments in the Metternichian tradition, coupled with resolute action (*"Festigkeit"*) in the tense post-1848 atmosphere, could regenerate Austrian prestige and interests. Military-diplomat Schwarzenberg's maxim was that "in politics one must be keen exactly as in war."[50] Austria would insist upon its treaty prerogatives with the Ottoman empire. Austria would cooperate with tsarist Russia wherever possible yet would resist total Romanov domination of the lower Danube. Austria would counter British political intrigues, but would cooperate with the British to promote mutually beneficial commercial expansion in the Orient. Austria would be a "good" if great power "neighbor" to its bordering Balkan princes. But within this traditional framework Schwarzenberg's Ballhausplatz would resolutely assert Austria's own influence and would foster Habsburg imperial prestige and political influence by promoting Austrian subjects' economic and material interests. Motivated by its own dynamic, Vienna would show the Habsburg flag and insist upon Austrian freedom of action as one of Europe's pentarchy of great powers. Therefore after 1850 from the Dalmatian littoral to the Danubian principalities *kaisertreu* Habsburg agents labored vigorously to counsel conservative local officials, to contain radical nationalism, to champion Austrian economic interests, all to safeguard the Habsburg emperor's cause. The stability Austria so prized in southeastern Europe would prevent any transformation of the status quo which Vienna could interpret as detrimental to the interests of the Habsburg empire.

At Schwarzenberg's death in April 1852 the status quo had been maintained in the Danubian principalities, Habsburg political and economic interests were being safeguarded, but true diplomatic "normalization" had not been achieved. Fear of revolution retained its primacy over the promotion of commercial expansion. Instability would continue along Austria's Balkan borders, especially in Bosnia and Montenegro but also in Wallachia and Moldavia, as Schwarzenberg's successors at the Ballhausplatz and Europe's great powers jockeyed for their respective treaty rights, commercial interests, protectorates and prestige in the Balkans and throughout the Orient. Such issues, within little more than à year of Schwarzenberg's death, would find Austria, Turkey, the Balkan borderlands, and the European powers drawn into the conflict known as the Crimean War.

NOTES

1. See J.A. R. Marriott, *The Eastern Question, an Historical Study in European Diplomacy*, 4th ed. (Oxford, 1940) and M. S. Anderson, *The Eastern Question 1774-1923* (London, 1966). On Austrian eastern policy see Adolf Beer, *Die Orientalische Politik Oesterreichs seit 1774* (Prague, 1883) and Karl A. Roider, Jr., *Austria's Eastern Question 1700-1790* (Princeton, 1982).

2. For Maria Theresa see "Second Memorandum" (February 1772) in C. A. Macartney, ed., *The Habsburg and Hohenzollern Dynasties in the Seventeenth and Eighteenth Centuries* (New York, 1970), 190-191. On Metternich see Paul W. Schroeder, *Metternich's Diplomacy at its Zenith 1820-1823* (Austin, 1962), 164-194; Ernest Molden, *Die Orientpolitik Metternichs 1829-1833* (Vienna, 1913); and Winfried Baumgart, *The Peace of Paris 1856* (Santa Barbara, 1981), 40 and 88. Baumgart, p. 40, cites a 9 February 1853 letter Metternich wrote to Buol: "fruits nourishing to our empire do not grow in any field in the Orient.... There is only one course we must cling to and that is *the political* which means in fact the maintenance of treaties and the prevention of a European war, from Oriental causes!"

3. Enno E. Kraehe, "Foreign Policy and the Nationality Problem in the Habsburg Monarchy, 1800-1867," *Austrian History Yearbook*, III (1967), Pt. 3, 22.

4. Ibid., 23.

5. On Schwarzenberg see Adolf Berger, *Felix Fuerst zu Schwarzenberg, ein biographisches Denkmal* (Leipzig, 1853); Eduard Heller, *Fuerst Felix zu Schwarzenberg, Mitteleuropas Vorkaempfer* (Vienna, 1933); Rudolf Kiszling, *Fuerst Felix zu Schwarzenberg, der Erzieher Kaiser Franz Josephs* (Graz, 1952); Adolf Schwarzenberg, *Prince Felix zu Schwarzenberg* (New York, 1946); Kenneth Rock, "Felix Schwarzenberg, Military-Diplomat," *Austrian History Yearbook*, XI (1975), 85-109; and Kenneth Rock, "A Time for Deeds and Courage: Schwarzenberg and the Austrian State after 1848," The Consortium on Revolutionary Europe, *Proceedings 1986* (Athens, GA, 1987), 395-412.

6. Bernhard Unckel, *Öesterreich und der Krimkrieg: Studien zur Politik der Donaumonarchie in den Jahren 1854-1856* (Luebeck, 1969), 18.

7. In addition to the works cited in notes 2, 5, and 6 above, see also Erzsebet Andics, *Das Beundnis Habsburg-Romanov. Vorgeschichte der zaristischen Intervention in Ungarn im Jahre 1849* (Budapest, 1963); Roy A. Austensen, "Felix Schwarzenberg: *Realpolitiker* or Metternichian? The Evidence of the Dresden Conference," *Mitteilungen des öesterreichischen*

(1977), 97-118; Heinrich Friedjung, *Oesterreich von 1848 bis 1860* (2 vols., Stuttgart, 1909-12); and Friedjung, *Der Krimkrieg und die oesterreichische Politik* (Stuttgart, 1907); Waltraud Heindl, *Graf Buol-Schauenstein in St. Petersburg und London 1848-1852* (Vienna, 1970); Josef Redlich, *Das oesterreichische Staats- und Reichsproblem* 2 vols. (Leipzig, 1920-26); Helmut Rumpler, *Die Protokolle des oesterreichischen Ministerrates 1848-1867. Einleitungsband* (Vienna, 1970); Paul Schroeder, *Austria, Great Britain, and the Crimean War* (Ithaca, 1972); Lawrence Sondhaus, "Austria and the German Question, 1848-1851: The Debate over Schwarzenberg's German Policy," (unpublished AHA paper, 1988); A. J. P. Taylor, *The Italian Problem in European Diplomacy 1847-1849* (Manchester, 1934); and Friedrich Walter, *Die oesterreichische Zentralverwaltung*, Pt. 3, 2 vols. (Vienna, 1964).

8. For Austria's involvement with the western Balkans and the South Slavs during the 1848 Revolutions and the Schwarzenberg era see, for example, Vladimir Dedijer, Ivan Bozic, Sima Cirkovic, and Milorad Ekmecic, *History of Yugoslavia* (New York, 1974), 310-321; Dimitrije Djordjevic, *Revolutions nationales des peuples balkaniques 1804-1914* (Belgrade, 1965), 77-85; and Djordjevic and Stephen Fischer-Galati, *The Balkan Revolutionary Tradition* (New York, 1981), 105-118; Michael B. Petrovich, *A History of Modern Serbia 1804-1918* 2 vols. (New York, 1976), I: 231-245; Gunther E. Rothenburg, *The Military Border in Croatia, 1740-1881* (Chicago, 1966), 57-85; and Kenneth Rock, "Loyalty and Legality: Austria and the Western Balkans, 1848-1853," in Ivo Banac, John G. Ackerman, and Roman Szporluk, eds. *Nation & Ideology: Essays in Honor of Wayne S. Vucinich* (New York, 1981), 121-148.

9. Russian ascendancy in the Danubian principalities rested upon the 1829 Treaty of Adrianople and the administrative statute known as the *Reglement organique*. The latter posited Ottoman sovereignty but real authority lay with the boyar landed oligarchy backed by Russian officials. A modest uprising in Moldavia was quickly suppressed in May 1848, but more serious national, agrarian, and social demonstrations occurred in Wallachia in June. The hospodar resigned, but by October 30 the Russo-Turkish occupation of Bucharest put the youthful insurgents to flight. See, for example, Radu R. Florescu, "Stratford Canning, Palmerston, and the Wallachian Revolution of 1848," *Journal of Modern History* 35 (September 1963): 227-244; and Florescu, "The Rumanian Principalities and the Origins of the Crimean War," *The Slavonic and East European Review* 43 (December 1964): 46-67. On related events in Transylvania see Keith Hitchins, *The Rumanian National Movement in Transylvania, 1780-1849* (Cambridge, MA, 1969), 181-281. On the Danubian grain trade and the river's commercial development see Vernon

John Puryear, *International Economics and Diplomacy in the Near East: A Study of British Commercial Policy in the Levant, 1834-1853* (Stanford, 1935); David F. Good, *The Economic Rise of the Habsburg Empire, 1750-1914* (Berkeley, 1984); and John R. Lampe and Marvin R. Jackson, *Balkan Economic History, 1550-1950; From Imperial Borderlands to Developing Nations* (Bloomington, 1982).

10. Timoni to Schwarzenberg, Bucharest, 9, 12, 23 January 1849; Eisenbach to Schwarzenberg, Iasi, 26 January, 12 February, 9 April 1849, Haus-, Hof- und Staatsarchiv, Vienna, Politisches Archiv (henceforth PA) XXXVIII (Konsulate) 90, 92.

11. Schwarzenberg to Timoni, Olmuetz, 24 January 1849; Timoni to Schwarzenberg, Bucharest, 22 January, 13 February 1849, PA XXXVIII 90.

12. Timoni to Schwarzenberg, Bucharest, 6 February, 13 March 1849, PA XXXVIII 90.

13. Timoni to Schwarzenberg, Bucharest, 20 March 1849, PA XXXVIII 90.

14. Timoni to Schwarzenberg, Bucharest, 30 March, 3 April 1849, PA XXXVIII 90.

15. Timoni to Schwarzenberg, Bucharest, 8, 15 May 1849, PA XXXVIII 90.

16. Schwarzenberg to Timoni, Vienna, 25 June 1849, PA XXXVIII 90.

17. Timoni to Schwarzenberg, Bucharest, 14 August 1849, PA XXXVIII 90; Dworzak to Schwarzenberg, Iasi, 24 august 1849, PA XXXVIII 92.

18. Schwarzenberg to Timoni, Vienna, 31 July, 11 August 1849, PA XXXVIII 90. Austria's demand for extradition rested upon the 1739 Treaty of Belgrade. Article XVIII stated: "Henceforth, asylum and refuge shall no longer be afforded to evil doers, or to discontented and rebellious subjects, but each of the contracting parties shall be compelled to punish people of this description (*ces sortes de gens*), as also robbers and brigands, even when subjects of the other party...." Cited by John H. Komlos, *Louis Kossuth in America, 1851-1852* (Buffalo, 1973), 35.

19. Schwarzenberg to Timoni, Vienna, 21 August 1849, PA XXXVIII 90.

20. Timoni to Schwarzenberg, Bucharest, 17, 24 August 1849, PA XXXVIII 90.

21. Timoni to Schwarzenberg, Bucharest, 26 August 1849, PA XXXVIII 90.

22. Timoni to Schwarzenberg, Bucharest, 4 September 1849; Schwarzenberg to Timoni, Vienna, 22 September 1849; PA XXXVIII 90. Italics in the original.

23. Schwarzenberg to Eisenbach, Vienna, 9 July 1849, PA XXXVIII 92.

24. Rescript, Vienna, 1 September 1849, PA XXXVIII 90. See also Istvan

Deak, *The Lawful Revolution. Louis Kossuth and the Hungarians 1848-1849* (New York, 1979), 338-341.

25. See Charles Sproxton, *Palmerston and the Hungarian Revolution* (Cambridge, 1919), 108-117; Harold Temperley, *England and the Near East: The Crimea* (New York, 1964), 260-268; Unckel, *Oesterreich und der Krimkrieg*, 46-51; and R. W. Seton-Watson, *Britain in Europe 1789-1914, A Survey of Foreign Policy* (Cambridge, 1955), 259-289.

26. Edmond Bapst, *Les Origines de la guerre de Crimée* (Paris, 1912), 91-118; Vernon John Puryear, *England, Russia, and the Straits Question 1844-1856* (Berkeley, 1931), 153-180; Donald Southgate, *"The Most English Minister ..." The Policies and Politics of Palmerston* (New York, 1966), 259-268.

27. Timoni to Schwarzenberg, Bucharest, 23 October 1849, PA XXXVIII 90.

28. Unckel, *Oesterreich und der Krimkrieg*, 51; Heindl, *Graf Buol*, 71-79, 83, 12n.

29. Unckel, *Oesterreich und der Krimkrieg*, 51.

30. On 16 October 1849 Nicholas I, responding to the Sultan's appeal and Fuad's St. Petersburg mission, dropped Russia's demand to extradite four leading Poles (Generals Józef Bem, Count Henryk Dembinsiki, Józef Wyzocki, and Count Ladislas Zamoyski). Provoked by Austria's severity in Hungary toward captured Magyar officers, impressed by British public support for Turkey, and pleased that Palmerston apologized for the British fleet's transgression of the 1841 Straits Convention, Russo-Turkish relations were re-established by 31 December 1849. Although some 3,000 common soldiers accepted Habsburg amnesty, Schwarzenberg and Ottoman ambassador Mussurus on 22 October agreed that the Hungarian refugee leaders be interned so that "in the future they could undertake nothing against the legal order in the K. K. states." Disagreement over the place and length of internment continued until 5 April 1850 when Vienna acquiesced to Constantinople's interning Kossuth and his associates far from Habsburg frontiers in Kuetahya, Anatolia. Austro-Turkish relations remained strained over the refugee issue and tensions rose again in September 1851 when Turkey released Kossuth to the Americans without Vienna's agreement. See Deak, *The Lawful Revolution*, 340-342; Komlos, *Louis Kossuth in America*, 33-39; and Unckel, *Oesterreich und der Krimkrieg*, 48-52.

31. Timoni to Schwarzenberg, Bucharest, 29 December 1849, PA XXXVIII 90; Schwarzenberg to Timoni, Vienna, 11 January 1850, PA XXXVIII 93. Transylvanian civil and military governor General Ludwig Wohlgemuth temporarily suppressed George Baritiu's *Gazeta de Transilvania* on 9 March

1850. See Hitchins, *The Rumanian National Movement*, 155-163, 277.

32. Schwarzenberg to Timoni, Vienna, 4 March 1850, PA XXXVIII 94.

33. Karl Krabicka, "Das oesterreichische Konsularwesen zwischen 1849 und 1859," (Unpublished doctoral dissertation, University of Vienna, 1953).

34. Instructions for the Imperial Agent and Consul General in Wallachia, Ministerialrat Ritter von Laurin, Vienna, 17 December 1849, PA XXXVIII 90.

35. Laurin to Schwarzenberg, Bucharest, 23 March, 1, 14, 19 April 1850, PA XXXVIII 93. Internuncio Stuermer had urged Vienna to warn Laurin that Ahmed Wefik Efendi, although a confidant of grand vizier Reshid Pasha and foreign minister Ali Pasha, was Paris-educated and bribable. Previously Turkish commissioner in Shumla, Bulgaria, Habsburg Vice Consul Roessler had noted his sympathy for Polish and Magyar refugees. Schwarzenberg to Laurin, Vienna, 6 April 1850, PA XXXVIII.

36. Laurin to Schwarzenberg, Bucharest, 10, 19, 26 April 1850, PA XXXVIII 93. Omer Pasha, born a Croat from Lika named Mihajlo Latas, had converted to Islam after fleeing to Bosnia to escape punishment while a Habsburg military cadet. He became one of mid-nineteenth century Turkey's most able commanders.

37. Laurin to Schwarzenberg, Bucharest, 8, 25 June 1850, PA XXXVIII 93.

38. Schwarzenberg to Stirbei, Vienna, 24 June 1850, PA XXXVIII 93.

39. Laurin to Schwarzenberg, Bucharest, 16 July 1850, PA XXXVIII 93. Vienna desired that Austrian textiles, glass, metalwares, and furniture compete favorably with western European exports to the Danubian principalities and the Near East. Minister of Commerce Baron von Bruck even spoke of the Danube River as "the thread of future Austrian history." By the 1850s Wallachian and Bulgarian ports had become points where Austrian merchants exchanged their goodsfor local raw materials, especially grain. Habsburg consuls championed *Kronstaedter Waren*, manufactures by Transylvanian Saxons, which for centuries had found markets southeast of the Carpathians. They sought to safeguard and enforce Transylvanian shepherds' winter grazing rights in Wallachia, Moldavia, and Bulgaria. Since Austria's consuls general in Bucharest and Iasi were preoccupied with political matters, by 1851 Bruck established nine new commercial agencies in Moldavia and eight in Wallachia to supplement the Habsburg consulate at Galati and vice consulates at Braila, Tulcea, and Giurgiu. Although Austrian trade did not expand as vigorously as Bruck had hoped, by 1855 Anton von Mihanovic, then Habsburg consul general in Bucharest, referred to Wallachia as an "Austrian geographical and commercial dependency." On Habsburg commercial expansion and controversial "protectorate" designs toward the Danubian principalities in the Crimean War era see Krabicka, "Das oesterreichische Konsularwesen," 40, 50-

52, 150-153; L. Boicu, *Austria si Principatele Romane in Vremea Razboiului Crimeii 1853-1856* (Bucharest, 1972), 31, 45-71; Paul Schroeder, "Austria and the Danubian Principalities, 1853-1856," *Central European History* 2(September 1969): 216-236; and Schroeder, "Bruck versus Buol: The Dispute over Austrian Eastern Policy, 1853-1855," *The Journal of Modern History* 40 (June 1968): 193-217; and Carey Goodman, "Austria's Danubian Diplomacy during the Crimean War" (The John L. Snell Prize Seminar Paper, University of Virginia, 1989).

40. Laurin to Schwarzenberg, Bucharest, 7 September 1850, PA XXXVIII 93.

41. Laurin to Schwarzenberg, Bucharest, 24 September 1850, PA XXXVIII 93.

42. Schwarzenberg to Laurin, Vienna, 8 October 1850, PA XXXVIII 93.

43. Eisenbach to Schwarzenberg, Iasi, 4 January 1850, PA XXXVIII 93.

44. Eisenbach to Schwarzenberg, Iasi, 20, 29 March, 5 April 1850; Schwarzenberg to Eisenbach, Vienna, 15 July 1850, PA XXXVIII 93.

45. Laurin to Schwarzenberg, Bucharest, 29 April, 3 June 1851, PA XXXVIII 95.

46. Laurin to Schwarzenberg, Bucharest, 24 October 1851, PA XXXVIII 95.

47. Schwarzenberg to Laurin, Vienna, 27 November 1851, PA XXXVIII 95. Austria, Wallachia, and Turkey concluded a treaty regulating the Transylvanian shepherds' winter grazing rights in 1855.

48. Instructions to the K. K. Agent and Consul General in Moldavia, Vienna, 12 June 1851, PA XXXVIII 95. Italics in the original. Testa had long been first interpreter at the Internuntiatur in Constantinople.

49. Testa to Schwarzenberg, Iasi, 6 October, 10 November, 5 December 1851, PA XXXVIII 95.

50. Cited in Heinrich von Srbik, *Deutsche Einheit: Idee und Wirklichkeit vom .Heiligen Reich bis Koeniggraetz* 4 vols. (Munich, 1935-1942), I, 386.

HITLER AND THE KAISER: THE GERMAN RESTORATION ISSUE, 1919-1934

HANS A. SCHMITT

In Germany the post-1918 status of monarchy differed greatly from the Russian scene. Here revolution swept away not only the Kaiser but also twenty-two state dynasties. The forces that engineered this overthrow were, however, Allied rather than domestic. Every student of these events knows that even Germany's Social Democrats were reluctant republicans.

This does not mean that German monarchy had not exhibited symptoms of malaise well before 1914. The German constitution of 1871 had been a compromise between national revolution and dynastic tradition. Like its immediate precursors, governing the operations of the Confederation of the Rhine, the Germanic and North German confederations, it was an "eternal" compact between German princes. In harmony with nineteenth-century traditions of German monarchical constitutionalism, it was, on paper, dominated by a Federal Council, where representatives of these princes might exercise an unqualified veto over every act of executive and legislative initiative. In such a system strengthening the national state endangered monarchy; preserving dynastic prerogatives reduced the national substance.

As it turned out, German state dynasticism in particular entered a period of decline as soon as the empire came into being. To the extent that federal powers grew as a result of the acquisition of colonies, the building of a *German* navy and the issuance of consolidated civil and criminal codes, state governments were reduced to administrative subdivisions of Germany. The German emperor and his chancellor usurped much of the power assigned to the community of monarchs.

This decline was reinforced by numerous scandals which tarnished the sheen of monarchical glamour. The dethronement of Louis II of

Bavaria, followed by the investiture of his insane brother Otto, the
homosexual proclivities of King Charles I of Wuerttemberg, which
would have led to a similar crisis had a sudden stroke not removed him
from the scene, highlighted some of the system's problems before the
nineteenth century had run its course. The investiture of Alfred, Duke
of Edinburgh, as duke of Saxe-Coburg-Gotha in 1893, confronted an
astonished and indignant German public with the disconcerting fact
that time-honored notions of legitimacy still allowed foreigners to make
at least local policy.[1]

Other succession problems, requiring the passage of legislation by
state parliaments, illustrate legislative advance at the expense of
dynastic power.   When thrones of very small states fell vacant,
furthermore, the most sensible solution, consolidation, produced
complex legal and political controversies.   If any of the states
disappeared, the number of votes in the Federal Council would be
reduced accordingly, increasing Prussia's preponderance. This question
first arose late during Bismarck's stewardship.   Recognizing that a
Federal Council reduced to a Prussian rubber stamp would increase the
power of the Reichstag and of democracy, the Iron Chancellor had only
one answer: the number of German states must never change.[2]

Under these circumstances one may well wonder how long it would
have taken the Bismarckian compromise to unravel had not World War
I hastened its destruction. But the events of November 1918 cut short
the process of organic political evolution. The kings, dukes and princes
departed, and their unpredictable primate suffered for his many sins by
being the only member of their caste forever exiled from Germany.

After 1918 legitimist principles called for the restoration of twenty-
two dynasties, but legitimism at the state level remained all but
invisible. Only in Bavaria did the local dynasty enjoy the requisite
popularity. Only Bavaria spawned a bona fide royalist party whose
history demonstrated all too clearly that legitimism was a position
difficult to sustain in a republican and democratic environment. If it
succeeded, it would owe its victory to the very political system it
abhorred. If it refused to compromise principle by operating under a
democratic constitution, it could not expect to influence public opinion.

Although an American observer concluded, after a visit to Munich
in 1922, that the Bavarian pretender, Prince Rupprecht, was "the
cleverest politician in Bavaria,"[3] neither the prince nor his supporters
found a solution to this dilemma. The *Königspartei* advocated the
return to power of a "people's king, equally accessible to peasants,

workers, civil servants and officers." But it refused to compete in parliamentary elections. This formula alienated some activist reactionaries who organized under different banners. Some were content to join the Bavarian Peoples Party, advocating states rights without commitment to any particular form of government. Some drifted into the conservative German Nationalist Peoples Party, and by the early 1930s others even found a home in the rising Nazi movement, whose authoritarian program harmonized with their own opposition to democracy. Throughout the Weimar era Bavarian monarchism was active, but restoration remained beyond its capacity.[4]

Efforts to restore the Hohenzollern to the German throne suffered from similar afflictions. Added to these was the handicap of the Kaiser's permanent and the Crownprince's temporary exile in Holland. As far as Wilhelm II was concerned, his claim alone was legitimate, but he would have agreed with Bavarian royalists that politicking in pursuit of its attainment constituted an unacceptable concession to republican mores. Neither he nor any of his sons could therefore condescend to lead a legitimist movement. But the tribulations of monarchy did not end there. While the state dynasties had been the more or less passive victims of revolution, Wilhelm had led Germany to disaster. Could his countrymen afford to give him a second chance?

To anyone seeking an answer to that question the Kaiser's conduct in exile was scarcely encouraging. Year after year he bombarded visitors with lectures designed to demonstrate that he could have prevented past defeats if only his ministers and diplomats had kept him properly informed. At the same time he insisted that Germany's current problems would vanish in a trice once he was allowed to return to power. During the Rhineland occupation of 1923 he was convinced that a restoration was needed to drive out the French. He predicted a dramatic break between Britain and France, which a German government could exploit only under his leadership. If these pronouncements demonstrated that Wilhelm refused to learn from experience, one must add the observation of the German minister to the Netherlands, Hellmuth Lucius von Stoedten, who concluded in 1926, after listening to the Kaiser's lecture on the follies of the Locarno treaty: "No one takes his remarks seriously anymore."[5]

But Wilhelm had fathered six sons, five of whom were to survive him, so that a restoration was not dependent on the exiled monarch. Stresemann, under whose aegis the Crownprince was allowed to return to Germany in 1923, believed that the oldest offspring was ready to play Louis Philippe, and willing to accept eventually a throne whose incumbent would be content to play the "people's monarch," also advocated by partisans of a Bavarian restoration.[6] In October 1923, the would-be Wilhelm III quietly left Holland for his estates in Oels in Silesia. Although he promised to stay out of politics, a promise he kept until Stresemann's death in 1929, he made no secret of his conviction that he, rather than his father, was best suited to lead a restoration. As he pointed out to an American correspondent: "My father has had his chance." After his repatriation, however, he was the first to realize that restoration was remote; neither he nor his progenitor had the popular following necessary to bring it off.[7]

Germany's monarchist movement, saddled with two unpopular pretenders, continued to struggle between despair and hope. In 1925 the election of Paul von Hindenburg to the presidency moved another devotee of the old regime into a key position in the new. But his election was the result of public veneration for a war hero; it constituted no national endorsement of the monarchy. Though Hindenburg may have viewed his administration as prelude to the Kaiser's return, he had not sworn to uphold the Weimar constitution. So seasoned and cynical an observer as Kurt von Schleicher predicted that "the old gentleman was far too religious not to take his oath on the constitution seriously."[8] Nothing illustrates the impasse more clearly than a letter from a diplomat, temporarily on loan to the new president to help cope with a sudden deluge of fan mail. "Most of the correspondents," he reported, "are simple souls--old women, children, *Stammtischler*, habitués of bowling and rifle clubs." Most importantly, however, not one of these correspondents ever "mentions the Kaiser."[9]

As a result legitimist forces in Germany scattered, as they had earlier in Bavaria. The monarchist veterans organization "Steel Helmet" (*Stahlhelm*), for instance, feared that Hindenburg's election would endow the republic with a counter-productive respectability. To prevent this, the organization initiated or supported constitutional amendments to dilute republican democracy. Many in its rank and file were increasingly looking for a Führer, rather than a Kaiser. In the presidential election of 1932, the leader of the *Stahlhelm's* populist wing, Theodor Duesterberg, became the nationalist candidate and even then an estimated forty per cent of the membership voted for Hitler. Only a few still supported Hindenburg.[10]

By this time the most serious advocate of restoration may have been Chancellor Heinrich Brüning, the most powerful supporter of the aged president. This conclusion is certainly conveyed by his memoirs and by the interesting and, in this instance, more reliable testimony of John W. Wheeler-Bennett, who reported that Brüning sought to overcome the handicap of Hohenzollern unpopularity by an imaginative maneuver. After Hindenburg's re-election he expected to prevail on the Reichstag to enact a constitutional amendment that would convert the chief executive into a regent. He hoped to obtain the requisite two-thirds majority with the aid of the conservative wing of the Nazi party.[11]

This design had two flaws. There was no evidence that any Nazi faction was ready to work with Brüning. There was ample evidence that Hindenburg's legitimist conscience would never accept a restoration by consent of the Reichstag. In any case the Brüning case made clear that the monarchist cause needed Adolf Hitler's support. How did *he* stand on this issue?

What Hitler genuinely believed is difficult to document. On the issue of monarchical restoration this remains as true as it does on other fundamentals, anti-Semitism not excluded. As a party, the NSDAP never took a position on restoration. Point 25 of the original program demanded "the creation of a strong central power in the Reich."[12] It is the only article dealing with political governance. Its implications are both anti-democratic and anti-federalist; one cannot be more precise than that. Programmatic pronouncements, whether emanating from Alfred Rosenberg, the party ideologer, Walter Darré, the prophet of blood and soil, or Joseph Goebbels, include no advocacy of a return to monarchy, but pay tribute to a small select group of representatives of past greatness, such as "our Bismarck," the Prussian reformer of the Napoleonic era, Karl von Stein, and--with monotonous regularity--Frederick the Great.[13]

Hitler proclaimed his devotion to the Frederician past as early as 1920, calling the king the "first worker" for the state, and referring to him in a number of speeches as "Frederick the Unique." More germane to our preoccupations, however, than the romance of Enlightening Despotism, are pronouncements about the Weimar present. They reveal Hitler as an opportunist, rejecting monarchy as a form of government, but ready to seize the coat tails of its partisans whenever that appeared advantageous. As early as 1919 Hitler began to advocate "redressing the wrong of 1918," an ingenious formula, because his own catalog of these wrongs included, among several grievances, the overthrow of the established order. Disgruntled conservatives, therefore,took "the wrong of 1918" to include what they wanted it to include, and assured the Nazi movement from the beginning of a sprinkling of monarchist support.

But Hitler cast his nets wide, and when he addressed audiences whom he suspected of being indifferent or hostile to legitimism, he expressed quite different feelings. For instance, he told a rally in 1921: "I am no monarchist. I do not thirst for monarchs such as the ones we have had."[14] An American visitor heard a different version: "The whole monarchic question is of fifth or sixth importance [sic]. The people can decide the question of monarchy or republic after a national government has come to power," he told Captain Truman Smith on November 20, 1922.[15] At other times he ascribed the establishment of the republic to the anonymous forces of history: monarchy had been overthrown because the dynasties had been unwilling to fight and die for their rights. It was not his duty to redress that verdict. On the eve of the 1923 Putsch he coined another neutral cliche: "The form [of government] is secondary, the content matters." The main task was to save Germany from the ravages of defeat and revolution.[16]

In prison, after the abortive Munich coup, Hitler turned to the uncongenial printed page as a means for disseminating his message. He continued to reject monarchy, but with slightly different accents. Hereditary government, he averred, conflicted with nationalism. During his adolescence in Linz, he reminisced, he had learned to understand the "difference between dynastic patriotism and populist nationalism. Even then I appreciated only the latter."[17] At the same time, he did not regret that Emperor Joseph II's attempted centralization and Germanization of the Austrian empire had failed. The indispensable foundation of a state was "an [indigenous] race capable of producing a civilization." Merely forcing everyone, the superior and the inferior, to speak German would have lowered "the racial quality of the German nation."[18]

Then Hitler went a step farther. Monarchs never qualified as state-builders. Their service attracted only "toadies and sycophants," men who denied their convictions to preserve their jobs, unwilling to take risks, let alone die for their masters. National-socialism, he went on, would not restore a government dominated by servility. Its aim was to "build a new state." While Hitler was dictating *Mein Kampf* to Rudolf Hess in prison, the populist *Deutsche Presse* put the case against restoration even more uncompromisingly: "The times of 1914 are irretrievably gone. Whoever seeks to restore them is unfit for leadership."[19]

Still, Nazi dickering with monarchist and dynastic partisans continued at least until 1934. German reactionaries continued to support Hitler because some of his more conciliatory formulae seemed to echo the 1920 program of the Bavarian Peoples Party which also insisted that "not the form [of the state] is decisive, but practical policies."[20] Secondly, some of Hitler's associates professed a continuing devotion to restoration. These included Ernst Röhm, in the early 1920s, a partisan of the Bavarian royal house, and Max Erwin von Scheubner-Richter, like Rosenberg a Baltic German, who seems to have had contacts to Prince Rupprecht, as well as Duchess Adelheid of Saxe-Coburg-Gotha, one of the earliest financial backers of Munich's populist militants. In the months before the Putsch, Scheubner-Richter sought to convince the Bavarian pretender that "in his heart Hitler was a monarchist" who would support restoration in return for Wittelsbach backing of his movement.[21] But the most important attraction the populist camp offered disgruntled and disoriented monarchists was General Erich Ludendorff, whose eccentricities rendered equivocation of the restoration issue respectable. Ludendorff, "a monarchist in [his] innermost convictions," had in 1918 been dismissed by the Kaiser in a particularly contemptuous manner.[22] His allegiance to Germany's monarchical past was, therefore, tempered by a bitter dislike of Wilhelm II, and prompted him to join conservatives who rated strength in government above legitimacy.[23]

Once Hitler emerged from prison, the wooing of princes and their supporters continued. His most persistent efforts were directed at members of the former imperial family. In 1926 he visited Crownprince Wilhelm at Cecilienhof Castle in Potsdam and reputedly assured him "that the restoration of the monarchy would constitute the apex of his career." His host appears to have treated him rather condescendingly, emphasizing that he was determined to remain above political battles. But the record reveals the Kaiser's eldest to have been well disposed toward the Nazi movement.[24] This also applied to his brother Oskar, who considered Hitler's followers "valuable," but their program in need of revision. Only August Wilhelm, the "intellectual" of the clan, some of whose "best friends were Jews," including Max Reinhardt, was fascinated by Nazi ideas of national community. In 1928 he drifted from the *Stahlhelm* into the SA, joining the party in 1930, indifferent to his father's objections. The Nazis found his adherence extremely useful, even though Goebbels considered him "somewhat senile" and wondered whether he could be "salvaged."

"Auwi," as he was generally known, was not aware of these reservations, and bravely mingled with the plain folks of the storm troops, while representing the party in the salons of Berlin society, often accompanied by another movement stalwart with access to high society, Hermann Göring.[25]

Goebbels was never happy about these flirtations with the Hohenzollern. In his opinion it was not fitting for representatives of a workers' party, and Hitler probably, if less consistently, shared these aversions. The Führer reserved his most emphatic strictures of monarchy for a "Second Book," written in 1928, but not published at the time. He reiterated the view that the Bismarckian empire, resting on dynastic loyalties, could not fully unite the German nation. According to Hitler, the First World War was lost because it was pursued for frivolous, petty aims such as the replacement in places like Lithuania and Finland of a "tsarist commissar" by a German princeling. Had it been up to the Führer, conquered eastern territories would have been divided into land grants for German soldiers. This would have transformed the war from a dynastic into a truly patriotic enterprise.[26]

It was just as well that these thought were left unpublished at the time. (For economic, not tactical reasons. *Mein Kampf* was selling badly, and the market was not crying for another volume from Hitler's pen.) The Nazi party attempted to appeal to all Germans (except Jews), but working class constituencies remained impervious to its propaganda, the majority remained faithful to the Social-Democrats and Communists. Courtship of blue-collar workers, particularly in large urban centers, culminating in the short-lived alliance with the Communists during the Berlin transport workers' strike of 1932, shocked and alienated both middle class and agrarian supporters. The November 1932 elections saw ten per cent of these former Nazi voters return to the conservative fold.[27]

While many of Hitler's hard-core followers responded to this setback by calling for an open endorsement of revolution, the leader kept his own counsel, and refused to be stampeded into a leftward course. After all, the Crownprince had publicly supported his presidential race against Hindenburg, and such Wilhelmine faithful as retired Admiral Magnus von Levetzow had openly sworn fealty to him. No wonder that Hitler suddenly professed to have rediscovered the virtues of monarchy, those of August Wilhelm's son Alexander in particular, especially when in the company of friends on whose indiscretion he could count. Before long many good conservatives were once again convinced that Hitler in power meant the return of the monarchy.[28]

Then came January 30, 1933, when plain citizen Adolf Hitler, "whose name was his only title," became head of the German government.[29] He now held power which he did not intend to share with anyone, but he also had to pose as the respectful junior partner of the venerable Hindenburg, whose emotional attachment to the monarchy had not diminished. As long as the "old gentleman" remained titular head of state, the game of equivocation continued.

Hitler felt his way carefully. His attacks on Marxism and Communism became strident and unceasing. Anti-Semitism, especially after the unfavorable publicity following the boycott of Jewish stores, became muted, and was camouflaged by a new emphasis on traditional values. In his first radio address on February 1, the Nazi leader paid tribute to past achievements of German history and promised "to respect everything contributed by past generations to ... creation of our state." While he told the *Daily Mail* six days later that a restoration of the Hohenzollern was out of the question, that statement was not included in a version of the interview published in Germany. The opening of the newly-elected Reichstag in Potsdam on March 21 was accompanied by ceremonies calculated to warm the hearts of monarchists. The royal box in the garrison church featured the Kaiser's chair left empty, surrounded by members of the family. Hitler and Hindenburg enacted their famous ritual handshake in the crypt holding the sarcophagus of Frederick the Great. As one officer of the old army, about to become a general in the new, Moritz Faber du Faur, remembered the event: "All uniforms converged: Hindenburg's spike helmet, the Hussar raiments of the Crownprince and of old [Fieldmarshall August von] Mackensen, brown and black [sic] shirts and the girls in uniform." Two days later when submitting his Enabling Act for the necessary approval by a two-thirds majority in the Reichstag, Hitler was careful to rule out restoration only "for the moment." In a subsequent meeting with the Kaiser's second son, Prince Louis Ferdinand, the chancellor still addressed him formally and respectfully as "royal highness."[30]

Once he had obtained dictatorial powers, Hitler, though still surrounded by monarchists in his cabinet, began to pursue a more open anti-monarchist policy. Up to a point he did so in harmony with Hindenburg, who in February 1933, vetoed restoration plans in

Munich, indicating that restorations at the state level threatened to "endanger the unity of the Reich."[31]

In retrospect it appears, but only in retrospect, that the mask dropped on April 20, when Germans were called to celebrate a new quasi-monarchical holiday, the Führer's birthday. Now the imperial house had to abandon its past reserve and do more than await re-investiture by national summons. Accordingly, the only member of the ex-Kaiser's entourage who had held a major position at court before 1918, Fritz von Berg-Markienen, last chief of Wilhelm's civil cabinet, asked Hitler point blank what plans he had to restore his master. The chancellor responded with the air of a courteous, frank and plain-spoken man. Once more he claimed the restoration of a *German* monarchy to be the culmination of his work. He agreed that the Hohenzollern were the only legitimate pretenders. But, he continued, the time was not ripe. Restoration at present would interrupt national-socialist reconstruction and produce difficulties abroad. He neither confirmed, nor contested, Berg's anxious response that any such postponement was tantamount to liquidating monarchist expectations. Berg had seen through Hitler's amiable procrastination, but what could he do about it?[32]

Still, Wilhelm's bureaucracy-in-exile did not give up the quest. Next, Court Chamberlain Wilhelm von Dommes requested and received permission to see the Führer. He reminded Hitler that the princes had worked hard to bring about the national revival over which he presided. Dommes insisted that the national government "would need the crown" to assure the survival of its achievements. He also used the opportunity to protest against recent anti-monarchist statements ascribed to various party officials. Hitler blamed these either on inaccurate reporting in the press, or on strategies designed to convert passionately anti-monarchist leftists to his cause. He professed sympathy with Dommes' concerns and once again agreed that Germany's long-range greatness could only be assured by dynastic government. Meanwhile, however, his work was not done. Bloody battles still impended. Would a monarch, such as the Crownprince [sic], be hard enough to fight them? Then he suddenly launched into a tirade asserting that the Kaiser had been a friend of the Jews. The outburst seems to have ended as suddenly as it began, but it seems to have left Dommes both helpless and speechless, doubtless the effect Hitler had sought to produce. In an instant the Führer became cordial again, and by way of a farewell urged the befuddled courtier to see him, or, in his absence, Rudolf Hess, if he had anything to discuss.[33]

When the Harvard historian, William L. Langer, visited the Kaiser in August 1933, he came away with the impression "that the imperial court rather expected ... Hitler's victory might be the prelude to an Hohenzollern restoration."   This view either reflected Wilhelm's undiminished capacity for self-delusion, or documented a brave attempt to keep a stiff upper lip in the face of constant adversity. Certainly the flood of tendentious books and pamphlets, spawned by the national revolution, left no doubt that a monarchical state was not part of the Führer's or his movement's vision of the future.[34]

By the beginning of 1934, however, two dissonant elements in the political atmosphere still created monarchist clouds on the firmament of Nazi power.   One was Hindenburg's monarchist allegiance; the other, and more immediate, challenge was posed by the ex-Kaiser's seventy-fifth birthday on January 27, 1934, the latter event stirring a brief flurry of monarchist activity and a corresponding nervousness in government circles.

At the exiled court the day produced a heavier than usual influx of family, princely bluebloods, and monarchist habitués from the homeland. It included the devoted Mackensen, who brought the ex-emperor a silver cup and "greetings from the old army," coupled with the wish that Wilhelm might soon return to his throne. For the first time since 1918 the German minister of war and his naval counterpart sent letters of congratulation on behalf of their services. The honoree enjoyed the fuss, and during the days that followed had extensive talks with his second and favorite grandson, Louis Ferdinand, informing him that his older brother's recent marriage to a commoner placed him in direct line of succession to the throne.[35]

In Germany, however, the day was marked by a sudden unforeseen crackdown on monarchist activities. Earlier in the month, a group of legitimists, headed by former Prussian minister of war, Karl von Einem, had founded a "German Kaiser movement." This organization was certainly a reflection of monarchist restlessness throughout the country. The German minister of the interior therefore issued a memorandum on January 13, apparently in response to numerous inquiries from state and provincial officials, outlining government views. "There is no place in the Third Reich for such [monarchist] propaganda," he observed. He approved of the "cultivation of historical memories" so long as they did not serve as a front for restoration efforts. This was also to apply to observances of Wilhelm's birthday.

There would be no public ceremonies, only private festivities that must eschew propagandistic overtones. When the United Patriotic Societies (*Vereinigte Vaterländische Verbände*), a monarchist front founded in 1919, nevertheless commemorated the feastday with a gala in the Marble Hall of Berlin's Zoological Gardens, a horde of storm troopers invaded the events, assaulted celebrants of both sexes, and administered bloody beatings to some old officers. The Association of German Officers dispatched a protest to Hindenburg, adding that the conduct of the assailants "reminded those present of the activities of unbridled communist rowdies of unhappy memory." Hindenburg demanded explanations from Hitler. Hitler promised an inquiry which predictably failed to identify the culprits.[36] By now the old, dying president had formulated his own justification for Hitler's delaying tactics. He had come to agree with the chancellor that any monarchy would remain a mere shadow until German power had been restored. The president did, therefore, nothing to keep the party in check.

On the first anniversary of his coming to power, Hitler made a speech that ruled out decisions on any long-range constitutional issue. Germany could only be led by a man endowed with a national mandate. As current incumbent of that mandate he would enact the reforms that promised to transform Germany forever. Four days later a government decree dissolved all monarchist organizations.

Continuing complaints from Doorn now found Hitler in a less gracious mood. His last interview with Dommes gave the Hohenzollern representative short shrift. The princes had fled the revolution, while he, Hitler, had fought it. Now he was uniting Germany, and the state dynasties would never be allowed to return. When Dommes objected that the ex-Kaiser could not desert the other princes, Hitler replied: "Why not? The Hohenzollern did it at other times." This time he did not invite the imperial emissary to return. There was nothing left to discuss.[37]

Now it became just a matter of waiting for Hindenburg to draw his last breath. On June 30, 1934, Hitler, the executioner of Röhm, his consorts and a host of other victims, became Germany's "fountainhead of justice," a function not claimed by anyone since the Middle Ages. When he gave the Reichstag his version of these bloody events, Göring, as the presiding officer of that rubber-stamp assembly, assured him: "All of us always approve what our Führer does."[38]

Two days before the sinking president expired, Hitler visited him on his estate at Neudeck. Only intermittently conscious, Hindenburg seemed preoccupied with his failure in 1918 to protect and preserve the monarchy. Attendants have claimed that in his last delirium he repeatedly begged his Kaiser's forgiveness. Hitler told the attending physician that he was not sure the old man recognized him: "For in the end he only addressed me as 'Majesty.'" The next day the Reichstag adopted a government bill that abolished the presidency after Hindenburg's death and appointed Hitler Führer and Chancellor. When that death finally came, on August 2, army and civil service were called upon to swear "by God, this holy oath" that they would give unconditional obedience to Adolf Hitler as head of state and nation. Some commented on the unseemly haste with which this crownless coronation proceeded. Rumors persisted that Hindenburg had exacted from Hitler a promise to restore the monarchy and left a "political testament" documenting that expectation. There is no conclusive evidence that he did.[39]

Hitler told Hermann Rauschning at the time that the German people would not recall the Kaiser unless he urged them to do so. "But I shall not do that," he added. On August 19, the German electorate, by a majority of 89.9 per cent of the vote, endowed the new head of state with a measure of authority no German prince had ever wielded.[40]

What other games Hitler continued to play, in a life dedicated as much to manipulating his supporters as to leading Germany, may be gathered from the memoirs of a military aide, who remembers that as late as 1937 Goebbels claimed to have only recently dissuaded Hitler from restoring the monarchy.[41] Today we can claim to know better. To Hitler the national state and monarchy may indeed have been irreconcilable. More importantly, he refused to play Mussolini's role of a dictator, wearing a legitimist fig-leaf in a state "only half Fascist," "with a royalist army."[42] His model was Stalin, the absolute ruler ready to exterminate enemies and rivals wherever they might appear.

NOTES

1. For an early estimate of the many imponderables involved in the Saxe-Coburg-Gotha settlement, see Prince Albert to Ernst II, March 16, 1857, in Hector Bolitho, ed., *The Prince Consort and his Brother* (London, 1973), 171. The events themselves are discussed fully by Elizabeth B. White, "The Saxe-Coburg Succession" (M.A. thesis, University of Virginia, 1977).

2. Bismarck to William II, September 17, 1888, *Lippe 2/1 Secreta* National Archives Microfilm T149, Reel 170, frames 485-89.

3. Robert Hessen, ed., *Berlin Alert: The Memoirs and Reports of Truman Smith* (Stanford, 1984), 50.

4. Falk Wiesemann, *Die Vorgeschichte der nationalsozialistischen Machtübernahme in Bayern 1932/33* (Beitrag zu einer historischen Strukturanalyse Bayerns im Industriezeitalter, v. 12) (Berlin, 1975),16-42; Kurt Sendtner, *Rupprecht von Wittelsbach, Kronprinz von Bayern* (Munich, 1954), 445-92.

5. Sources for the above include an undated Lucius *Aufzeichnung* from 1926; Lucius to Stresemann, November 2, 1926; and Alexander von Senarclens-Drancy to Lucius, October 31, 1927, all in *Lucius von Stoedten Privatakten*, National Archives Microfilm T291, Reel 11, Frames 99-108, 638 and 838-41; Sigurd von Ilsemann, *Der Kaiser in Holland: Aufzeichnungn des letzten Flügeladjutanten Kaiser Wilhelms II*, ed. by Harald von Königswald, 2 vols. (Munich, 1967-68), composed of excerpts that emphasize both commentaries on current events and the prospects of restoration, *passim*; Percy Ernst Schramm, "Notizen über einen Besuch in Doorn (1930)." in *Spiegel der Geschichte. Festgahe für Max Braubach* (Münster, 1964), 942-50; and Otto Ernst, *Zwölf Monarchen im Exil* (Vienna, 1932), 57-70. For more affectionate accounts, see Viktoria Luise, *Mein Leben* (Munich, 1965), 263-65, and Louis Ferdinand, *The Rebel Prince: Memoirs of Prince Louis Ferdinand* (Chicago, 1952), 228-35.

6. Paul Herre, *Kronprinz Wilhelm: Seine Rolle in der deutschen Politik* (Munich, 1954), 175-179, 185.

7. The German Foreign Office took the position that granting "a German citizen permission to enter Germany" was a domestic matter. The world-at-large seemed to agree. Cf., National Archives Microfilm T120; Adolf von Maltzan to German Embassy, Paris, November 10, 1923; Stresemann to same, November 12, 1923, Roll 3753, Frames L003864-66; Crownprince to Miss Sylvia Cushman, January 1, 1924, Prussian Secret State Archives (Berlin),

Brandenburg-Preussisches Hausarchiv, Folder 53/164; Herre, *Kronprinz*, 185-89.

8. Andreas Dorpalen, *Hindenburg and the Weimar Republic* (Princeton, 1964), 84, 92-93; Arnold Brecht, *Aus nächster Nähe. Lebenserinnerungen 1884-1927* (Stuttgart, 1966), 457; Otto Meissner, *Staatssekretär unter Ebert-Hindenburg-Hitler* (Hamburg, 1950), 147; Wolfgang Ruge, *Hindenburg: Porträt eines Militaristen* (Cologne, 1981), 215-16.

9. Rudolf von Holzhausen to Lucius, July 22, 1925, *LPA*, T291/11/106-08.

10. Volker Berghahn, *Der Stahlhelm: Bund der Frontsoldaten 1918-1935* (Beitr. zur Geschichte des Parlamentarismus und der politischen Parteien, v. 33) (Düsseldorf, 1966), 64-74, 120-124, 210-220.

11. John W. Wheeler-Bennett, *Wooden Titan: Hindenburg in Twenty Years of History* (New York, 1936), 352-55.

12. See Walter Hofer, ed., *Der Nationalsozialismus: Dokumente 1933-1945* (Frankfurt, 1957), 28-31.

13. E.g. Alfred Rosenberg, "The Folkish Idea of the State,": and Walter Darré, "Marriage Laws and the Principles of Breeding," both in Barbara Miller Lane and Leilah J. Rupp, eds., *Nazi Ideology before 1933: A Documentation* (Austin, 1978), 64, 69, 111; Elke Frohlich, ed., *Die Tagebücher von Joseph Goebbels* (Munich, 1987-), I: 44, 208,363, 420, 579, 1198-99.

14. Eberhard Jäckel & Axel Kuhn, eds., *Hitler-Sämtliche Aufzeichnungen 1905-1924* (Quellen und Darstellungen zur Zeitgeschichte, v. 21) (Stuttgart, 1980), 148, 175, 218, 467.

15. *Berlin Alert*, 61.

16. Jäckel & Kuhn, *Hitler*, 757, 988, 1017-18, 1027; *Der Hitler Prozess vor dem Volksgerichtshof München* (Munich, 1924), 85.

17. Adolf Hitler, *Mein Kampf*, 2 vols. (Munich, 1925-27), I: 11.

18. Ibid., I: 79; II: 429-33.

19. Ibid., I: 258-61; II: 554. For the quote from the *Deutsche Presse*, see NSDAP, Hauptarchiv, Reel 63, Frame 148.

20. Quoted by Wiesemann, *Vorgeschichte*, 16.

21. Sendtner, *Kronprinz Rupprecht*, 527-28; Charles B. Flood, *Hitler, the Path to Power* (Boston, 1989), 318; *Hitler Prozess*, 79-80.

22. "Niederschrift des Obersten von Haeften über die Entlassung Ludendorffs," reprinted in Brecht, *Aus nächster Nähe*, 492.

23. *Hitler Prozess*, 69, 291. See also Ludendorff's "Die völkische Bewegung," *Völkischer Beobachter*, November 1, 1923.

24. It is difficult to tell how much the imperial princes knew about the confused populist position in regard to the referendum on dynastic expropriation, held on June 20, 1926: Ulrich Schuren, *Der Volksentscheid zur*

Fürstenenteignung 1926 (Beitr. zur Geschichte des Parlamentarismus und der politiswchen Parteien, v. 64) (Düsseldorf, 1978), especially, 182-84; Frederick C. West, *A Crisis of the Weimar Republic: A Study of the German Referendum of June 20, 1926* (Memoirs of the American Philosophical Society, v. 164) (Philadelphia, 1985), 180 concludes correctly that "the [Nazi] party's role throughout the ... properties' controversy was an inconspicuous one." It is noteworthy that regions providing the least support for expropriation produced the largest majorities for the Hitler government in the elections of March 5, 1933 (cf. Eliot B. Wheaton, *The Nazi Revolution, 1933-1935* (Garden City, 1969), 270-71.

25. Victoria Luise, *Mein Leben*, 267-72; Herre, *Kronprinz*, 195-96; Willibald Gutsche & Joachim Petzold, "Das Verhältnis der Hohenzollern zum Faschismus," *Zeitschrift für Geschichtswissenschaft*, 29 (1981): 919-20; Fröhlich, ed., *Tagebücher von Joseph Goebbels*, I: 405-06, 473-78, 488-93, 502-10. On Wilhelm's reaction to Auwi's membership in the NSDAP, see Ilsemann, *Kaiser in Holland*, II: 142.

26. Fröhlich, ed., *Tagebücher von Joseph Goebbels, II*: 76; Gerhard L. Weinberg, ed., *Hitler's Zweites Buch: Ein Dokument aus dem Jahr 1928* (Quellen und Darstellungen zur Zeitgeschichte, v. 7) (Stuttgart, 1961), 105, 146, 169, 184.

27. Thomas Childers, "The Limits of National Socialist Mobilization: The Elections of November 6, 1932, and the Fragmentation of the Nazi Constituency," in Thomas Childers, ed., *The Formation of the Nazi Constituency 1919-1933* (London, 1986), 238-55.

28. Henry Ashby Turner, ed., *Hitler aus nächster Nähe. Aufzeichnungen eines Vertrauten 1929-1932* (Frankfurt, 1978), 86-98; Levetzow to Hitler, December 30, 1932 in Gerhard Granier, *Magnus von Levetzow* (Schriften des Bundesarchivs, v. 31) (Boppard, 1982), 334-35. For the text of the Crown Prince's declaration, and Hitler's response, Max Domarus, *Hitler Reden und Proklamationen, I: Triumph 1922-1938* (Würzburg, 1962), 103. On the ephemeral candidacy of Prince Alexander we have the recollections of Otto Dietrich, *Hitler*, trans. by Richard and Clara Winston (Chicago, 1955), 23 and *The Ribbentrop Memoirs*, introduction by Alan Bullock (London, 1954), 12. Anneliese von Ribbentrop professes to remember such an expression of preference as late as "the summer of 1933," a time from which Hermann Rauschning also recalls Hitler treating other Hohenzollern with pronounced courtesy. Cf. *Gespräche mit Hitler* (Vienna, 1973), 73.

29. The Hitler paraphrase from a 1932 speech, Domarus, *Hitler Reden*, 135.

30. Domarus, *Hitler Reden*, 191-96, 201, 229-32, and Norman H. Baynes, *The Speeches of Adolf Hitler, April 1922-August 1934*, 2 vols. (Oxford, 1942),

I: 272. The quotes from Faber du Faur and Louis Ferdinand in *Macht und Ohnmacht: Erinnerungen eines alten Offiziers* (Stuttgart, 1953), 46-47 and *Rebel Prince*, 240-41.

31. Five days before the Reichstag fire, War Minister von Blomberg visited Munich to make sure that the local Riechswehr command would nip a local restoration in the bud, and on March 9 Hitler replaced the Bavarian government of Heinrich Held with a state commissioner of his own choice. See Wiesemann, *Vorgeschichte*, 162-240; Wilhelm Hoegner, *Der schwierige Aussenseiter* (Munich, 1959), 79-80; Dorpalen, *Hindenburg*, 403; Sendtner, *Kronprinz Rupprecht*, 547-58. On cabinet discussions of the Munich episode, consult Heinz Minuth, ed., *Die Regierung Hitler 1933/34*, 2 vols. (Akten der Reichskanzlei) (Boppard, 1983), Nos. 34 and 60.

32. Memorandum "Stellungnahme Hitler's zur Monarchie," May 15, 1933, G. St. A., BPH, 53/167/2, published in Gutsche & Petzold, "Verhältnis der Hohenzollern zum Faschismus," 935-36.

33. "Besprechung mit Staatsekretär Lammers," September 26, 1933; and Memorandum of meeting with Hitler, October 24, 1933, ibid., loc. cit., 53/167/1 and 3, repr., ibid., 936-39.

34. William L. Langer, *In and Out of the Ivory Tower* (New York, 1977), 160-161. For contemporary comments symptomatic of Nazi attitudes towards the monarchy, see Walter Gehl, *Der nationalsozialistische Staat* (Breslau, 1933), 51-52; Hanns Johst, *Standpunkt und Fortschritt* (Schriften an die Nation, v. 53) (Oldenburg, 1933), 58-60; Otto Kollreuter, *Der Aufbau des deutschen Führerstaates* (Grundlagen, Aufau und Wirtschaftsordnung des deutschen Führerstaates, I, 2, 18) (Berlin, 1933), 16-17, 33-34, and Wilhelm Stuckart, *Nationalsozialismus und Staatsrecht* (Ibid., I, 2, 15) (Berlin, 1933), 29-32.

35. Ilsemann, *Kaiser in Holland*, II: 247-50; *Rebel Prince*, 252-53. Later that year Hitler reputedly promised Louis Ferdinand an internship in the Chancellory to prepare him for possible future duties. Herre, *Kronprinz*, 221.

36. NSDAP, HA, Reel 7a, 138: H.D. Hohn to Rudolph von Blomberg, January 21, 1934 on the new organization. Regarding the events of January 27, 1934 and their aftermath, see *Regierung Hitler*, Nos. 287, 299, 331.

37. Dorpalen, *Hindenburg*, 476; Dommes to Hitler, February 2, 1934, Dommes memorandum of conversation with Hitler, April 27, 1934, G. St. A., BPH, 53/167/4-6; Domarus, *Hitler Reden*, 353-63.

38. Domarus, *Hitler Reden*, 392-425. On Hitler as supreme lawgiver, see Carl Schmitt's commentary on the events of June 30, 1934, reprinted in Hofer, *Der Nationalsozialismus*, 105-06.

39. Domarus, *Hitler Reden*, 429-39; Ferdinand Sauerbruch, *Das war mein*

Leben (Bad Wörishofen, 1951), 519-20.

40. Rauschning, *Gespräche mit Hitler*, 162; Domarus, *Hitler Reden*, 444. See also the symptomatic comment by Matthes Ziegler, "Urgeschichte oder Frühgeschichte?" *Nationalsozialistische Monatshefte*, 54 (September, 1934), 77.

41. Nicholaus von Below, *Als Hitler's Adjutant 1937-1945* (Mainz, 1980), 55-57.

42. *Hitler's Secret Conversations, 1941-1944*, with an introduction by H. R. Trevor Roper (New York, 1953), 41.

A REASSESSMENT OF THE PRESUMED FIFTH COLUMN ROLE OF THE GERMAN NATIONAL MINORITIES OF EUROPE

VALDIS O. LUMANS

Early on September 20, 1938, from safe haven inside Germany, Konrad Henlein, the leader of the Sudeten German national minority of Czechoslovakia, ordered several units of Sudeten German agents, trained and equipped in Germany, to instigate inside Czechoslovakia at least ten incidents between the afternoon of the twentieth and the morning of the twenty-first.[1] The reaction of Czech authorities to these provocations was expected to intensify what was becoming known as the Sudeten Crisis, and would enable Adolf Hitler to escalate demands of the Prague government--or perhaps provide him a pretext for invasion. These Sudeten Germans were serving the Third Reich and its Führer as a "fifth column," willing to betray their own state of Czechoslovakia, and in the interests of a foreign power, to help in its destruction.

Incidents such as these would earn for the estimated 10,000,000 Volksdeutsche (ethnic Germans) living throughout Europe as citizens of non-German states, a general reputation for serving the Third Reich as "fifth columns."[2] But this generalization ignores the fact--which this paper emphasizes--that neither as individuals, nor collectively as minority groups, did all Volksdeutsche serve the Third Reich in this capacity.[3] All sooner or later were expected to serve the Reich, but the form of service varied from one minority group to another, from one individual to another.

The primary factor determining the Third Reich's policy towards the German minorities and thereby prescribing the nature of Volksdeutsche service to the Reich was Hitler's foreign policy. Although he proclaimed--and many believed--that the revision of the

Versailles settlement was his chief foreign policy goal, a return to prewar borders would not have satisfied him. His ultimate goal was to create a new German Reich, bringing together all Germans, Reich as well as Volksdeutsche, which would become the dominant force in a new, racially reconstructed Europe.[4] Essential to this scheme was the acquisition of Lebensraum, additional living space, where racially pure Germans and other Germanics could expand and thrive. In Hitler's view Lebensraum, located primarily in Eastern Europe and the Soviet Union, could be acquired only through aggressive diplomacy, expansion and war.[5]

Acquiring the Lebensraum thus became Hitler's ultimate foreign policy goal, and revisionism, along with other considerations such as the interests of the minorities, were secondary--to be pursued only when they coincided with and advanced the primary objective. Since securing the needed Lebensraum was a complicated matter and would take time, Hitler pursued his ultimate goal in stages, each with its own immediate objectives. As he proceeded on this course, moving from stage to stage, the host states of the German minorities assumed new significance in his schemes, and the services expected of their respective German minorities as groups, and of their Volksdeutsche as individuals, were modified accordingly, always in consideration of his latest diplomatic requirements.[6] Beginning in 1936 Hitler's quest progressively became more aggressive, inevitably leading to war.

In his drive for expansion Hitler expected all Germans, including Volksdeutsche, to contribute. He claimed Volksdeutsche loyalties belonged to the Reich and to himself, not to their own states. Many Volksdeutsche agreed, and stood ready to serve the Reich, but encouraged by his constant denunciation of the Versailles settlement, which for many Volksdeutsche was responsible for their minority status, in return for their allegiance and services they expected his support for their revisionist ambitions, essentially some sort of unification with the new Reich. They would, however, soon discover that his support was forthcoming only when their objectives coincided with his immediate goals. Having taken his revisionist rhetoric as a serious commitment, they expected an imminent unification of all Germans in the new Reich. Although this remained Hitler's steadfast, ultimate goal, his immediate actions and policies did not always pursue this goal. Indeed, they often seemed contradictory. The result was disbelief and disappointment. One of Hitler's most difficult tasks--or rather, the task of his subordinates--was to retain the loyalty and services of Volksdeutsche in the face of what appeared to many of them a betrayal.

The earliest service the Volksdeutsche provided the Reich was espionage work,[7] usually for either the party's *Auslandsorganisation* (AO), or the *Sicherheitsdienst* (SD), Himmler's security office. It was not until 1937, and especially in 1938, that the Reich began making demands on entire minority groups. The first Volksdeutsche to serve the Reich as a group were the estimated 200,000 Germans of the Italian South Tyrol,[8] who would indirectly help Hitler in the Austrian Anschluss of March, 1938. These former Habsburg subjects, whose land had been transferred to Italy as part of the post-war settlement, hoped and agitated, with encouragement and support from the Reich, for an eventual return to German rule. But their wishes and Hitler's plans clashed. By late 1937 Hitler had decided that friendship with Mussolini, an important cornerstone of his foreign policy, was an absolute prerequisite for a successful Anschluss. Since South Tyrolean unrest complicated his relationship with Mussolini, Hitler ordered them to cease their campaign for revision. What he expected of them was not collaboration aimed at reclaiming the South Tyrol, but rather cooperation, intended to please Mussolini and secure his approval for the annexation of Austria.[9]

Following the Anschluss the South Tyroleans, encouraged by this event, but to the great displeasure of Mussolini, resumed their agitation for revision. When efforts to quiet them failed, Hitler decided to eliminate them as a source of friction by resettling them.[10] The operation began in the fall of 1939, and by the time it was completed in December, 1942, more than 80,000 South Tyroleans had served the Reich in this matter.[11] They were the first Volksdeutsche to realize as a group that their loyalty to the Reich and the Führer did not guarantee their interests would be served. They also learned that there were many ways in which they might serve the Reich. Instead of using them as a "fifth column," Hitler ordered them to cooperate with Italian authorities. When that order became too difficult to follow, they served him best by leaving.

Following the Anschluss the Sudeten Germans of central and western Czechoslovakia were called on to serve the Reich, many functioning as the classic "fifth column." By then Konrad Henlein's movement, the *Sudetendeutsche Partei* (SdP), had emerged as the principal German minority organization. In May, 1935 it had legitimized its position with nationwide electoral success, winning the largest vote of any single party in Czechoslovakia.[12] Henlein and the SdP, with Reich encouragement, pursued revisionist goals, at first for greater autonomy, but eventually for the transfer of the predominantly German areas of Czechoslovakia to the Reich. The Anschluss raised their hopes, as the Sudeten Germans realized that annexation might also be in store for them.[13]

Unlike the revisionist goals of the South Tyroleans, those of the Sudetenlanders coincided rather than conflicted with Hitler's foreign policy plans, which targeted Czechoslovakia for total destruction. On March 28, shortly after the Anschluss, Hitler assured Henlein that he would deal with Czechoslovakia in the near future and instructed him to apply pressure to the Prague government by loudly publicizing Sudeten German grievances and demanding justice.[14] The Sudeten Germans were to make demands until the Czechs refused any more concessions, and their apparent intransigence would justify Reich intervention. On the following day channels for Henlein's collaboration were established in the way of permanent liaisons between the minority and Reich authorities.[15] Through them the Reich instructed Henlein and directed the minority.[16]

The crisis peaked on September 12, as Hitler denounced Czech treatment of the Sudeten Germans at the party rally at Nuremberg. Two days later Henlein fled to Germany and from there began transmitting orders to his agents inside Czechoslovakia, who succeeded in intensifying the crisis.[17] Only the intervention of Hitler's friend, Mussolini, prevented war from breaking out. Instead, the infamous Munich conference convened, which resulted in the transfer of the Sudetenland to the Reich.

Although all Sudeten Germans did not participate in these events, many did, including their officially recognized leadership. As a result a large share of the responsibility for the first partition of Czechoslovakia can justifiably be attributed to the Sudeten German minority. Following the transfer of the Sudetenland the Germans living in what remained of the state contributed to its final demise. Berlin ordered further provocations, which resulted in more charges against the Prague government, followed by Reich military intervention in March 1939.[18] The destruction of Czechoslovakia, to which many of its Volksdeutsche had contributed, was complete. In the process they achieved their revisionist objective of returning to German rule, but only because their goal happened to coincide with Hitler's goal of destroying Czechoslovakia.

Although the Sudeten Germans as a group contributed to the destruction of Czechoslovakia, the charge of collaboration cannot be leveled against all of Czechoslovakia's Volksdeutsche. The Carpathian Germans of Slovakia did not play the role of a "fifth column" either in Czechoslovakia or in the successor state of Slovakia.[19] These residents of the formerly Hungarian half of the Habsburg Empire organized the *Karpathendeutsche Partei* in 1929, which in 1933 affiliated with Henlein's movement. Under the leadership of Franz Karmasin they hoped to benefit from their association with the larger and more influential Sudeten group.[20] But in 1938 Karmasin and his constituents found themselves ignored. They mistakenly had presumed that Hitler's concern for the Sudeten Germans extended to all Germans of Czechoslovakia. It did not. Their situation was far more complex than that of the Sudeten Germans. Whereas the latter had to overcome only Czech resistance as an obstacle to their revisionist objectives, the Carpathian Germans, who also hoped to come under German rule, not only encountered the resistance of the central government in Prague, but also had to deal with Slovak national aspirations as well as the ambitions of the Hungarians, who intended to reacquire Slovakia. Although the dismemberment of Czechoslovakia released them from Prague's rule, the Reich's subsequent policy towards Slovakia and Hungary conflicted with their aspirations. This became clear when after the October 6 declaration of Slovakia's autonomy Reich officials told Karmasin that at least for the time being Slovakia's Germans would not come under direct German rule.[21]

What remained of their hopes was shortly dashed when in March 1939 Hitler consented to Slovak independence, and Slovakia became the Reich's first client state in Eastern Europe.[22] Although the Carpathian Germans received considerable autonomy within the new state, they were disappointed.[23] Karmasin nevertheless accepted the Führer's assignment for his minority, in order to help maintain good relations with Slovakia and to keep it a client state with as little effort as possible during the coming war years. These Volksdeutsche were expected to practice cooperation rather than subversion. They would serve the Reich, but not as a "fifth column."

After the destruction of Czechoslovakia Hitler turned towards the Memelland, which Lithuania had seized from Germany after the war. The majority of its estimated 60,000 German residents wanted nothing less than its return to the Reich.[24] Several local groups, including two Nazi factions, were prepared to serve the Reich to achieve this objective. It was presumed that sooner or later Hitler would take back the Memelland, but while he was preoccupied with the Anschluss and then Czechoslovakia, he preferred not having to deal prematurely with Lithuania. The transfer of the Sudetenland to Germany raised the level of activism in the Memelland and hopes for an imminent return to the Reich.[25] German activists began acting as a "fifth column" without being asked, much to the consternation of Reich authorities.[26]

Following elections in December 1938, when over ninety percent of the Memelland electorate voted for Nazi candidates, a clear mandate for a return to the Reich, Hitler summoned minority leader Ernst Neumann to Berlin for a conference on January 2. Hitler informed him that he would shortly act in regards to the Memelland and ordered Neumann to establish contacts with the Reich and await further instructions.[27] The minority, including its recognized leadership, stood at the Reich's disposal, prepared to do its bidding. But before the Memelland Germans had the opportunity to act as a "fifth column," Reich diplomats arranged for a transfer of the territory. The Lithuanians were relieved that Hitler seemed satisfied with acquiring the Memelland and had no apparent intention of exploiting local unrest as a pretext for destroying their state. Indeed the fate of most of Lithuania's Volksdeutsche living in the interior was not raised as an issue. The return of the Memelland was clearly an instance of limited border revision, prompted by the clamoring of unruly Volksdeutsche. It was also a case of a "fifth column" mobilizing without being summoned to do so.

By early 1939 another German minority, the estimated 1,200,000 Germans of Poland, were being prepared to participate in their country's destruction, many of them directly as "fifth column" agents, collaborating closely with Reich authorities.[28] Since most of the collaborationists participated on an individual basis, recruited for their specific missions by different Reich agencies and interests, it is difficult to attribute general responsibility to the minority as a whole, certainly not to the degree one can in the case of the Sudeten Germans, or even the Memellanders. Another reason why one cannot without reservation describe the collective role of the German minority in Poland as a "fifth column" was the lack of political and organizational unity within the group. Unlike the Sudeten Germans, most of whom belonged to Henlein's movement and had voted for the SdP, the Volksdeutsche of Poland never managed to unite to the same degree.

The consequences of disunity, especially the inability to control the minority according to the Reich's foreign policy needs, became apparent during the Sudeten crisis. Various activists, in particular those associated with the *Jungdeutsche Partei* (JDP), the group closest to Henlein's in ideology, clamored for a resolution in Poland similar to that in Czechoslovakia.[29] From the Reich side numerous organizations were recruiting Volksdeutsche as their agents in anticipation of using their services inside Poland. For instance, military intelligence was seeking informers for its spy network, and the SD was reconfirming its contacts as well as secretly organizing a Selbstschutz militia. The Reich Foreign Ministry became quite alarmed as it learned of these uncoordinated, clandestine activities, fearing that they could provoke serious Polish reaction.[30]

By February 1939 Reich officials were already drawing parallels between the situation in Poland and that in Czechoslovakia.[31] A major difference, however, unknown to but the very highest, was the fact that neither the minority issues nor any sort of negotiations interested Hitler. With Czechoslovakia he had missed an opportunity to destroy it by war, and this time, with Poland, he would not let the opportunity escape him. Nor would Hitler call on the minority leadership as he had in Czechoslovakia to participate significantly in these events. He wanted no Polish Henlein. Hitler would resolve the Polish matter not at the conference table but rather on the battlefield. The expected role of Poland's Volksdeutsche as individuals would be to prepare for the various assignments charged to them by their Reich patrons, but as a group, to maintain calm and discipline and abstain from forcing the issue prematurely through unexpected incidents.

Just such an incident occurred only a week before the attack on Poland, when the leader of the JDP, Rudolf Wiesner, offered to mediate the disputes between Poland and Germany, the very last thing Hitler wanted. Certain Reich authorities, by then aware of Hitler's intentions not to negotiate and to resolve the issue by force, removed Wiesner before the Poles learned of his offer. The fewer opportunities the Poles had to negotiate, the better for Hitler. Although Wiesner did not get his opportunity to play Henlein, beginning on September 1, 1939 many of his fellow Volksdeutsche actively assisted the Reich and its forces in the destruction of Poland, as agents of the Reich military, of the SD, and as members of various local armed units. As such they helped the Reich destroy Poland, an accomplishment coinciding with their own revisionist ambitions of returning to German rule.

It appears that Hitler's foreign policy and his corresponding policy towards those German minorities that came into prominence as he pursued his prewar course of aggression, with the two exceptions of the minorities in the South Tyrol and Slovakia, coincided with the revisionist goals of each minority. But with the outbreak of war more often than not Hitler's needs conflicted with minority aspirations. Rather than being called upon as the Reich's accomplices to help in the subversion and destruction of their states, most Volksdeutsche were expected to cease resistance towards their states, give up their revisionist hopes for some sort of unification with the Reich, and serve the Reich by cooperating with their regimes. If cooperation was difficult, or if their continued presence left potential for trouble, they served the Reich best through their removal. This became apparent on October 6, 1939, when Hitler announced plans to remove Volksdeutsche from Eastern Europe by resettling them in the Reich and its recently conquered territories.[32]

Hitler's announcement shocked Volksdeutsche abroad and their supporters inside the Reich. He was apparently reversing his policy towards the minorities. Rather than supporting their revisionist claims, Hitler now seemed to be retreating and abandoning these claims. The fate of the South Tyroleans would become the fate of Volksdeutsche elsewhere. Beginning with the Baltic Germans of Estonia and Latvia, Volksdeutsche were summoned to the Reich in order to remove them as potential points of friction in Hitler's relations with Stalin, the leader of the Soviet Union.

Hitler had decided to resettle the Volksdeutsche of Latvia and Estonia in late September, after Stalin informed him that he was about to assert his influence in these states, influence Hitler had conceded in a secret clause of the August 23, 1939, Nazi-Soviet Friendship and Non-Aggression Treaty.[33] This clause divided much of Eastern Europe into German and Soviet spheres of interest, with Estonia and Latvia allocated to the Soviet sphere. Lithuania, originally in the German sphere, would shortly be transferred to the Soviet zone in exchange for parts of Poland. Hitler knew that once Stalin asserted his influence, which meant seizing the Baltic States, the local Volksdeutsche, faced with sovietization, would seek his help. He would then face the dilemma of having to choose between defending them and thereby alienating his ally, Stalin, or allowing Stalin to do as he pleased in these states, thereby abandoning these Germans, whom he, as the Führer of Germans everywhere, was committed to protect. Rather than facing this choice, Hitler decided to remove the Baltic Germans.

The Baltic Germans, many of whom had looked forward to an eventual unification with the Reich, had not expected this development. As with other minorities, the prewar annexations heightened their expectations, and with the German invasion of Poland, they even believed military moves against the Baltic states a possibility. Activists, especially the youth, were prepared to serve the cause if called upon, but the summons did not come.[34] Rather than calling on the Baltic Germans to help establish German rule in their states, Hitler ordered them to give up such notions and resettle. The majority heeded his call and departed in the fall of 1939, but many remained.[35] In the summer of 1940, when the Soviets invaded the Baltic States and forced them to seek admittance into the Soviet Union, those that had disobeyed the Führer in 1939 pleaded for one more change to leave.

Hitler, now facing the situation he had wished to avoid in 1939, of having to choose between protecting the Baltic Germans and maintaining the Stalin alliance, consented to a second resettlement from Estonia and Latvia as well as a resettlement of Volksdeutsche from Lithuania, whose relocation had not seemed urgent in 1939.[36] Resettlement also was the service the Volksdeutsche of eastern Poland and northern Rumania performed for the Reich. In the winter of 1939-1940 Hitler resettled Volksdeutsche from those parts of eastern Poland the Soviets had seized in the September campaign.[37] In the fall of 1940 he removed others from northern Rumania, from Bukovina and Bessarabia, territories also claimed by Stalin.[38]

When Hitler launched his campaigns in the West in 1940, the German minority in North Schleswig, the southernmost borderland of Denmark, served the Reich but not as a "fifth column." Its services were determined by Denmark's role in Hitler's plans for the future. The majority of these estimated 40,000 Volksdeutsche, who became a minority as the result of a 1920 plebiscite transferring the region from Germany to Denmark, wanted to return to the Reich.[39] In hopes of fulfilling this ambition, the minority leadership drew closer to the new Reich and by 1938 it had accepted National Socialism as its creed. In return it expected an imminent return to the Reich. After all, North Schleswig, which had belonged to the Reich, had a better claim to annexation than the Sudetenland, which had not. Like the Memelland, also annexed by the Reich, it belonged to a small state which was in no position to resist Hitler's demands. Although local activists were willing to help in the process, these Volksdeutsche were not destined to become pretexts for Reich aggression against Denmark.

What Hitler had in mind for Denmark was to enlist it as a partner in the creation of the new racial order in Europe. In his mind the Danes, as Scandinavians, would help create a "Nordic Community of Fate," bringing together the supposedly racially superior Germanic peoples as the nucleus of the new Europe. Hitler did not wish to alienate his future racial partners, and therefore the Germans of North Schleswig had to cease their revisionist demands.[40] Rather than create trouble, they were expected to cooperate with the Danes.[41]

Even with the Reich's invasion of Denmark on April 9, 1940, Hitler remained adamant that Denmark, although conquered, must be ruled as leniently and benevolently as possible. In accordance with this policy, on the day of the invasion Reich authorities instructed the minority to drop the border issue, even though it was within the Reich's power to seize North Schleswig. For the next two years the Reich sought Danish cooperation through relatively lenient occupation policies and worked diligently to keep the minority under control and to prevent it from unduly antagonizing the Danes. Reich authorities even frowned on the minority's ties to the indigenous Danish Nazi movement which, although ideologically close to National Socialism and enthusiastic about the Nordic idea, was unpopular with the majority of Danes.[42] Consequently there was no extensive, organized German "fifth column" in North Schleswig, neither at the time of the invasion, nor for the first two years of the occupation. By the time the Reich realized that its policy of trying to persuade the Danes to cooperate was futile and shifted to a stricter occupation regimen in late 1942, there was little need of a "fifth column." Subsequent Reich demands on the local Germans hardly differed from those imposed on the Danish population.

In the campaign against France, beginning in May 1940, one cannot properly speak of a German minority participating as a "fifth column." Although certain German sources claimed more than 1,500,000 Germans living in Alsace and Lorraine, the French government regarded the entire population of the two provinces as French. They had permitted no German political organizations on the basis of nationality in these provinces and had allowed no formal ties with the Reich.[43] Although several Reich agencies established some contacts in France, their services were limited to gathering intelligence. Little effort was made to organize or "nazify" these people.[44] Thus when the German forces invaded France, they received assistance from individuals, but there was no organized movement among the local Germans that justified a collective "fifth column" label. Indeed, as the splits in the French national fabric became more apparent with the German invasion, French defeat, and the subsequent occupation, the contributions of even individual Germans to the Reich's cause diminished in overall importance.

Observing German successes elsewhere, one by one, the states of Southeastern Europe, Hungary, Rumania, Bulgaria and Yugoslavia, acknowledged German superiority and accepted closer ties to the Reich. Hitler was determined to keep them, like Slovakia, in some degree of subordination with a minimum of effort and resources. He never abandoned, however, his ultimate goal of germanizing the area, which was destined to become part of his new order.[45] But that was for the more distant future, and while he pursued more immediate goals, in the West and shortly in the Soviet Union, he appreciated the support these states could provide him, economic, political and perhaps even military.

Just as Slovakia provided a model for what Hitler expected of the states of Southeastern Europe, its German minority became a prototype for the German minorities of Hungary, Rumania and Yugoslavia, some of the largest, most active and best organized in all of Europe.[46] These Volksdeutsche were expected to cooperate and remain loyal to their states, rather than serve the Reich as disloyal "fifth columns" working for their destruction.

The major exception to the Reich's policy in the Southeast came in the spring of 1941, when a coup overthrew the pro-Nazi government in Yugoslavia and replacedit with a pro-Western regime. Following the coup anti-German unrest and demonstrations occurred throughout Yugoslavia. Although minority leader Sepp Janko pledged loyalty to the new regime and ordered his constituents to abstain from any provocative actions, tensions mounted.[47] As the government called up reservists and increased military inductions, the minority leadership inquired in Berlin whether or not Volksdeutsche should comply with these orders. Hitler, who had already decided to invade Yugoslavia, ordered them to evade reporting for duty and to go into hiding or flee the country.[48] As the situation intensified, several Reich offices suggested orchestrating Volksdeutsche cries of help as pretexts for Reich military action.[49] Nothing came of this idea, since incidental appeals for help made little difference to Hitler, who by then was indifferent to world opinion and needed no justification.

Even though the Volksdeutsche of Yugoslavia did not serve as pretexts for the invasion, they nevertheless provided considerable assistance to the invading German forces by providing intelligence, serving as translators, guides, and even trying to join German military units.[50]   Although many assisted the Reich, by no means did all Volksdeutsche collaborate.   But since Volksdeutsche assistance was widespread and apparently had the support and consent of the minority leadership, one could argue that the label of "fifth column" aptly described this group's collective role in Yugoslavia's destruction.

The pro-Reich sympathies of these Volksdeutsche became even more evident with the German occupation and the subsequent dismemberment of Yugoslavia. Those not annexed to the Reich or transferred to either Hungary or Italy became residents of one of the two successor states, Serbia-Banat and Croatia, where they became a privileged elite. In return for this status they were expected to serve the Reich. Those living in Serbia-Banat under direct Reich military rule collaborated in every way.[51] Those residing in Croatia as subjects of the new Croatian state, enjoyed status comparable to that of the Volksdeutsche of Slovakia. In the interest of maintaining good Reich-Croatian relations they were expected to act as loyal subjects while providing whatever services the Reich required of them.[52] Although both groups, by virtue of their participation in Yugoslavia's partition and their wartime activities could be considered "fifth columns" in respect to Yugoslavia, because of their cooperation with the authorities of Serbia-Banat and Croatia--the question of their legitimacy aside--the Volksdeutsche living there remained loyal subjects.

One last group served the Reich in the destruction of their country, the German minority in the Soviet Union. Since Stalin had permitted absolutely no contacts between this minority and the Reich, it was not until the German invasion of the Soviet Union in June 1941 that these Volksdeutsche first made contact with the Reich. As the German armies advanced into Russia, they encountered only a few able-bodied Volksdeutsche men, whom the Soviets had overlooked in their efforts to deport all Soviet Germans to Central Asia. Not until the German armies reached the eastern Ukraine did they discover large enough groups of Volksdeutsche to enlist in their military effort. These, however, were more than willing to serve the Reich in any capacity, most importantly as interpreters and guides. Several "Selbstschutz" militia units were eventually organized. Their primary purpose was to defend German settlements from partisans, but eventually they participated alongside Reich forces, mostly on missions with SS security units performing their varied duties in the occupied territories.[53]   One cannot deny that these Volksdeutsche were serving the invading forces and contributing towards the destruction of their country, but in consideration of their experiences in the Soviet Union and the relatively small numbers of them serving the Reich, the label of "fifth column" for this minority seems hardly appropriate.

In conclusion, as one reviews the different German minorities and the services they performed for the Reich, it is clear that although they all served the Reich, not all served it as the classic "fifth column." Not all Volksdeutsche were active, subversive collaborationists, certainly not as individuals, nor collectively.   Only the Sudeten Germans of Czechoslovakia, the Volksdeutsche of Poland, and the Germans of Yugoslavia actively assisted the Reich significantly in the destruction of their own states.   But when evaluating Volksdeutsche contributions to the Reich one must not overlook other services, such as practicing restraint and subordinating their own interest to those of Hitler's foreign policy.   Important also were the contributions of those sacrificing their homes and homelands by resettling.   So too were the services of the Volksdeutsche living in the client states during the war years, performing services which for the most part were not directed against their states and therefore by definition not subversive.   All of these services, performed by Volksdeutsche individually as well as collectively, contributed to Hitler's purposes.   "Fifth column" activities, although important in some instances, were not the only services the Volksdeutsche of Europe performed for the Reich.   Indeed, in a final tally they were the exception, not the rule.

NOTES

1. "Adolf Hitler's Richtlinien für das Sudetendeutsche Freikorps vom 18 September 1938, in Václav Král, *Die Deutschen in der Tschechoslowakei, 1933-1947: Dokumentsammlung* (Prague, 1964), No. 226, 312-13; and Henlein's order to the Freikorps, 20 September 1938, Order No. 6, No. 229, 316-17.

2. Wilhelm Winkler, *Statistisches Handbuch der europäischen Nationalitäten* (Vienna, 1931) and *Deutschtum in aller Welt: Bevölkerungsstatistische Tabellen* (Vienna, 1938). According to Winkler, who relied on official statistics, some 10,000,000 Volksdeutsche lived throughout Europe: Czechoslovakia, 3,318,445; Poland, 1,190,000; Lithuania-Memelland, 100,000; Yugoslavia, 700,000; Hungary, 500,000; Rumania, 750,000; Latvia and Estonia, 80,000; Danzig, 400,000; Alsace-Lorraine, 1,500,000; Italy, more than 200,000; Belgium, 70,000; Soviet Union, 1,240,000; Denmark, 30-40,000.

3. Among the first to attribute general responsibility for subversive activities to the minorities were Henry Wolfe, *The German Octopus: Hitler Bids for World Power* (Garden City: 1938), 18; anonymous writer of *The Brown Network: The Activities of the Nazis in Foreign Countries* (New York, 1936) 11; and Franz Neumann, *Behemonth: The Structure and Practice of National Socialism, 1933-1944* (New York, 1966), 163.

4. For a thorough discussion of the development of Hitler's foreign policy refer to Gerhard L. Weinberg, *The Foreign Policy of Hitler's Germany: Diplomatic Revolution in Europe, 1933-36* (Chicago, 1970) and Hans-Adolf Jacobsen, *Nationalsozialistische Aussenpolitik, 1933-1938* (Berlin, 1968).

5. Adolf Hitler, *Mein Kampf,* trans. by Ralph Manheim (Boston, 1943), 140.

6. Foreign Minister Joachim von Ribbentrop complained about the problems the minorities caused Reich foreign policy and referred to the issues as the "gloomy problem." Annelies von Ribbentrop, ed., *Joachim von Ribbentrop: Zwischen London und Moskau* (Leoni, 1954), 88.

7. For example, refer to documents preceding the Austrian Anschluss, in National Archive Microfilm of Records of Private German Individuals, Series T-253, reel 49.

8. The best study of the Tyrol situation, including the role of the German minority, is Conrad F. Latour, *Südtirol und die Achse Berlin-Rom, 1938-1945* (Stuttgart, 1962); see also his article, "Germany, Italy and the South Tyrol, 1938-45," *The Historical Journal* 8 (1965): 95-111.

9. Behagel, VDA, to Ministerialdirektor Fischer, Munich, February 22, 1938, Microfilm series T-253, reel 59, frame 516257. Hereafter microfilm will be

cited as follows: Series/reel/frames. Refer also to relevant sections in Hans-Adolf Jacobsen, ed., *Hans Steinacher, Bundesleiter des VDA, 1933-1937: Erinnerungen und Dokumente*, Schriften des Bundesarchivs, No. 19 (Boppard am Rhein, 1970), especially "Zur Lage der deutschen Volksgruppen in Sudtirol."

10. Memo of meeting at Reich Foreign Ministry, May 19, 1938.Microfilmed Records of the German Foreign Ministry and Reich Chancellery, T-12-/2529/520256-259.

11. "Gesamtzahl der Umsiedler," January 1, 1943, National Archives Microfilmed Records of the Reichsführer SS and Chief of the German Police, T-175/194/2733184; RKFDV Report of 1942, April 30, 1943, Bundesarchiv (Hereafter, BA) R49 14.

12. Jacobsen, *Steinacher*, 585-90. See also Radomir Luza, *The Transfer of the Sudeten Germans: A Study of Czech-German Relations, 1933-1962* (New York, 1964), 74-79, and Smelser, 120.

13. Henlein, "Aufruf," March, 1938, in Král, 156.

14. Foreign Ministry memo, March 28, 1938, in Král, 162-63; "Bericht Konrad Henleins über seine Audienz beim Führer," Král, 163.

15. Memo of Reich Foreign Minister of meeting on March 29, 1938, in Král, 163-64.

16. Lorenz memo, June 3, 1938, in U. S. Department of State, *Documents on German Foreign Policy, 1918-1945: Series D, 1937-1945*, Vol. 2, Document Nos. 237, 384. (Hereafter cited as *DGFP*). See also Lorenz memo, June 21, 1938 in Král, No. 159, 234; Luig, VoMi, memo to Foreign Ministry, June 9, 1938, in Král, No. 154, 231; Behrends, VoMi, to Altenburg, Foreign Ministry, August 12, 1938, in Král, No. 172, 254-57.

17. Altenburg memo, September 14, 1938, *DGFP*, D, 2, No. 472, 757-58; "Adolf Hitler's Richtlinien für das Sudetendeutsche Freikorps vom 18 September 1938," in Král, No. 226, 312-13; and Henlein's order to the Freikorps, September 20, 1938, Order No. 6, in Král, No. 229, 316-17.

18. Schliep memo, Pol. Abt. V, November 9, 1938, *DGFP*, D, 4, No. 109, 138.

19. For a thorough discussion of the experiences of the Carpathian German minority of Slovakia, see Valdis O. Lumans, "The Ethnic German Minority of Slovakia and the Third Reich, 1938-45," *Central European History* 15 (September 1982): 266-296.

20. Jorg K. Hoensch, *Die Slowakei und Hitlers Ostpolitik: Hlinkas Slowakische Volkspartei zwischen Autonomie und Separation, 1938-1939*, No. 4 in Beitrage zur Geschichte Osteuropas (Köln, 1965), 172-73. See also Henlein in Asch to Karmasin in Bratislava, October 15, 1937, in Král, No. 76,

130-31.

21. Lorenz (not Werner), Foreign Ministry, memo re. conversation with Luig, VoMi, to Foreign Minister, October 15, 1938, T-120/402/1022/309240-248; also draft of October 31, 1938, T-120/402/1022/309262-263; and undated draft, T-120/402/1020/309227-229.

22.. Minutes of February 12, 1939 meeting, International Military Tribunal, *Trial of the Major War Criminals before the International Military Tribunal* (Nuremberg, 1949), hereafter IMT), vol. 3, 149. See also Hoensch, 129-31, 226, 285-88; and Yeshayahu Jelinek, *The Parish Republic: Hlinka's Slovak People's Party, 1939-1945* (New York, 1976).

23. Karmasin to Henlein, March 16, 1939, Král, No. 282, 384-85.

24. Akademie für Deutsches Recht, "Die Deutsche Volksgruppe in Litauen," March, 1939, T-120/1305/2334/476769-774; also "Übersicht über die Entrechtungen und Benachteiligungen der deutschen Volksgruppen in . . . Litauen," 1939, T-120/1305/2334/486810-813. For an excellent discussion of Memel and Lithuania, see Martin Broszat, "Die memeldeutschen Organisationen und der Nationalsozialismus, 1933-1939," *Vierteljahrshefte für Zeitgeschichte* 5 (July, 1957): 273-78; also Walter Hubatsch, "Das Memelland und das Problem der Minderheiten," in *Die Deutschen Ostgebiete zur Zeit der Weimarer Republik*, Studien zum Deutschtum im Osten, No. 3 (Cologne, 1966).

25. Woermann memo, July 23, 1938, *DGFP*, D, 5, No. 349, 462; Weizsacker telegram to Consul General, Memel, September 28, 1938, *DGFP*, D, 5, No. 353, 469.

26. Memo Grundherr, Pol. VI, "Report to the Foreign Minister on the Memel Question,' December 1, 1938, *DGFP*, D, 5, No. 369, 494-95; Memo Doertenbach, Pol. VI, December 5, 1938, *DGFP*, D, 5, No. 371, 494-95.

27. Grundherr to Zechlin, January 2, 1939, Report of meeting attended by Ribbentrop, Lorenz, Neumann, Grundherr, and Hewel, *DGFP*, D, 5, No. 381, 506-09. This meeting was preceded by a forty-minute audience for Neumann with Hitler and Ribbentrop.

28. Among the better studies of the German minority in Poland are Theodor Bierschenk, *Die Deutsche Volksgruppe in Polen* (Würzburg, 1954); Richard Breyer, *Das Deutsche Reich und Polen, 1932-1937: Aussenpolitik und Volksgruppenfragen* (Würzburg, 1955); Martin Broszat, *200 Jahre deutsche Polenpolitik* (Munich, 1963); Broszat, *Nationalsozialistische Polenpolitik, 1939-1945* (Stuttgart, 1961); and relevant sections in Jacobsen, *Nationalsozialistische Aussenpolitik*.

29. Refer to Eva Seeber, "Der Anteil der Minderheitsorganisation 'Selbstschutz' an der faschistischen Vernichtungsaktionen im Herbst und

Winter 1939 in Polen," *Jahrbuch für Geschichte der sozialistischen Länder Europas* 13 (1969): 3-34.

30. Schwager memo, Kultur A, October 27, 1938, T-120/1178/2168/470991-992; also Foreign Ministry memo to Kultur B, November 15, 1938, T-120/1178/2168/470995.

31. "Recht und Unrecht; die Lage des Deutschtums in Posen und Pomerrellen, Anfang, 1939 . . .," February, 1939, T-120/1305/2334/486704.

32. Hitler's speech before the Reichstag, October 6, 1939, Dietrich A. Loeber, ed., *Diktierte Option: Die Umsiedlung der Deutsch-Balten aus Estland und Lettland, 1939-41* (Neümunster, 1972), 79-81.

33. Schulenberg in Moscow to Foreign Ministry, Berlin, September 25, 1939, *DGFP*, D, 8, No. 131, 130.

34. Frohwein, Reich Minister in Tallin to Foreign Ministry, Berlin, October 7, 1938, T-120/1305/2334/486644-647.

35. "Die Aufgaben des RFSS als RKFDV," T-175/194/2733378-397; Chief of Sipo-SD, EWZ Nordost, Posen, January 1, 1940, report on Baltic Resettlement, Microfilmed Records of the Deutsches Ausland-Institut, T-81/290/2414094-100.

36. Twardowski memo for State Secretary, October 24, 1939, Loeber, No. 177, 260-61; Ribbentrop to Weizsäcker, undated, *DGFP*, D, 10, No. 22, 23. The majority of Lithuania's Volksdeutsche lived in a strip of land near the German border. When Hitler exchanged Lithuania for parts of Poland with Stalin, it was understood that the strip remained in Germany's sphere, and therefore Reich authorities did not consider the resettlement of these people. Only after the Soviets insisted on having this strip of land in the summer of 1940 did the Reich proceed with their resettlement.

37. *Das Schwarze Korps*, February 15, 1940, 4; RKFDV, "Gesamtzahl der Umsiedler," January 1, 1943, T-175/194/2733184; Chief of Sipo-SD, EWZ, November 15, 1944, T-81/264/2381873.

38. "Die Ostumsiedlung: Übersicht," Jahresbericht 1942, BA R49 14.

39. Richard Bahr, *Volk Jenseits der Grenzen: Geschichte und Problematik der deutschen Minderheiten* (Hamburg, 1933), 300; Joachim Joesten, *Rats in the Larder: The Story of Nazi Influence in Denmark* (New York, 1939), 147; Great Britain, Naval Intelligence Division, *Denmark, B. R. 509* (London, 1944), 519. See also Akademie für Deutsches Recht, "Die deutsche Volksgruppe in Dänemark," March, 1939, T-120/1305/2334/486785-789; "Übersicht über die Entrechtungen und Benachteiligungen der deutschen Volksgruppen in Dänemark," 1939, T-120/1305/2334/486801-802.

40. For an interesting discussion of this notion, see the section in Jacobsen, *Aussenpolitik*, "Nordische Schicksalgemeinschaft," 483-95; also memo of

conference between Hitler and Quisling, August 16, 1940, in *DGFP*, D, 10, No. 352, 491-95; also memo of conversation between Hitler and Danish Foreign Minister Scavenius, November 27, 1941, *DGFP*, D, 13, No. 510, 861-64. See also "Die Schicksalstunde des Nordens," Schulungsbrief der NSDAP-Nord Schleswig, No. 12, Reich Legation in Copenhagen to Foreign Ministry, Berlin, March 25, 1942, T-120/1378/2714/D531595-598.

41. Sven Tagil, *Deutschland und die deutsche Minderheit in Nordschleswig: Eine Studie zur deutschen Grenzpolitik 1933-1939* (Stockholm, 1970), 132.

42. Rimann, VoMi, to Foreign Ministry, Kultur A, January 23, 1941, T-120/2423/4696H/E226696-699; VoMi, "Deutsche Volksgruppe in Nordschleswig," October 26, 1942, National Archives, Transcripts of Case 8, USA v. Ulrich Greifelt, et al., US Tribunal at Nuremberg, Document NO-3526, Prosec. Doc. Book IIB.

43. Gottfried Fittbogen, *Was jeder Deutsche vom Grenz-und Ausland-deutschtum wissen muss*, 8th ed. (Munich and Berlin, 1937), 16-17, considered Alsace 95% German (1,152,800), and Lorraine 73% (655,211). Paul Gauss, *Das Buch vom deutschen Volkstum: Wesen-Lebensraum-Schicksal* (Leipzig, 1935), 7, estimated that 1,580,000 Germans lived in these two provinces.

44. VoMi, West-Referent Weekly Report, January, 1938, T-253/49/504266; and Report of January 8, 1938, T-253/49/504267-268.

45. Two outstanding studies of these minorities are Geza C. Paikert, *The Danube Swabians: German populations in Hungary, Rumania and Yugoslavia and Hitler's Impact on their Patterns* (The Hague, 1967), and the more recent Anthony Komjathy and Rebecca Stockwell, *German Minorities and the Third Reich: Ethnic Germans of East Central Europe between the Wars* (New York, 1980).

46. Winkler counts 758,226 Germans in Rumania in 1931, p. 11;and 66-67, 478, 630 in Hungary, pp. 66-67. Gauss estimated 700,000 Germans in Yugoslavia, p. 7.

47. Carstanjen, VDA, Graz, to Foreign Ministry, March 29, 1941, T-120/2415/4670H/E221510; Abwehrabteilung II to Chef Z Ausl., March 28, 1941, T-120/2415/4670HE221505-506.

48. OKW, Amt Ausland, Abwehr, to Foreign Ministry, March 28, 1941, T-120/2415/4670H/E221506.

49. Louis de Jong, *The German Fifth Column in the Second World War*, trans. C. M. Geyl (Chicago, 1956), 232 refers to a letter from Berger to Himmler, dated April 3, 1941.

50. Lorenz telegram to OKW, to be transmitted to RFSS, the Foreign Minister and to VoMi, April 16, 1941, PA AA, Inl. IIg, 251.

51. VoMi, "Deutsche Volksgruppe in Serbien und Banat," October 26, 1942,

NO-3526, Prosec. Doc. Book IIB; VoMi, "Volksgruppenorganisationen in Restserbien, NO-3526, Prosec. Doc. Book IIB.

52. "Bestandaufnahme der Deutsche Volksgruppe in Kroatien," May 26, 1942, T-81/307/2434886; "Deutsche Volksgruppe in Kroatien," October 26, 1942, NO-3526. Prosec. Doc. Book IIB. See also Ladislaus Hory and Martin Broszat, *Der Kroatische Ustascha-Staat, 1941-1945* (stuttgart, 1964), 70-71; and Johann Wuescht, *Jugoslawien und das Dritte Reich: eine dokumentierte Geschichte der deutsch-jugoslawischen Beziehungen von 1933 bis 1945* (Stuttgart, 1969), 267-68.

53. Ohlendorf Testimony, in U. S., Chief Counsel for War Crimes, *Trial of War Criminals before the Nuremberg Military Tribunals* (Washington, 1949-1953), (hereafter *TWC*) Vol. 4, Case 8, p. 854; *TWC*, 4, Case 8, 669; Behrends to Naumann, Chief of Einsatzgruppe B, July 6, 1942, NO-5095, Prosec. Exh. No. 741, *TWC*, 4, Case 8, 850; RFSS, Brandt Memo, April 20, 1942, NO-2278, Prosec. Doc. Book VA; Lorenz Testimony, pp. 2632-33; VoMi, Sonderkommando R, May 21, 1944, BDC SSO Siebert.

The John L. Snell Prize Seminar Paper

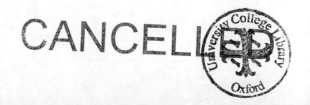

AUSTRIA'S DANUBIAN DIPLOMACY DURING THE CRIMEAN WAR

CAREY GOODMAN

> One glance over the map of Europe will show us on the western side of the Black Sea the outlets of the Danube, the only river which springs up in the very heart of Europe .... The Power which holds the outlets of the Danube necessarily holds the Danube also, the highway to Asia, and with it controls a great deal of the commerce of Switzerland, Germany, Hungary, Turkey, and above all, of Moldavia and Wallachia.[1]

Karl Marx, 1854

For over a century historians have excoriated the Crimean War diplomacy of Austrian Foreign Minister Karl Count von Buol-Schauenstein. In several studies over the last two decades, however, historian Paul Schroeder has masterfully reinterpreted the policies of the beleaguered Buol. Discarding the old assumptions that Buol was either rashly aggressive or continuously vacillating between east and west, Schroeder argues that Buol's inspiration was defensive and remained consistent from its formulation in early March 1854 through the peace of March 1856. Schroeder insists that Buol's policies, though admittedly leading to adverse consequences, were the best plays possible with the poor hand Austria had been dealt. Yet there remains one area of Buol's Crimean War diplomacy that Schroeder has not reinterpreted: the foreign minister's Danubian diplomacy.

While still at the negotiating table in Paris in March 1856, Buol wrote his emperor, Franz Joseph, that this waterway's "liberation" was the most striking justification of Austrian policies during the Crimean War.[2] This study examines the role of the Danube in Austria's Crimean War diplomacy, attempting to clarify its rank in the hierarchy of Austrian goals and achievements between 1853 and 1856. More precisely this paper focuses on the commercial significance of this river in Habsburg diplomacy, rather than its strategic importance.

In March 1854 several ministerial meetings were held in Vienna to formulate general guidelines for Austrian policy during the imminent hostilities. During these meetings, argues Schroeder, Buol outlined his view of Austria's position and proposed the responses that he would adopt until peace was restored. In particular, Austria needed to defend itself from the threat of Russia dominating the principalities, inspiring revolutions, and unilaterally carving up the Ottoman Empire.   As Schroeder notes, "There were also dangers from Prussia--in the short run, that she would tie Austria's hands and contravene her action in this crisis; in the long run, that she would undermine and destroy Austria's position in Germany."[3] The danger to Austria that Buol described most flamboyantly, however, was the Russian threat to the Danube. In concluding his much-studied memorandum of 21 March 1854, the foreign minister wrote that even if the western powers forced Russian to give up its extensive ambitions in the Near East, it was unlikely that the Danube would be removed from Russia's control. Buol stated that it was his innermost conviction that if the Danube, "this lifeline of Germany," remained in Russian possession, and if Austria did not successfully protest, then this power would continue to haunt both Austria and the rest of Germany like a nightmare.[4]

In light of these threats Buol proposed a three-part response in this same memorandum: adopt a stance of armed neutrality, create an alliance with the West if necessary, and win the support of Prussia and the German Confederation. For Austria to turn its back on Russia and to join hands with Britain and France against her was a radical step that Franz Joseph could not condone lightly. Schroeder states, "There is every reason to believe that Buol's fears were genuine. Nothing indicates that Buol deliberately concocted or exaggerated them in order to persuade the emperor to accept his proposal, as . . . Bismarck so often did with William I".[5]

Flowing from the Black Forest to the Black Sea, the Danube is Europe's second-longest river and one might readily accept that the Danube was the Habsburgs' economic lifeline to the rest of the world. This claim by Marx was frequently repeated by Austrian leaders of his day. Diplomatic historians have accepted this as well,[6] arguing that "a Danube under Russian control would mean the strangulation of the Habsburg monarchy; this was the opinion even of Buol's opponents at court, the great aristocrats who sighed for a new Holy Alliance."[7]

But reality belies a map's two-dimensional deception and nothing illuminates this better than a description of the river as it was in the mid-nineteenth century. From its headwaters in southwestern Germany through much of Austria, shallows, rapids, undergrowth, and strong winds made the river "a gigantic torrent" and hindered river traffic.[8] Besides these natural obstacles on the upper Danube, stone bridges blocked the transit of larger boats, and in fact, some still do.[9] Some of the most serious hindrances to navigation occurred where the Danube passed through the Carpathian Mountains. The river rushed over rocky cataracts as it dropped almost one hundred feet in as many miles, requiring most cargo and passengers to be unloaded, portages around the obstacles, then reloaded to continue the journey. Shortly before it joined the Pruth River, about one hundred miles from the sea, the Danube became accessible to maritime shipping. Ocean-going vessels, however, were continually confronted by the obstacles that the delta of the Danube presented. Here the river divided and three separate channels wandered into the Black Sea. They were notorious for silting up at their mouths. Naturally occurring mud and sand bars reduced the waterway to just a few feet in depth at the confluence of river and sea, impediments that had to be removed by man for commerce to thrive.[10] The disease-ridden marshes of the delta also encouraged travelers to avoid the Danube's mouths altogether by taking an overland route across the Dobrudjan plateau, a day's journey depicted by Hans Christian Andersen after he made this trek in 1841.[11] Altogether these impediments made the Danube "an economically uninteresting river" until early in the nineteenth century,[12] and clearly it was not naturally an efficient highway to Asia, or to anywhere else.

In the first half of the nineteenth century technology had already begun to change life on the river and overcome some of the adversities nature presented. In the summer of 1818 a steamship made its first trial run on the Danube.[13] In 1831 the Danube Steamship Company began freight and passenger service within Austrian borders, and began operating on the lower Danube after 1834. After 1846 the firm enjoyed a state-granted monopoly on Habsburg steamship routes, and by 1856 its one hundred ships carried one-half of all traffic between the Austrian capital and Braila, a port on the lower Danube.[14] This rapid development of commerce on the river might partially explain the conception that the Danube represented an economic lifeline for the Habsburg monarchy, but was it valid?

The development of steam power was a mixed blessing for Danubian trade because this technology also gave rise to new competitors. For example, raw silk from the Ottoman Empire would cross the Mediterranean on French steamships from Marseilles rather than being sent up the Danube as in the past.[15] Nevertheless, the premier historian of the economic causes of the Crimean War, Vernon John Puryear, conceded that "the Danube [was] the greatest commercial waterway of eastern Europe."[16] He qualifies this statement, however, by stating that Austria's "most important sea outlet was the Adriatic. The route of the Danube, the Black Sea, and the Straits, although a continuous waterway to world markets, was thus a secondary economic outlet" that remained relatively undeveloped before the Crimean War.[17] The Danube Steam Navigation Company's routes on the lower Danube were never profitable and this was part of the Austrian government's motivation in arranging the sale of the Danube Company's six maritime steamships to the Austrian Lloyd, which was based in Trieste, in 1845.[18] In 1841 26 percent of Austria's foreign trade was transported by water. Of that, only 10 percent of the overseas trade was carried by the Danube, that is, 2.5 percent of total foreign trade. Trieste, on the other hand, accounted for 62 percent of the seaborne trade.[19]

Physical and commercial realities leave little doubt that the Danube was no economic lifeline, but this assertion denies neither that the river had economic importance, nor that Russian control of the mouths presented problems for Austria. Russian influence on the Danube was realized in the Treaty of Adrianople (1829) that provided the court of St. Petersburg with complete territorial control of the two northern branches of the Danube's mouth, and joint control with the Ottomans of the southernmost branch.[20] The 1840 Convention of St. Petersburg, a treaty between Austria and Russia, theoretically guaranteed for the first time free navigation on the Danube to ships of all flags for ten years.[21] This convention applied to the Danube the principles for free navigation of international rivers as established by the Congress of Vienna.[22] Secondly, the Russian government pledged to clear the sand banks from the mouth of the Sulina channel. But Russia did not live up to its pledges, and the accumulating silt presented a frustrating obstacle to the heavier steamships, which by 1850 accounted for about one-half of the traffic through the Sulina mouth.[23]

Russian neglect irritated not only Austrian interests, but also those of Great Britain. British interests in the lower Danube were negligible at the beginning of the nineteenth century,[24] but they increased "phenomenally" in the following decades.[25]   In the 1840s a Prussian consul in Jassy wrote of the flood of British manufactures into the Principalities, Moldavia and Wallachia, that was squeezing out German products.[26] The year after the corn laws were ended in Britain (1846), British grain imports from the Principalities reached almost 5 percent of total grain imports.[27]   In fact, British interests in the lower Danube were so extensive that in 1853 almost twice as many British ships sailed into the mouth of the Sulina as Austrian ships, 205 to 111.[28] Because of these increasing interests, the tide of British and Austrian complaints rose as the navigable depth at Sulina fell,[29] and Puryear argues that just prior to the Crimean War similar British and Austrian commercial interests tended to throw the two into cooperation against Russia.[30]

Austrian dissatisfaction with Russian handling of the Sulina became clearly evident in 1850.   When faced with the need to prolong the 1840 convention, Austria and Russian renewed it for only one year rather than the ten-year term that it originally enjoyed, a result, some say, of Russia's refusal to accept Austrian demands for guarantees concerning the channel.[31]   And even this new agreement was apparently allowed to lapse when it expired in September 1851.[32]

These three factors--growing, yet still limited, value of the river as a transportation network; a regime at the mouth of the river that hindered this growth; and tangible grounds to believe that another great power would cooperate in rectifying the situation--all seemed to justify Austrian demands for change if an opportunity presented itself, as it did in the Crimean War.   In July 1853, 50,000 Russian troops began their occupation of the Principalities, and in October the armed conflict between the two actually began *on* the Danube when Ottoman batteries fired on Russian ships.[33]   Austrian diplomatic correspondence makes quite clear the strategic importance of the Danube during the first months of war.   The river represented a line that if crossed by the Russians would push Austria from its stance of friendly neutrality to one of armed neutrality seeking an understanding with the sea powers, Britain and France,[34] a point made quite clear by Franz Joseph to Tsar Nicholas I.[35]

Whereas the Danube immediately became strategically important, it did not automatically become commercially controversial.   Indeed there were few commercial reasons to protest Russian control of the Danube, besides the perennial problem at the mouths, because when hostilities began in October 1853, Russia continued to allow neutral ships access to the Danube, as long as they did not carry supplies for the Ottomans.[36] Occasional mishaps had occurred, such as the Russian firing on the Austrian Danube steamer "Pesth" on 3 November 1853, but the Austrian internuntius in Istanbul, Karl Ludwig Freiherr von Bruck, dismissed this isolated incident as the recklessness of an individual Russian commander rather than an effort to deter Austrian shipping.[37]

Nevertheless, calls for Austria to act against Russia on behalf of the monarchy's commercial interests on the Danube came relatively quickly. In early March 1854 French leaders reportedly urged Austria to join the western powers in the imminent conflict in order to protect all that Franz Joseph held dear: his majesty's throne, the independence of his state, the universal church, and the liberation of Austria's great commercial artery, the Danube.[38] Then in late March Buol laid out his policies for Austria in the memorandum described above in which he echoed, but altered, the message from Paris by calling for the liberation of Germany's lifeline.

Austrian diplomatic correspondence would increasingly emphasize the German nature of the Danube over the next two years, raising the important question, why did Buol and others use this rhetorical device? Buol's three-point plan for facing Austria's challenges provides a partial explanation. One element of this plan was to win the support of Prussia and the German Confederation, which meant that Buol had to persuade the German states that this was their war, too. Claiming that German interests were at stake on the Danube was a potentially persuasive argument. Taking a broader perspective, Paul Schroeder writes that the dangers Austria faced added up for Buol to a great crisis in which the principles, the honor, the integrity, and the very existence of Austria as a Great Power were at stake. His fundamental fear was not simply that particular Austrian interests might be affected but that Austria might cease to be a Great Power if she failed at this juncture to act like one.[39] Acting like a great power included defending German interests on the Danube. Thus it is clear that Austrian statesmen had compelling political motivation, if not convincing economic reasons, for defining the Danube as Germany's lifeline.

These two issues--relations with the German states and relations with other great powers--were intricately related because Austria's status in the European states system was dependent upon her status in Germany. As international tensions mounted, therefore, support from Germany became ever more imperative for Austria. In January 1854, while negotiations with Russia remained barren, Franz Joseph instructed his foreign minister to arrange an agreement with Prussia and the states of the confederation. But when in late March Britain and France declared war on Russia, Austria was still without allies. Fortunately for the Habsburgs, Prussian King Frederick William IV was amenable to Austrian overtures and a bilateral alliance was signed on 20 April 1854.[40] Article two of this treaty called for the joint defense of German rights and interests against any and all infringement, implying, but not actually specifying, protection of interests on the Danube.[41]

Rejecting the logic of this agreement, one historian writes quite explicitly that Germany--neither Prussia nor the middle states--had any significant interests on the lower Danube. The German portion of exports to the Danubian principalities had continually declined in comparison to the Austrian share. More fundamentally, geographic, political, and economic realities, especially the dynamic of the Zollverein, impeded the projection of German influence on the lower Danube.[42] In more concrete terms, the states of Hanover, Mecklenburg, and Oldenburg, along with the Hanseatic cities, altogether sent only twenty-three ships into the Sulina channel in 1853, and Prussia added only four more.[43]

At least one Prussian of that day agreed with this assessment. Otto von Bismarck was well aware that the Danube did not live up to its purported significance. Bismarck was serving as Prussia's envoy to the diet of the German Confederation when, after becoming partners through the April treaty, the Austrian and Prussian governments decided to send a joint declaration to the diet to explain their position in the oriental crisis and to request the confederation's support for this position. Austria's aim was to have its political interests recognized as synonymous with universal German interests, or as noted above, showing the Germans that this was their war, too. For this purpose a direct German interest in the eastern question had to be established, and this interest became embodied in the principle of freedom of commerce and navigation on the Danube. The declaration sent to Frankfurt, the diet's meeting place, argued that economic expansion into the lands on the lower Danube and the orient, and success in the competition there with other leading nations, were essential for German economic well-being. Bismarck would have none of this. The mouth of the Danube, he believed, was of very little consequence to Germany; the Adriatic and England's control of Ionian islands were ten thousand times more important. To his mind, Austria did indeed have direct interests in the oriental question, but Prussia did not. Prussia's true interest lay in using this issue as a means of dislodging Austria from it presidial position in Germany, a sentiment that Buol attributed to many in Berlin. Bismarck therefore called for the portion of the declaration concerning the Danube's importance to be stricken, so as to impede Austria's effort to win German support. Although his opposition proved in vain, Bismarck clearly saw Austria's Danubian diplomacy for what it was: a means and not an end.[44]

Leaders of other German states debated the question of real or inflated value of the Danube as well, most notably at Bamberg in 1854. Representatives of the German middle states met in this Bavarian city to formulate a response to the new Austro-Prussian alignment and to define the vague German interests that they were being asked to protect. Some of these politicians, however, had more grandiose ambitions, such as elevating the status of the middle states in German and European politics during this time of crisis. For example, Bavaria's Minister-President Ludwig Count von der Pfordten prepared a pre-conference memorandum which specified the German interests, as he saw them, that Austria and Prussian should defend in resolving the eastern question. In addition to protecting Christians in the Ottoman Empire and preserving the monarchy in Greece (a special Bavarian interest), his memorandum stated that the British and French entrenchment on the Turkish straits presented a more ominous threat to Germany's material interests than did the Russian occupation of the Principalities, which the sea powers were intent on removing. Germans were concerned not only with freedom on the Danube, but also with free access through the Turkish straits and on the Black Sea. This memorandum became the basis for discussion at the conference, and with it Pfordten attempted to belittle the Austrian agenda and to stake the middle states' claim to an independent political role.[45]

During the Bamberg conference Minister Reinhard Baron Dalwigk zu Lichtenfels of Hesse-Darmstadt reportedly called for modifications of the regime of the Danube, suggesting that Austria serve as a co-protector of the Principalities in the interest of German commercial and transportation needs. Foreign Minister Friedrich Ferdinand Count von Beust of Saxony--Saxony along with Württemberg being "pro-Russian citadels"[46]--opposed this essentially pro-Austrian proposal. The participants of the conference agreed that the "German Rights and Interests" as expressed in the April treaty needed more precise definition. Although Beust wanted to insert a clarification of these interests--specifically, demanding free commerce and transportation on the Black Sea and the straits, as well as the Danube--this addition was stricken from the final 3 June 1854 "Bamberger Note." The majority of the German representatives opposed its inclusion because it seemed dangerous to impart to the note an anti-Austrian, anti-western accent.[47]

This did not entirely satisfy Franz Joseph who was convinced of the necessity of a united German stance, and therefore called on Frederick William IV for a te-à-te in Teschen (Silesia) on 8 June. The perception of solidarity between these two German powers, inspired by this meeting, served as a catalyst for the dissolution of the Bamberger front, and by 24 July all of the confederation's states, with the exception of Mecklenburg, had signed on to the Austro-Prussian alliance.[48]

Just as Vienna tried to use the Danube to win over the German state, so did rival European powers use the river in their attempts to woo Austria. In January 1854 a Russian envoy in Vienna offered the Habsburgs, in exchange for Austrian acquiescence in Russian aggression across the Danube, gains in the Balkans and "a share for Austria in Russia's protectorate over the Principalities or a promise of immediate action to clear the Danube mouth."[49] A few months later Russia tried to win concessions from the Austrians before evacuating the Principalities by promising "to guarantee complete freedom of trade on the lower Danube."[50] In late May 1854 French Foreign Minister Edouard Drouyn de Lhuys offered the Habsburgs more generous rewards for joining the war against Russia: the Danube delta would be placed under the protectorate of Austria which would become the "concierge" of the river in the name of Germany and Europe, and he promised overt French assistance to maintain free navigation on the river.[51]

In May 1854 the French ambassador to Vienna, Francois Adolphe Baron Bourqueney, informed Buol that, among other issues, the question of Danube navigation would necessarily be resolved in the final peace settlement. This was the first step in the formulation of the Four Points note which was eventually agreed to by Austria, France, and Britain on 8 August 1854 as the basis for peace with Russia.[52] Clearly, Buol desired to revise the Russian regime at the Danube's mouth. Unclear, however, is his conception of what should replace Russian mismanagement. In early July Buol suggested that a convention, cosigned by Russia, would be sufficient to liberate the Danube. This convention would place the removal of all impediments to Danubian commerce and navigation under European control, and Russian adherence to the convention's provisions should be supervised by the powers.[53] The dearth of specifics, including his glaring omission of which state would have suzerainty over the Danube's outlets after the war, leaves Buol's true intentions unfathomable. The fact that other Austrian statesmen also had opinions on the river's future only increases uncertainty about Austrian policy. The man generally regarded as the Habsburg monarchy's expert on the eastern question, Anton Count Prokesch von Osten, wanted to stipulate specifically that an Austrian establishment at the mouth of the Danube should be the guarantor of free navigation.[54]

The most extensive Austrian proposals were developed by Bruck, who had taken up his current post as Austrian internuntius in Istanbul in June 1853.[55] A few months later Buol instructed him to ascertain ways and means of alleviating the sad condition at the Danube's mouth. Bruck did not report his proposals for improving navigation on the Sulina channel until May 1854. In essence he called for a modified renewal of the 1840/1850 agreement, a concept similar to proposals that he had submitted in 1850 while serving as commerce minister under Felix zu Schwarzenberg. Bruck advocated new treaties that would create a Danubian commission consisting of representatives of the three riparian states, Austria, the Ottoman Empire, and Russia, allowing the first two powers to supervise and guarantee Russia's opening of the Danube's mouth for shipping. He defended these proposals as a means of furthering Austrian interests there, while at the same time not hindering the more general European interests.[56] Bruck had himself negotiated a similar treaty for free navigation of the Po River in July 1849.[57]

Although Habsburg statesmen desired an extension of Austrian influence on the Danube, up to this time none was advocating an end to Russia's political control of the Danube's outlets. Instead they sought amelioration of the problems through limited international oversight. Austria was to protect this "German lifeline" not by controlling it, but through cooperation. This fundamental agreement, however, was not a clearly defined program, and the contents of the Four Points note accepted on 8 August reflect this indecision concerning the river's future. Point Two called very simply, and very vaguely, for clearing all obstacles to navigation from the mouth of the Danube and the "application of the principles established by the Acts of the Congress of Vienna."[58] Although the Russians would reject the Four Points in their entirety, they had no compunctions about the uncontroversial Danubian clause. The Austrian minister to St. Petersburg quoted Russian Foreign Minister Karl Robert Count von Nesselrode as saying, "As for the question of the Danube, there is certainly no difficulty, it is a secondary matter."[59] Though acceptable, as originally formulated Point Two was far from definitive and Buol himself called for a conference to clarify the Four Points, which he felt were essentially "Drouyn's program, not Austria's."[60]

The other powers had few fixed attitudes about the Danube either, their aims varying among individual representatives and changing over time as well. Britain exemplifies this point. In March 1854 Palmerston considered giving the Principalities and the Danubian mouths to Austria,[61] but later suggested returning them to Turkey.[62] Lord John Russell swayed between extravagant and conservative war aims, on the modest side placing the Sulina channel of the Danube under Turkish control with European assurances that it would be kept open for navigation.[63]

The debate about the Danube's "liberation" would go on until the peace conference in Paris finally hammered out a solution. In the interim, however, a little-studied aspect of the Crimean War, the Anglo-French blockade of the mouths of the Danube, transformed the fundamental issues under discussion, at least as far as Austria was concerned. On 1 June 1854 the combined British and French naval forces had established an effective blockade at the mouths of the Danube.[64] The blockade applied only to ships going into the Danube, not to those coming out, and was nominally intended to prevent supplies from reaching the Russians.[65] Intent aside, it presented a real and immediate blow to Austrian economic interests, for it restricted Danubian commerce far more absolutely than had Russian neglect in the past or Russian policy during the war.

The damaging nature of this Anglo-French action was especially apparent to the Austrian internuntius in Istanbul, Bruck, and he, more vigorously than any other Habsburg representative, demanded that they quit this obstructive policy. Bruck's views are significant because he wasa businessman who had earned his living and status from maritime shipping.[66] After the Russians withdrew from the Principalities and Austrian forces began to occupy them in mid-August 1854, Bruck perceived no obstacle to lifting the blockade. He wrote Buol that the sea powers now had no reason to keep closed this commercial route so important for central Europe and that Russia would not object to the resumption of shipping. Bruck also argued that the Austrian government could win international praise by negotiating an end to the blockade because releasing the Principalities' pent up grains would reduce grain prices on European markets. For the internuntius an immediate resumption of traffic on the Danube was both politically possible and essential.[67]

As the year wore on the commercial problems created by the blockade became more acute. On 2 October Bruck forwarded to Buol a petition from Austrian shippers that urgently requested immediate negotiations with England and France to lift the blockade.[68] Buol responded to his insistent subordinate that as desirable as this goal might have been from a commercial perspective, one had to consider the difficulties this would raise for the sea powers. The Austrian occupation of the Principalities provided only a temporary cease-fire, and Turkish and Russian troops remained in the Dobrudja and Bessarabia, that is, in the immediate vicinity of the Sulina channel. Given these conditions, ships traveling through the channel could provoke renewed conflict, thereby re-opening a theater of operations for the sea powers to be concerned with.[69] Such a distraction would have been unwelcome indeed as Anglo-French forces had begun their primary offensive only a month before, landing in the Crimea in mid-September.

On the same day that Buol sent this response to Istanbul, which developed at length the argument summarized here, he also sent a confidential letter to Bruck expressing his serious concerns about the internuntius' behavior in his post. The foreign minister cited the storm of complaints about Bruck that the English and French had battered him with, and he charged Bruck with disregarding the policies outlined by the emperor and himself. In particular his concerns focused on two themes: that Bruck claimed Austria should have exclusive influence in the Principalities, and that he publicly professed his sympathies for Russia and his disdain for closer ties to the sea powers.[70] This scolding leaves no doubt about Bruck's preference for Russia over an alliance with Britain and France, and yet the prejudices it identifies did not necessarily impair Bruck's ability to determine what constituted the Habsburg monarchy's best economic interests.

It seems that his concern for Austrian commercial interests encouraged Bruck to continue pressing Buol to have the blockade lifted. In late October the internuntius wrote that over one hundred Austrian vessels were waiting in harbors for the opening of the Danube. Given both these conditions and the state of affairs around the river's mouth, he argued that the Austrians had both the right and the duty to request that the blockade be lifted. The spiraling grain prices in Austrian territories on the Adriatic presented further incentive for its removal. Bruck questioned the friendly intentions of those who relentlessly throttled Austrian commerce and unfavorably compared their actions to Russian behavior during the war which hindered Danubian traffic as little as possible. Bruck's convictions evoked a rare moment of poignancy in this usually uninspiring correspondent: "The roles of liberator and oppressor," he wrote, "have in this case been reversed."[71]

In fact, in mid-October Buol had instructed his envoys in London and Paris to request confidentially that the sea powers lift the blockade, arguing rather lamely that this would render an important service to European commerce,[72] but his appeal had no apparent effects. During the following two months the situation and Buol's lethargy became intolerable for Bruck, driving him to take matters into his own hands.[73] The blockade was especially exasperating to him because it prohibited Austrian businessmen from sailing Austrian ships loaded with grain purchased by Austrians to Austrian ports. What did this neutral commerce have to do with Britain and France's war against Russia? He made these complaints known to the British ambassador in Istanbul, Lord Stratford de Redcliffe, who, toward the end of 1854, expressed sympathy for the apparently unwarranted distress caused by the blockade. Stratford suggested that Bruck prepare a memorandum containing specific suggestions for relieving this affliction without prejudicing the sea powers' efforts against Russia.[74]

Bruck did exactly that, sending in mid-December a copy of his memorandum to both the British and French representatives in Istanbul, and to Buol in Vienna. He outlined the problem as he saw it: the blockade, justifiably imposed following the Russian occupation of the principalities, lost its justification when those forces quit Moldavia and Wallachia. Almost scornfully he chided that he would not treat the question of whether or not the sea powers had ever enjoyed the right to impede neutral shipping as they had for the last six months, but instead wanted to examine ways in which the blockade against Russia could be maintained without crippling the commerce of the lower Danube. His relatively simple plan proposed allowing commercial vessels to visit non-Russian ports on the Danube, and in particular to allow grain shipments form those ports. The sea powers' consuls in those towns could supervise this trade and their warships stationed in the Black Sea could continue to interdict contraband trade. In defense of his plan he suggested that the blockade had even been counterproductive to the western powers' war efforts by, for example, depriving the capital of their Ottoman ally of the grain normally flowing from the Principalities.[75]

Bruck's impetuosity spurred Buol to action. On *Silvesterabend*, New Years Eve day, the foreign minister related Bruck's tale to Hübner in France and Colloredo in Britain, instructing both to convey these proposals to the respective governments in hopes of diminishing the inconvenience to commerce resulting from the blockade.[76]   During January 1855, though, the art of persuasion was not practiced solely in Paris and London; a veritable lobbying campaign on behalf of Bruck's proposals converged on Buol. Besides additional correspondence from Bruck,[77] Buol also received a note from the Austrian commerce minister (Bruck's successor in the post) to support the internuntius' plan because the monarchy would benefit commercially from its adoption.[78] Another letter written on behalf of the monarchy's (purportedly) largest ship owner requested that Buol press for the implementation of Bruck's plan. These supplicants had more a personal interest in the matter than the commerce minister, because the Trieste businessman they were representing had four of his own ships plus five other vessels ready to carry his grain out through the Sulina channel. They quite openly stated that their business interests demanded the free use of the Danube.[79]

Within a month of Buol's 31 December entreaty to his envoys, Bruck's plan bore fruit.[80] On the last day of January Hübner concluded his telegram to Buol about the negotiations' progress with the words, "Je concidère la chose comme faite."[81] And indeed the next day it was done when Drouyn de Lhuys informed Hübner that Bruck's plan had been accepted and that the French and British governments were sending orders to their Black Sea fleets lifting the blockade for ships that were not sailing to enemy ports on the Danube and that were leaving loaded from those ports.[82] Less than three weeks later the sea powers went a step further. On 18 February the French and British naval commanders in the Black Sea signed a declaration officially lifting the blockade, while warning, "that cruizers [sic] will be stationed off the mouths of the said river to seize vessels laden with contraband of war."[83]

Ironically, for some Austrians the "liberation" of the Danube did not mean freeing it from Russian control, because for almost eight months of the Crimean War the sea powers held the river's outlets. Though theoretically and nominally imposed against Russia, in practice the blockade had applied very direct pressure on the Habsburg monarchy. To this writer's knowledge it is unprecedented to suggest that the blockade was aimed as much at Austria as at Russia, but there are sound reason for doing so. This novel interpretation conforms to the logic so frequently encountered in Crimean War diplomacy, namely that the Danube was a primary motivating force in Austrian minds. Various attempts by great powers to use the Danube as bait to lure Austria into an alliance have already been noted; with the blockade they were simply wielding stick rather than carrot. Unintentionally supporting this argument, Schroeder has noted that the sea powers' failure to capture Sebastopol in short order caused them to increase pressure on Austria to support them against Russia.[84] Rejecting Buol's October demands to relax the blockade would seem to be a logical extension of this effort. Economic coercion was certainly not beneath Britain's dignity; in 1853 at least one English diplomat suggested forcing Austria into the western camp by shutting down her Adriatic trade.[85]

The blockade's imposition is not the only suspicious factor here; the reasons given for and timing of the blockade's lifting also raise questions. The diplomatic correspondence preceding the blockade's termination repeatedly and specifically refers to Bruck's plan as the inspiration that broke through half a year's diplomatic inertia. Why would the Austrian internuntius at Istanbul, who only two months before had been so roundly criticized by western statesmen and his own foreign minister, now be so widely praised? Were Bruck's arguments truly ingenious enough to remove the scales from British Foreign Secretary Clarendon and Drouyn de Lhuys' eyes, enabling them to see that interfering with Austrian commerce was inappropriate, and inspiring them to lift the blockade? Perhaps more than to Bruck, credit should go to the 2 December 1854 signing of a treaty by which Austria formally joined the Anglo-French alliance.[86] While some historians have called this treaty a "diplomatic revolution,"[87] others have acknowledged an inability to perceive what Austria gained by revolting.[88] Chronology and logic point to one benefit, the lifting of the blockade, though the evidence marshaled here scarcely constitutes a definitive proof of cause and effect.

The information here, however, does reveal a great deal about Buol. His actions, or rather his inaction, indicates that he subordinated

Austria's commercial interests to the higher necessity, as he perceived it, of joining with Britain and France. For Buol the economic distress caused by the blockade provided insufficient justification for vigorous protest against the sea powers, as he said explicitly and forcefully when rebuking Bruck in October, despite the fact that this temporary regime imposed on the Danube's outlets by the west was more detrimental than Russian control had ever been. The number of ships entering the mouths of the Danube had increased steadily in the years prior to the war, reaching 2,490 in 1853, but plummeted to 680 in 1854.[89] Schroeder writes, "For Buol, the main question was always one of controlling, not the Principalities, but the general outcome of the war."[90] Substituting "the Danube" for "the Principalities" would undeniably be correct. The blockade episode strongly supports the thesis that the Danube had no dominant role in Austrian diplomacy, as so many historians have insisted, but was instead subordinated to other Austrian interests.

Solid evidence from the ongoing negotiations to end the war buttresses this thesis. The Habsburgs came closest to achieving paramountcy on the Danube during the Vienna conference of March-June 1855. From this time until the final peace treaty was signed in Paris the Austrian effort to control the river suffered notable setbacks. Though many have studied this prolonged peace process few have emphasized Buol's retreat from stances he had taken on the Danube as he repeatedly sacrificed Austrian interests to appease Britain and France.

After Russia agreed in late November 1854 to discuss the Four Points as a potential framework for peace, British, French, and Austrian officials modified the points to serve as the basis for a conference to be held in Vienna. According to a memorandum signed by these three powers on 28 December, Point Two was modified so as to read:

> .. . it would be desirable that the course of the Lower Danube, beginning from the point where it becomes common to the two River-bordering States, should be withdrawn from the Territorial Jurisdiction existing in virtue of Article III of the Treaty of Adrianople [Russian jurisdiction]. In every case the Free Navigation of the Danube could not be secured if it be not placed under the control of a Syndicate authority, invested with powers necessary to destroy the obstructions existing at the Mouths of that River, or which may hereafter be formed there.[91]

Immediately prior to the Vienna conference, during a meeting of the allies on 7 March 1855, the Austrian representatives essentially approved the new Point Two, but wanted to specify the details of another issue which had been discussed previously but not included in this revised version: stationing warships at the mouth of the Danube to guarantee free navigation. Prokesch argued for granting only the three riparian states--Austria, Russia, and the Ottoman Empire--the right to station ships at the Danube's mouths. The French quickly repudiated this demand, insisting that all the signatory powers should enjoy this privilege. The Vienna conference, which began on 15 March 1855 and ran through early June, resolved the issue. In the conference's fourth session, on 21 March, Prokesch accepted the French objections in one section of an extensive program that he laid before the assembled diplomats.[92] Buol and Prokesch's goal of insuring relatively greater Austrian authority on the river by minimizing the number of states exercising real powers had been conceded without a fight. This represented only the first of many retreats by the Austrians.[93]

Prokesch's memorandum expanded on the revised second point and provided guidelines for discussions in the conference. Its most important feature was the suggestion to create a temporary European commission, consisting of all the contracting states, that would be charged with establishing the legal principles for navigation on the lower Danube and with organizing a permanent executive commission to consist solely of riparian states. The British plenipotentiary challenged this latter provision, arguing that Britain should be included in the permanent commission due to her economic interests in Danubian commerce. Buol hid his *realpolitische* opposition to British intrusion behind the legalistic argument that the seminal 1815 acts provided for riparian regulation of commerce and navigation on international rivers. Buol won on this point, but the British countered by successfully inserting the clause "ne sera dissouté que d'un commun accord" in the article concerning the European commission; that is, it would only be dissolved by general agreement.[94] Nevertheless, the Austrians appeared successful because the delegates accepted the Prokesch memorandum on 23 March.[95]

The Austrians were successful on another point as well. They insisted on confining the application of the 1815 principles to the lower Danube only, excluding the portions of the river under Habsburg control. The Austrians insisted "that conditions on the upper river were satisfactory and needed no regulation; [and] that she [Austria] intended to introduce complete liberty of trade in all her dominions, including free navigation of the Danube."[96] As far as the Danube was concerned, the Vienna conference had gone well. In fact, "the whole settlement was favorable to Austria," especially because Britain was to help clear the physical obstructions from the mouth, but had won no permanent position on the river.[97] Prokesch rejoiced, "Europe itself will stand watch on this European river which is one of Germany's lifelines."[98] But Prokesch's celebration was premature. Future retreats on two important issues raised in Vienna--the role of the committees and geographic extent of internationalization--would temper this joy as more Europeans than Austria had bargained for became watchmen on the Danube.

The Vienna conference as a whole failed to achieve its objective--peace--not because of the Danube but because of Russian unwillingness to accept the harsh Point Three concerning the Black Sea. After Sebastopol fell in September 1855, however, Buol's desire for peace encouraged him to prepare a new initiative based once again on a modified version of the Four Points. After much secret negotiation between Vienna and Paris, Buol offered to present these peace proposals to Russia in the form of an ultimatum, the rejection of which would be grounds for Vienna to sever relations with St. Petersburg. One new feature in these proposals was particularly onerous for the Russians: the cession of a large part of Bessarabia which would remove Russia from the banks of the Danube.[99] Point Two of the proposals asserted that the freedom of the Danube and its mouths would be assured by European institutions in which all powers signing the treaty would be equally represented, while making exceptions for the special interests of the riparian.[100]

Buol's next task was to win his emperor's support for this new ultimatum. On 9 November 1855 he submitted an outline of the agreement he and the French ambassador had prepared. He argued that a peace based on these proposals would benefit Austria and Germany because it would create a new regime on the Danube. The nightmare so long vexing Austria--Russian control of the Danube's outlets--would permanently disappear as the Danube became a German stream all the way to its outlet. Support from Germany was essential for persuading Russia to accept the changes--the cession of part of Bessarabia in particular--that would make this new Danubian regime possible. Prussia had to be turned from its misguided policy and motivated to support austria. Bavaria had to be won over as well, and this was best accomplished by promising Munich a seat on the commission regulating navigation on the river. Taking a broader view of the central European scene, Buol insisted that simple cooperation with the cabinets in Berlin and Munich would be much less beneficial for insuring Austria's dominance in Germany than the electrifying charge that would be sent all over Germany by the news that Franz Joseph had decided to take strong action to remove all Russian influence from the Danube.[101]

This document has received considerable scrutiny by other historians.[102] It is one of those fundamental pieces of evidence, much like his 21 March 1854 memorandum, that seems to justify historians' representation of the Danube as a primary and vital Austrian interest. The foreign minister was working hard to persuade his emperor of the virtues of his relatively harsh proposals, and he was "fearful that Franz Joseph would not consent to having them presented to Russia in his name."[103] With this argument Buol confessed that a fundamental reason to support his plan was the propaganda value it would have in Germany. Just as Buol had tired to recruit the German states with the liberation of the Danube, he was now trying to entice Franz Joseph. Buol's blatant appeal worked; it persuaded Franz Joseph. On 16 December 1855 Austria sent Russia its ultimatum. The second point stated that the freedom of the Danube and its outlets would be assured by European institutions in which all powers signing the treaty would be equally represented, except for the special interests of the riparian, which would be regulated according to the principles established by the Congress of Vienna relative to river navigation. Each of the contracting powers would have the right to station one or two light warships at the mouths of the river to enforce the principle of free navigation.[104]

Taken by hand to St. Petersburg, the ultimatum did not reach the Russian court until late in December, giving Austria a chance to round up German support for the initiative. Prior to its dispatch on the sixteenth, the ultimatum had been kept secret from the other German capitals. "Buol, aware of the anger his ultimatum would arouse in Germany and the *Schadenfreude* that would greet a failure," once again employed the Danube in his attempts to garner backing.[105] On the day the ultimatum left Vienna Franz Joseph wrote to the king of Bavaria, requesting the latter's support for these peace proposals. He concluded by directly stating that the complete freedom of the mouth of the Danube would certainly be compensation for whatever sacrifices this support would entail.[106]

For the most part, however, appeals based on this presumptive importance of the Danube fell short of the mark, leaving the new peace plan open to criticism. Probably the most devastating critique came from Württemberg's Foreign Minister Karl Eugen Baron von Hügel. He rejected the notion that the Danube was a commercial artery of any consequence. After the completion of projected railroad from Belgrade to Istanbul and from Rustchuk to Varna, all trade to and from the orient would be concentrated on these routes. It was therefore irresponsible, Hugel reportedly said, to demand that Russia cede territories because of its proximity to the Danube, especially since the Russians were likely to reject these demands, thereby causing the entire peace process to collapse.[107] Furthermore, Württembergers "insisted that the lower Danube was Hungarian, not a German, stream."[108] Saxony's Foreign Minister Beust also rebuked the proposed Russian cession of Bessarabia. Beust argue that the German diet had approved the four Points back in December 1854 and that those proposals satisfactorily protected German interests. The plan to remove Russia from the Danube in order to guarantee free navigation was little more than a ploy to diminish Russian influence in the Principalities.[109] The Bavarians were somewhat more supportive, but Minister-President Pfordten criticized Point Two for allowing all of the contracting parties to station ships at the Danube's mouth, questioning the right of France and England--non-riparian states--to enjoy this privilege.[110] In sum, the courts of these states blew away the smoke beclouding Austria's rhetoric about "Germany's lifeline" and, seeing clearly the paltry rewards offered, could deny their support for all or parts of the Austrian ultimatum.[111]

Again, this is not to suggest that the Danube had no significance. From St. Petersburg the Austrian ambassador wrote that there were no longer any illusions in the Russian capital about the maritime Danube's importance for Austrian and German commerce, nor about the need to remove the obstacles to navigation. Despite the unpleasant Bessarabian cession, one could foresee the reaction that a Russian rejection of the ultimatum would have in Germany.[112'] This was one of the many reasons, albeit a minor one, that Russia unconditionally accepted the Austrian ultimatum on 16 January 1856, setting the stage for peace talks. Also highlighting the river's significance, only days later in Paris, Hübner told Napoleon III that "the mouth of the Danube, this represents German interests, it is the price of our action, it is our trophy, in no way will we give this up . . "[113] But these Russian views overestimated Germany's assessmentof the Danube; Bismarck correctly claimed that the phrase "German interests" lost its effect when unaccompanied by the resolve to preserve the peace for Germany.[114]

Yes, the Danube was significant, but only in a limited way, and for ascertaining these limits Buol's actions speak louder than his envoy's words.   The foreign minister himself led the retreat on two key diplomatic fronts, the role of the Danubian commissions and the extent of the river's internationalization.   Both of these issues had been addressed in the March 1855 Vienna conferences, but they took on more serious dimensions as the Paris peace talks grew near.   Franz Joseph brought up the former while convening with his ministers to formulate instructions for the Austrian plenipotentiaries to the Paris conference.   The emperor emphasized the necessity of delineating the rights and responsibilities enjoyed by the riparian states and the contracting European powers.   He desired for the peace to define exactly and explicitly the institutions regulating the Danube.[115]

Franz Joseph's Commerce Minister, Georg Graf von Toggenburg, provided a detailed explication of this concern in his 19 February memorandum. Having removed the Russian regime at the mouth of the Danube, everything now depended on the European institutions that would replace the Russians. In particular, a commission composed of all the great powers would be more likely to play politics with Danubian regulation than one consisting solely of riparian states, and thus the former could pose a threat to Austrian interests. Toggenburg realized that political complications and previous negotiations might make a European commission unavoidable. It was essential to limit both the duration of this body's existence and the extent of its responsibilities. A European commission was to be set up with well-defined duties, and it was explicitly stated and agreed that this European commission would not be permanent. A contradictory British proposal to make this a permanent commission had been rejected, and had only achieved the stipulation that general agreement was a prerequisite for its dissolution. Although this left no doubt that the European commission was intended to enjoy only a transitory life, the commerce minister wrote that it was of decisive importance that this limited time period and dissolution be defined more explicitly than they had been in 1855.[116]

Buol had his marching orders for the Paris congress which began on 25 February 1856, orders which mapped out both his target--

Austrian ascendancy on the Danube--and the pitfalls that lay between him and this goal. But those giving orders underestimated the foe and Buol was routed in short order. In the congress's fifth session, on 6 March, the foreign ministers of France and Britain "proposed just what Buol wanted to avoid. According to their ideas, the original commission on which all the powers would sit, . . . would remain in existence indefinitely. That is, it could be dissolved only by mutual consent, and Britain, as Clarendon remarked, would never let it be dissolved."[117] Buol had predetermined this defeat by allowing that clause, "ne sera dissoute que d'un commun accord," to be incorporated in early 1855.[118]

A more hotly contested front than the commission question opened up the same day when the president of the congress, French Foreign Minister Walewski, demanded that the 1815 Vienna principles concerning free shipping be applied to the entire Danube, rather than just the lower Danube as accepted in 1855.[119] Most Austrians, and especially the emperor, strongly opposed placing the Austrian portions of the Danube under international control. The French and British, however, would accept no less, threatening to close the lower Danube to Austrian shipping if the upper Danube remained exempt.[120] On 13 March, fearing a collapse of the peace negotiations, Buol and Hubner prepared two correspondences, with Buol adding a third private letter, designed to convince his emperor that Austria truly had no choice but to accede to the west's demands.[121] Buol led the retreat and Franz Joseph followed, reluctantly accepting the entire river's internationalization.

In the long run, this strategic withdrawal was less harmful to Austrian interests than was imagined, because "the introduction of the new regime on the entire course of the river was a theoretic one, Austrian applied her own norms on her sector of the river, up to 1921."[122] Much more damaging to Austrian aspirations on the Danube was Buol's inability to prescribe a definitive termination for the "temporary" European commission. Although Article 18 of the Treaty of Paris (30 March 1856) stated that this body should have finished its work within two years,[123] the British and French took advantage of the dissolution clause and were able to dominate the international commission that controlled the maritime Danube up to the First World War. While the European commission lived on, "the riparian commission, intended to be permanent, never functioned as an administrative commission."[124] Because the Austrian statesmen only grudgingly gave up their intention to dominate the entire river they continue to engage in Danubian diplomacy.[125]   But this crucial Crimean War phase was over; the outlets of the Danube that had been liberated from Russia were delivered over to new masters, albeit more efficient ones.

The traditional overemphasis of the Danube's importance for Austria is unjustified.[126]   Despite assertions to the contrary, the river was no Austrian economic lifeline, much less a German one; Austrian statesmen did not universally seek to terminate Russian control from the Danube's outlets, though most sought to modify it.   The Danube's "liberation" was not the primary thrust of Austrian foreign policy. These misperceptions concerning the Danube's significance derive in large measure from the words of Habsburg Foreign Minister Buol. Assertions of his--as when he wrote that the freedom of this great waterway would be judged as the most striking justification of Franz Joseph's Crimean War diplomacy--have long nourished the myth of the primacy of Danubian policy.   The moral to the story is that Buol's inflation of the Danube's import and his many calls for, and celebration of, the Danube's liberation were little more than political rhetoric.

Buol consistently backed away from concrete Austrian interests on the Danube in favor of accommodation with the west, as the history of Austria's Crimean War diplomacy makes abundantly clear.   He "won" the opening and development of the Sulina channel, but at what price? The Russian regime was replaced by one dominated by Britain and France, but the 1854-55 blockade of the Danube's mouths had demonstrated the callous disregard for Austria's commercial interests that these two could adopt.   One might contend that Buol's retreats from the Danube were simply expressions of his realistic view that Austria had little choice but to subordinate its interests to those of Britain and France.   Or one might argue, as Winfried Baumgart does, that the foreign minister's Danubian diplomacy demonstrates "how thoroughly Buol's ideas were rooted in European rather than merely Austrian attitudes."[127] But in fact both of these arguments only support the notion that the Danube was a secondary Austrian interest.

Several factors motivated Buol's rhetorical aggrandizement of the Danube. His politics required him to persuade a leery emperor to break with an old ally. He had to compete in the multi-polar struggle for mastery in Germany. Finally, the results of his overall diplomacy were so bleak--Austria is generally considered the greatest loser of the Crimean War[128]--that he had to hyperbolize whatever achievements were in sight, even if they fell short of recognized Austrian goals.

These factors encouraged Buol to trumpet a not-so-vital interest as essential to central Europe's economic future. Whereas Karl Marx may have misrepresented the Danube's role out of ignorance, Buol did so quite consciously. Contrary to Paul Schroeder's assertions, as least one of the dangers that the foreign minister presented in March 1854 as warranting adoption of his wartime diplomacy was exaggerated, if not concocted altogether. For Buol the Danube was little more than a diplomatic tool with which he tried to cobble together the peace he so dearly desired.

NOTES

1. Karl Marx, "England and Russia," in *The Eastern Question: A Reprint of Letters Written 1853-1856 Dealing with the Events of the Crimean War*, ed. Eleanor Marx Aveling and Edward Aveling (London, 1897; repr., New York, 1969), 201-2.

2. Karl Count von Buol-Schauenstein to Franz Joseph, Vienna, 9 March 1856, *Akten zur Geschichte des Krimkriegs*, Series. 1. *Osterreichische Akten zur Geschichte des Krimkriegs* (Munich, 1979), 3:488 (hereafter cited as *AGKK*).

3. Paul Schroeder, "A Turning Point in Austrian Policy in the Crimean War: the Conference of March, 1854," *Austrian History Yearbook* 4-5 (1968-69): 164.

4. Buol to Franz Joseph, Vienna, 21 March 1854, *AGGK*, 1:688-93. Also, see Bernhard Unckel, *Österreich und der Krimkrieg. Studien zur Politik der Donaumonarchie in den Jahren 1852-1856* (Lübeck, 1969),125-26; Paul W. Schroeder, *Austria, Great Britain, and the Crimean War: The Destruction of the European Concert* (Ithaca, NY, 1972), 157-59; and Norman Rich, *Why the Crimean War? A Cautionary Tale* (Hanover, NH, 1985), 113-14.

5. Schroeder, "Turning Point," 164.

6. A. J. P. Taylor, *The Struggle for Mastery in Europe 1848-1918* (Oxford and New York, 1954), 55 and 228; and M. S. Anderson, *The Eastern Question 1774-1923* (London, 1966), 125.

7. David Wetzel, *The Crimean War: A Diplomatic History* (Boulder, 1958), 85.

8. Heinrich Benedikt, *Die wirtschaftliche Entwicklung in der Franz-Joseph Zeit* (Vienna and Munich, 1958), 104.

9. One old bridge in the center of Regensburg is presently classified as an historical monument and prohibits through shipping now as it did in the middle nineteenth century. Wolfgang Götzer, *Der völkerrechtliche Status der Donau zwischen Regensburg und Kelheim* (Frankfurt am Main, 1988), 5 and 23.

10. Joseph P. Chamberlain, *The Danube* (Washington, 1918) 7.

11. Hans Christian Andersen, *A Poet's Bazaar; A Journey to Greece, Turkey and Up the Danube*, trans. Grace Thornton (New York, 1988), 139-44.

12. Götzer, *Status der Donau*, 33.

13. Helmut Pemsel, *Die Donauschiffahrt in Niederosterreich* (St. Pölten and Vienna, 1984), 60.

14. David F. Good, *The Economic Rise of the Habsburg Empire, 1750-1914* (Berkeley, 1984), 30; John R. Lampe and Marvin R. Jackson, *Balkan

Economic History, 1550-19500: From Imperial Borderlands to Developing Nations (Bloomington, 1982), 106-8; Robert A. Kann, *A History of the Habsburg Empire 1526-1918* (Berkeley, 1974), 286-87.

15. Ronald E. Coons, *Steamships, Statesmen, and Bureaucrats:Austrian Policy towards the Steam Navigation Company of the Austrian Lloyd, 1836-1848* (Wiesbaden, 1975), 131.

16. Vernon John Puryear, *International Economics and Diplomacy in the Near East. A Study of British Commercial Policy in the Levant, 1834-1853* (Stanford, 1935), 7.

17. Puryear, *International Economics*, 6-13.

18. Coons, *Steamships*, 108, 115-17.

19. Puryear, *International Economics*, 186.

20. Unfortunately, a significant article on this subject has come to my attention too late to have been incorporated in this essay: Manfred Sauer, "Österreich und die Sulina Frage 1829-1854," *Mitteilungen des Österreichischen Staatsarchivs* 40 (1987): 185-236.

21. Text of the convention in Edward Hertslet, ed., *The Map of Europe by Treaty* (London, 1875-91), 2:1016-20. Also see, Spiridon G. Focas, *The Lower Danube River*, trans. Rozeta J. Metes (Boulder: East European Monographs, 1987), 201-5.

22. Articles 108-14 of the Vienna Final Act of 9 June 1815.

23. Lampe and Jackson, *Balkan Economic History*, 100.

24. Henry Hajnal, *The Danube, Its Historical, Political and Economic Importance* (The Hague, 1920), 151.

25. Puryear, *International Economics*, 202-6.

26. Hajnal, *Danube*, 152-33.

27. Richard C. Frucht, *Dunarea Noastra: Romania and the Great Powers and the Danube Question* (Boulder: East European Monographs, 1982), 5-6.

28. Hajnal, *Danube*, 156-57.

29. Anderson, *Eastern Question,* 110; Chamberlain, *Danube*,18-24; Frucht, *Danube Question* 13-14; Lampe and Jackson, *Balkan Economic History*, 101.

30. Puryear *International Economics*, 207.

31. Hajnal, *Danube*, 63.

32. A thorough study of the 1850 negotiations and the treaty's lapse in 1851 has not come to my attention, but the topic certainly merits investigation because the existing literature does little more than confuse. Lampe and Jackson state that the convention was not even renewed in 1850, *Balkan Economic History*, 101, but the protocol prolonging it is readily available for inspection in Hertslet, *Map of Europe*, 2:1142.

33. Anderson, *Eastern Question*, 128.

34. Buol to Franz Joseph, Vienna, 16 January 1854, *AGKK*, 1:510; and protocol of ministerial conference, Vienna, 23 January 1854, *AGKK*, 1:521-22.

35. Franz Joseph to Nicholas I, Vienna, 5 February 1854, *AGKK*, 1:570-72.

36. Puryear, *International Economics*, 212; Bruck to Buol, Buyukdere, 2 October 1854, Haus-Hof-und Staatsarchiv (HHStA), Politisches Archiv XII (PA), Carton 52, Varia, Blokade der Donau-Mündungen, ff. 13-14 (reproduced on microfilm, Alderman Library, University of Virginia).

37.Bruck to Buol, Constantinople, 10 November 1853, HHStA, PA XII, 47, Berichte, ff. 193-96; Bruck to Buol, Constantinople, 17 November 1853, HHStA, PA XII, 47, Berichte, ff. 247-49.

38. Joseph Alexander Count von Hübner (Austrian minister to France) to Buol, Paris, 5 March 1854 *AGKK*, 1:649-50.

39. Schroeder, "Turning Point," 166.

40. Unckel, *Österreich*, 114-25.

41. Helmuth K.G. Rönnefarth, comp., *Konferenzen und Verträge*, 2nd ed., part 2 (Wurzburg, 1958), 3:308-9.

42. Michael Simon, *Die Aussenpolitik Hessen-Darmstadts während des Krimkrieges* (Frankfurt am Main, 1977), 38-40.

43. Hajnal, *Danube*, 156-57.

44. Arnold Oskar Meyer, *Bismarcks Kampf mit Österreich am Bundestag zu Frankfurt (1851 bis 1859)*(Berlin and Leipzig, 1927), 218-21.

45. Simon, *Aussenpolitik Hessen-Darmstadts*, 76.

46. Schroeder, *Austria*, 229.

47. Simon, *Aussenpolitik Hessen-Darmstadts*, 77-78.

48. Unckel, *Österreich*, 135-36.

49. Schroeder, *Austria*, 139-40.

50. Ibid., 176.

51. Hübner to Buol, Paris, 31 May 1854, *AGKK*, 1:185-87. Also see, Schroeder, *Austria*, 103.

52. Schroeder, *Austria*, 183.

53. Buol to Hübner, Vienna, 2 July 1854, *AGKK*, 1,2:23.

54. Prokesch to Buol, Frankfurt, 7 August 1854, *AGKK*, 1,2:330-32.

55. Karl Ludwig von Bruck to Buol, Constantinople, 16 June 1853, HHStA, Vienna, PA XII, 47, Berichte, ff. 302-6.

56. Bruck to Buol, Constantinople, 18 May 1854, *AGKK*, 2:151-55.

57. Hertslet, *Map of Europe*, 2:1095-1103.

58. Ibid., 1216.

59. Count Valentin Esterhazy to Buol, St. Petersburg, 21 August 1854, *AGKK*, 1,2:369-70.

60. Schroeder, *Austria*, 192-96, 203.

240 Essays in European History

61. Rich, *Cautionary Tale*, 108; Schroeder, *Austria*, 150.

62. Schroeder, *Austria*, 204.

63. Ibid., 203-4.

64. Albert Chiari (Austrian consul in Galatz) to Buol, Galatz, 14 March 1855, PA XII, 52, Varia, Blokade der Donau-Mündungen, ff. 77-78.

65. Bruck to Buol, Constantinople, 5 June 1854, HHStA, PA XII, 52, Varia, Blockade der Donau-Mündungen, ff. 1-2.

66. Charmatz, Richard, *Minister Freiherr von Bruck, der Vorkämpfer Mitteleuropa* (Leipzig, 1916); Hannes Androsch and Helmut Haschek, "Karl von Bruck, ein österreichisches Schicksal", *österreichische porträts* (Salzburg and Vienna, 1985), 164-92.

67. Bruck to Buol, Constantinople, 21 August 1854, HHStA, PA XII, 52, Varia, Blokade der Donau-Mündungen, ff. 9-10.

68. The petition was written in Italian, as were many from merchants in Constantinople. Bruck to Buol, Constantinople, 2 October 1854, HHStA, PA XII, 52, Varia, Blokade der Donau-Mündungen, ff. 13-14.

69. Buol to Bruck, Vienna, 16 October 1854, *AGKK*, 2:507-8.

70. Buol to Bruck, Vienna, 16 October 1854, *AGKK*, 2:508-9.

71. Bruck to Buol, Buyukdere, 26 October 1854, HHStA, PA XII, 52, Varia, Blokade der Donau-Mündungen, ff. 27-30.

72. Buol to Colloredo, Vienna, 16 October 1854, PA VIII, England, 40, Weisungen, Diversa, f. 40; Buol to Colloredo and Hübner, Vienna, 16 October 1854, PA XII, 52, Varia, Blokade der Donaumündungen, ff. 17-18.

73. Colloredo to Buol, London, 27 November 1854, HHStA, PA XII, 52, Varia, Blokade der Donau-Mündungen, ff. 40-45; Bruck to Buol, Constantinople, 13 November 154, HHStA, PA XII, 52 Varia, Blokade der Donau-Mündungen, ff. 46-48; Bruck to Buol, Constantinople, 20 November 1854, HHStA, PA XII, 52, Varia, Blokade der Donau-Mündungen, ff. 51-52; Hubner to Buol, Paris, 10 January 1855, *AGKK*, 2:684.

74. Bruck to Buol, Constantinople, 14 December 1854, PA XII, 52, Varia, Blokade der Donau-Mündungen, ff. 61-64.

75. Memorandum by Bruck, Constantinople, n.d., PA XII, 52, Varia, Blokade der Donau-Mündungen, ff. 65-72.

76. Buol to Hubner and Colloredo, Vienna, 31 December 1854, PA XII, 52, Varia, 1855, III. Blokade der Donau-Mündungen, ff. 1-2.

77. Bruck to Buol, Constantinople, 18 January 1855, Constantinople, PA XII, 52, Varia, Blokade der Donau-Mündungen, ff. 13-15.

78. Andreas Freiherr von Baumgartner (commerce minister) to foreign minister, Vienna, 21 January 1855, PA XII, 52, Varia, Blokade der Donau-Mündungen, ff. 19-22.

79. [Illegible] to Buol, no place, n.d. (presented on 23 January 1855), PA XII, 52, Varia, Blokade der Donau-Mündungen, ff. 23-24.

80. Hübner to Buol, Paris, 10 January 1855, *AGKK*, 1,2:684.

81. Telegram, Hübner to Buol, Paris, 30 January 1855, PA XII, 52, Varia, Blokade der Donau-Mündungen, f. 29.

82. Hübner to Buol, Paris, 1 February 1855, PA XII, 52, Varia, Blokade der Donau-Mündungen, ff. 31-32.

83. Albert Chiari (Austrian consul in Galatz) to Buol, Galatz, 14 March 1855, PA XII, 52, Varia, Blokade der Donau-Mundungen, ff. 77-78.

84. Schroeder, *Austria*, 206.

85. Ibid., 87.

86. For the text of this treaty see, Hertslet, *Map of Europe*, 2:1221-24.

87. Rich, *Crimean War*, 144-45. Rich himself does not, but he notes the significance which others have attached to it.

88. Schroeder, *Austria*, 225-27.

89. Hajnal, *Danube*, 156-57.

90. Schroeder, *Austria*, 212.

91. Hertslet, *Map of Europe*, 2:1225-26.

92. Text of Prokesch's memorandum in, *British and Foreign State Papers, 1854-1855* (London, 1865), 45:71-73.

93. Protocol of the 21 March session, *State Papers*, 45:68-71; Unckel, *Österreich*, 200-5.

94. *State Papers*, 45:74-75.

95. Unckel, *Österreich*, 205-6; Focas, *Danube* 232-34.

96. Chamberlain, *Danube*, 26-27; 31, n.4.

97. Ibid., 28-29.

98. Memorandum, Prokesch von Osten, Vienna, n.d. [23 March 1855], *AGKK*, 1,2:827.

99. Rich, *Crimean War*, 157-69; Schroeder, *Austria*, 311-13; Wetzel, *Crimean War*, 174-76.

100. Anonymous memorandum, [Vienna?], n.d. [6 November 1855?], *AGKK*, 1,3:97. Either a French version of the preliminary peace proposals or, more likely, an Austrian revision of the French plan.

101. Buol to Franz Joseph, Vienna, 9 November 1855, *AGKK*, 1,3:103-4.

102. Unckel, *Österreich*, 232-33, Schroeder, *Austria*, 314-15; Rich, *Crimean War*, 168-69.

103. Rich, *Crimean War*, 168.

104. Austrian ultimatum, Vienna, 16 December 1855, *AGKK*, 1,3:162-63.

105. Schroeder, *Austria*, 330-31.

106. Franz Joseph to Maximilian I, Vienna, 16 December 1855, *AGKK*,

1,3:171-73.

107. Eduard Baron von Lago to Buol, Stuttgart, 28 December 1855, *AGKK*, 1,3:194-95.

108. Schroeder, *Austria*, 332.

109. Franz Graf Kuefstein to Buol, Dresden, 30 December 1855, *AGKK*, 1,3:208-9.

110. Apponyi to Buol, Munich, 26 December 1855, *AGKK*, 1,3:190-91; Rudolph Graf Apponyi to Buol, 7 January 1856, *AGKK*, 13:219-20.

111. The Habsburg envoy in Berlin responded to this ingratitude for Austria's defense of German interests by administering a sardonic tongue-lashing to the Wurttemberg and Saxon envoys there. Count Georg Esterhazy to Buol, Berlin, 24 January 1856, *AGKK*, 1,3:284-85.

112. V. Esterhazy to Buol, St. Petersburg, 12 January 1855, *AGKK*, 1,3:235-36.

113. Hübner to Buol, Paris, 19 January 1856, *AGKK*, 1,3:268.

114. Meyer, *Bismarcks Kampf*, 228.

115. Minutes of ministerial conference, Vienna, 11 February 1856, *AGKK*, 1,3:369-71.

116. Toggenburg to Buol, Vienna, 19 February 1856, *AGKK*, 1,3:391-96.

117. Schroeder, *Austria*, 359.

118. Chamberlain, *Danube*, 32.

119. Buol and Hübner to Franz Joseph, Paris, 7 March 1856, *AGKK*, 1,3:479-81; Winfried Baumgart, *The Peace of Paris 1856: Studies in War, Diplomacy, and Peacemaking*, trans. Ann Pottinger Saab (Santa Barbara, 1981), 126-28. Also see Focas, *Danube*, 236-42.

120. Buol and Hübner to Franz Joseph, Paris, 13 March 1856, *AGKK*, 1,3:511-15;.

121. Buol and Hubner to Franz Joseph, Paris, 13 March 1856, *AGKK*, 1,3:511-15; Buol and Hübner to Franz Joseph, Paris, 13 March 1856, *AGKK*, 1,3:516-17; Buol to Franz Joseph, Paris, 13 March 1856, *AGKK*, 1,3:518-19.

122. Focas, *Danube*, 251.

123. Hertslet, *Map of Europe*, 2:1259.

124. Chamberlain, *Danube*, 34.

125. Barbara Jelavich, *Russia and the Formation of the Romanian National State 1821-1878* (Cambridge, 1984), 67; Anderson, *Eastern Question*, 142.

126. E.g., Rich, *Crimean War*, 168.

127. Baumgart, *Peace of Paris*, 126.

128. Rich, *Crimean War*, 198.

Contributors

Michael Graham is assistant professor of history
at the University of Akron.

Carey Goodman is a graduate student in history at the
University of Virginia.

John Haag is associate professor of history at the
University of Georgia.

George O. Kent is professor of history emeritus at the
University of Maryland.

Enno E. Kraehe is William W. Corcoran professor of history
emeritus at the University of Virginia.

Jere H. Link teaches at the Westminister School in
Atlanta, Georgia.

Valdis O. Lumans is professor of history and department
chair at the University of South Carolina, Aiken.

Barbara A. Niemczyk is assistant professor in the Russian
Department at Dickinson College.

Bruce F. Pauley is professor of history at the University of
Central Florida.

Kenneth W. Rock is professor of history at
Colorado State University.

Hans A. Schmitt is professor of history emeritus at the
University of Virginia.

Andre Spies is associate professor of history and department chair
at Hollins College.